750

Ferruccio Busoni

Ferruccio Busoni (1866–1924), world-famous as a virtuoso pianist, was also one of the most outstanding composers this century has seen. But, as in the case of Mahler, his career as a concert pianist tended to deflect attention from his genius as a composer, which in Great Britain has not yet found proper recognition.

H. H. Stuckenschmidt, a noted German musicologist and critic, gives a vivid account of Busoni's childhood in Italy—his Italian father and German mother were both musicians—and his musical education and development in Germany, where he spent the greater part of his life. During his concert tours, Busoni travelled the world relentlessly. The letters he wrote to his Finnish-born wife and his many friends, while on tour, show him to be concerned not only with musical problems but with the wider fields of aesthetics and philosophy within the European framework.

As a teacher Busoni had a lasting influence on his pupils, and the author draws on many recollections that reflect the complexity of the man and the importance of the musician. This sympathetic study and illuminating interpretation of Busoni's eclecticism and wide range of musical imagination must ensure the rightful level of his reputation as an outstanding composer.

This translation by Sandra Morris is the first in English of what must be considered the definitive work on Busoni.

H. H. Stuckenschmidt

Ferruccio Busoni

Chronicle of a European

Translated by Sandra Morris

Calder & Boyars   London

First published in Great Britain in 1970 by
Calder and Boyars Limited, 18 Brewer Street, London, W1

Originally published by Atlantis Verlag AG, Zürich as
Ferruccio Busoni, Zeittafel eines Europäers
© Atlantis Verlag AG Zürich, 1967
© This translation Calder & Boyars Limited, 1970

ISBN 0 7145 0234 0 cloth edition
ISBN 0 7145 0235 9 paper edition

Printed in Great Britain by
Clarke, Doble & Brendon Limited,
Plymouth

Gratefully and respectfully dedicated to
Her Majesty Queen Marie-José of Italy

Contents

List of Illustrations

Life of Busoni

'After a desperate struggle, witnessed by a crowd of relatives' he first saw the light of day. That was how Ferruccio Busoni, writing in 1909, described his birth. Empoli is a modest little Tuscan town on the left bank of the Arno, nearer to the main town of Florence than to Siena in the south and Pisa in the west. The Busonis were not Tuscans but probably came over from Corsica by way of Leghorn. Busoni's father, Ferdinando, was the outsider in a family that, from time to time, had achieved success in the middle-class business world. Born in 1834, from the time he was a child music and literature were his only interests; and in spite of his father's disapproval, he developed into a virtuoso performer. His instrument was the clarinet, and in the early days he played mainly in a brass band in Leghorn. Quarrelsome by nature, and therefore not endowed with the team-spirit essential for playing in a band, his ambition was to be a soloist. After a short period as clarinettist in the local orchestra and teacher at the Instituto Musicale in Novara, he took up the nomadic life of a concert performer, with a glittering repertoire which included as many operatic fantasias as original compositions for the clarinet. Ferdinando Busoni must have been an outstanding player; this much is testified not only by his famous son but also by the honorary membership of the Accademia Filarmonica in Bologna conferred on him at the age of thirty. At a concert given in Trieste in 1865, he was accompanied by the woman who was later to become his wife, the pianist Anna Weiss. 'She was German on her father's side, although her mother was Italian', her son wrote later. Like many people born in Trieste, she was brought up as bilingual, with a definite preference for all things Italian. Born in 1833, she first played in public at the age of fourteen and at twenty-one gave three concerts in Vienna where she was praised for her rendering of Liszt. The elegant bearded virtuoso clarinettist, an *homme à femmes*, with the reputation of a Don Juan, swept her so completely off her feet that she decided then and there to become his wife. Her father,

13

Joseph Ferdinand Weiss, a painter and craftsman with some experience of the world, promptly showed the romantic suitor the door. But Anna got her own way, and in a short time she was Frau Busoni. Ferdinando added her maiden name to his own, and as Anna Weiss-Busoni, she played with him in many towns throughout Italy. As late as the end of March 1866 she is supposed to have played for Franz Liszt in Rome. On 1st April, an Easter Sunday, after a difficult confinement she gave birth in Empoli to a son who was christened Ferruccio Dante Michelangiolo Benvenuto. He remained their only child, and the parents did all they could to develop his talents as quickly and thoroughly as possible. The bond between them was very close, as is so often the case in middle-class Italian families, and it was a long time before Ferruccio was able to break away from them. There is certainly a hint of criticism in the observation he makes in the autobiographical fragment dating from 1909 : 'From the time I was seven my parents began to concentrate on me entirely and gradually withdrew from their own artistic activities.' The nomadic existence of this little family began eight months after his birth. By the end of the 'sixties they settled in Paris. Ferruccio, who had previously been in Trieste with grandfather Weiss, now joined his parents. These were the final years of the Second Empire, a period of social brilliance when the rich bourgeoisie made their own cultural contribution in an effort to outrival the court. Ferdinando's virtuosity achieved more success than he had ever known in his own country. He played at private concerts given by influential families, received enthusiastic press notices and was on the point of giving up his nomadic life. His good fortune was interrupted by rumours of war. Even before France and Prussia declared war in 1870, the Busonis left Paris. Anna and her child went to live with grandfather Weiss at his large house in Trieste. They spent two years with the seventy-year-old man who shared his home with a tyrannical housekeeper, a *serva padrona*, who deeply resented the daughter. Busoni was later to speak highly of the talents and determination of this man who had begun his career as a cabin-boy and achieved prosperity and social prestige.

Meanwhile Ferdinando, permanently estranged from his father-in-law, continued to pursue his nomadic carer as a clarinettist. It was a hard time for Anna. The young couple separated by circumstances beyond their control. The husband she worshipped and the young child's father away, goodness knows where. In her father's house, the jealousy of a woman who did everything she could to stir up trouble between old Weiss and his daughter. One can well imagine the young pianist, who had caused quite a stir with her precocious compositions, taking refuge in music. Her child, Ferruccio, lived in a tense atmosphere of family quarrels and continually strained relationships. But he also shared the comfort that his mother found at the keyboard. In Paris he had already played around with glissandos. It was during this period, between the time he was four and six, that he first felt excited and, at the same time, peculiarly disquieted by the large wooden piece of furniture that stood in one of his grandfather's enormous rooms, and from which one could entice sounds simply by touching the white keys. Slowly little Ferruccio became familiar with the mysterious mechanism. One day, to his mother's astonishment, he was playing melodies by ear. She immediately reacted in the proper way by beginning to teach the boy, showing him fingering and making him practise scales. After a couple of months mother and son were playing four-handed exercises by Anton Diabelli. So at the very beginning of his career he was exposed to music that combined the traditions of both Italy and Austria, to a composer whom Beethoven has immortalized in one of his great works in variation form.

Trieste was a town of mixed races and cultures; cosmopolitan because of its position as a free-port, Italian in its language and culture, Austrian by nationality, Istrian in its hinterland and Slav in its population. The environmental influences of early childhood make a deep impression, help to form a person's character and way of thinking. Busoni's intellectual attitude, gravitating as it did between different nations and cultures, must surely be ascribed not only to dissimilar parents but also to the people and languages among which he spent the first years of his life.

Even his few years in Paris had left their mark; whenever the Frenchwomen stopped open-mouthed in the street to fondle the lovely child, Ferruccio would babble away in French. So later in Trieste he may well have picked up Slav words from his Slovenian and Croatian aunts and cousins.

His mother also taught this exceptionally intelligent child to read and write; his first letter to his father written entirely on his own is dated 11th August 1872. Here he tells him how he spent his day : after school a piano lesson, homework, and in the evening letter writing. As a reward for his diligence Ferruccio's mother presented him with Carl Czerny's exercises for the piano. In addition he was taught the violin.

In his autobiography Busoni describes the dramatic moment when they met his father quite by chance. It was during the 1872–73 season, and his mother had taken the child to a puppet theatre where the marionettes were operated mechanically without wires. Ferruccio was deeply impressed by a drinking scene during which the entire contents of a bottle of wine disappeared through the mouth of the little mechanical actor. On the way home a man with a large beard and high boots suddenly appeared in front of them with a well-trained poodle on a chain and looking every bit like a lion tamer. When the parents had greeted one another, the father took the child in his arms and with tears in his eyes stammered, 'Ferruccio!'

After this Ferdinando stayed in Trieste. The strenuous period during which he dedicated himself to teaching Ferruccio began in two rooms in the Via Geppa. No pianist himself and rhythmically unsure into the bargain, he forced the child to practise four hours a day without a break. Ferruccio later spoke of the quite indescribable energy of his sire, his strictness and pedantry, the sudden bursts of temper when he used to box his ears and shout at him till he brought tears to his eyes, only to reassure him once again how much he loved him. Barely a year after beginning this intense musical training the boy was so advanced that his parents allowed him to perform publicly in Trieste. The programme for this concert which took place on

24th November 1873 at the Schiller Society is described by Busoni's biographer Edward Dent. A week before his eighth birthday he made his second public appearance, playing two fugues by Handel, Schumann's *Knecht Ruprecht* and a work in variation form by Hummel. That same year he studied and played Mozart's Concerto in C minor, in his own view 'very precisely and with fine detail'.

In the autumn of 1875 Ferdinando took a bold step. He travelled to Vienna with the nine-year-old boy to introduce him to the great world of music in three roles: as pianist, composer, and improviser on themes provided by his audience. Busoni has described vividly how they stayed at the Hotel Erzherzog Carl, a meeting-place for all the most aristocratic and eminent people, where the young lad played for the great Anton Rubinstein. Ferdinando embarked on this Viennese adventure with very little money and no command of the German language and he frequently had to ask strangers for a couple of gulden to pay for the bare necessities. In actual fact Ferruccio was to have given his first concert soon after their arrival in Vienna. It eventually took place on 8th February 1876 and was a great success. Not only with the public but also with the demanding and influential Viennese critics. One of them called him the Tom Thumb of the musical world and a most enchanting miniature version of Liszt, Rubinstein and Brahms. The most important critic of the time, Eduard Hanslick, wrote an article on the child which appeared in the *Neue Freie Presse* on 13th February 1876. In this he said: 'It is a long time since an infant prodigy appealed to us as much as little Ferruccio Busoni. Precisely because there is so little of the infant prodigy about him and so much that suggests a good musician, not merely an inexperienced amateur but also a real composer. At the piano the child immediately shows a definite feeling for music; his playing is fresh and spontaneous, with the kind of musical awareness that is difficult to define but immediately recognizable: incapable of being confused by subjective emotions, always hitting on the right tempo and stresses, grasping the feel of the rhythm, clearly distinguish-

17

ing the different voices in a polyphonic movement, in short able to feel and shape a piece musically. He plays everything from memory with complete assurance, even ensemble pieces in several movements, such as Haydn Trios (in which Arthur Nikisch was violinist). The comportment of his body and hands is relaxed, easy and free; his touch is resonant even though there is not much strength behind it as yet, his technique correct. Consequently there is nothing puppet-like about his performance, it is not just something he has been taught; on the contrary the boy seems to find it all an amusing game and often looks quite openly at the audience instead of at the keys.' Hanslick then goes on to write about the six short original piano pieces which the child played : 'These reveal the same musical awareness which we enjoyed so much in his playing; not a sign of precocious sentimentality or contrived effect, just sheer pleasure in the play of notes, in lively figuration and little combinatorial techniques. Nothing operatic, not a trace of a dance rhythm, on the contrary a remarkable seriousness and maturity which suggests a devoted study of Bach.'

Hanslick's reference to Bach cannot fail to surprise anyone who is familiar with the period and its musical climate. The young Busoni had received his musical training in Trieste at the beginning of the 1870s. Apart from occasional violin lessons his parents had taught him themselves. Anna's repertoire as a pianist consisted of virtuoso pieces by Franz Liszt and Sigismund Thalberg and included piano concertos such as the one by Mozart in D minor and the one by Carl Maria von Weber in E flat major. In Paris she won acclaim for her chamber music rendering, a brilliant and lyrical performance of Schumann's Quintet in E flat. When teaching the child she used the current teaching manuals by Czerny and Diabelli. She had also received a thorough grounding in composition; one of her teachers was the cathedral choirmaster and organist, Luigi Ricci, who originally came from Naples although later settled in Prague. Yet it appears that Bach had no place either in her repertoire or in her extensive teaching activities. In fact it was Ferdinando who introduced the boy to Bach. A year before his own death Ferruccio Busoni wrote the epilogue to his Bach Edition, and here to our surprise we find a reference to this very point: 'I have my father to thank for my good fortune, because during my childhood he insisted on my studying Bach at a time and in a country that did not rank the master much higher than a Carl Czerny. My father was a simple virtuoso clarinettist who loved to play fantasias on *Il Trovatore* and the Venice Carnival; his musical training had been incomplete, he was an Italian and an admirer of the *bel canto*. How did such a man, ambitious on behalf of his son, happen to hit upon exactly the right thing? The only way I can explain it is as a mysterious revelation. Moreover, by this means he trained me to be a "German" musician and showed me a path that I have never entirely abandoned even though I always retained the Latin characteristics that were inherent in my nature.'

Incidentally, Hanslick's accurate assessment was not based exclusively on the six short compositions that Busoni performed. He also had the opportunity to admire the child's much-praised ability to improvise on a given theme. In his article Hanslick goes on to say: 'The pieces are all short, as befits a talent that is still only half-fledged, short but good; not so good however as to make one suspect the help of a master. I have no doubt whatsoever as to the authenticity of his compositions, especially since I myself gave the boy several motifs on the piano which he immediately worked out imaginatively in the same serious manner, mostly in an imitative and contrapuntal style.'

Seldom since Mozart, Beethoven and Liszt, has the creative and interpretive talent of a child musician won such authoritative support as this. Thus the months spent in Vienna laid the foundations of Ferruccio's future career. He also made personal and social contacts which in some cases lasted a lifetime. One of the most socially influential families in Vienna at the time was that of the philosopher Theodor Gomperz, a Brünner by birth, who had held the chair in classical philology at the university since 1873. His two sisters, Josephine von Wertheimstein

19

and Baroness Sophie Todesco, belonged to the moneyed aristocracy of Austria. They immediately took a liking to the little virtuoso and from the time they first met in Vienna in 1875 provided him with financial support. Ferruccio struck up a childhood friendship with Jella, Sophie Todesco's daughter, that was to last a lifetime. She later married and became Baroness Oppenheimer. Caroline Bettelheim, a famous singer in the past, was also related to the Gomperz family. In Vienna the Busonis not only attended concerts but also performances at the Royal Opera House. It was here that Ferruccio had his first introduction to Mozart's works for the stage which he immediately began to study with the help of piano arrangements. However the excitement and strain of the February concert seem to have been too much for the child. That same month, February 1876, Ferdinando took him back to Trieste where Ferruccio went on busily composing, and in addition to his musical studies continued with the German he had begun in Vienna.

It is one of the paradoxes of Busoni's early development that the urge to draw his attention to German music came entirely from his father, a straightforward typical Italian virtuoso whose brilliant musical skill was directed solely towards worldly success and whose way of life conformed with the popular image of the artist; whereas the Latin elements in his spiritual education were provided by his half-German mother whose literary taste revealed a marked preference for the French style. In Vienna Ferruccio had learnt to admire Mozart opera; in Trieste his mother took him to a performance of Verdi's *Rigoletto*. After seeing *Rigoletto* in Vienna in 1908 Busoni wrote to his wife in Berlin: 'I have only seen the opera once before, when I was very young, probably nine years old. I can still remember my mother telling me the story one evening in Via Geppa in Trieste (a version adapted for children). Even as an adult I have never forgotten the opening festal music, the whispered Abduction Chorus, and the sound of the wind raging conveyed by voices behind the wings.'

After a summer holiday in Gmunden the family, this time including the mother, returned to Vienna where Ferruccio heard

Franz Liszt play and was introduced to him. Although the boy was delicate and could not take the cold winters in Vienna, they returned to the imperial city once again after a second vacation in Gmunden carrying them over to the summer of 1878. There is a letter of introduction from Anton Rubinstein dating from this period, advising them to let the child quietly carry on with his studies and not force him to perform in public. October 1878 found them in Graz. There they finally found a teacher to whom they could entrust Ferruccio's training as a composer. After an introduction by the composer Wilhelm Kienzl, young Busoni was gladly accepted by Dr. Wilhelm Mayer who was writing music under the pseudonym W. A. Rémy. In 1898 Busoni wrote an obituary to Mayer-Rémy in which he said: 'The undersigned . . . remembers with gratitude and sorrow the immense pleasure that he derived from lessons with Mayer. With his witty and elegant delivery he knew how to hold the attention of his young pupils; his universal erudition enabled him to elucidate, embellish and bring to life points in music and the history of music by drawing upon the entire history of civilization, giving character sketches of the masters where relevant, and making his own highly personal remarks on the side, some factual, some in jest and some poetical . . . A deep love, an infinite respect, an unshakable faith, were the inspiration of his life . . . his admiration for the genius of Wolfgang Amadeus Mozart. Next in his esteem came Bach; he was inexhaustible in his continued analysis, elucidation and poetic interpretation of the preludes and fugues of *The Well-Tempered Clavier*.'

Mayer-Rémy was a stout apoplectic man of forty-five when Busoni first came to him at the beginning of 1880. He quickly recognized the thirteen-year-old boy's exceptional talents and expected him to be punctilious and thorough in following the course in composition. In fifteen months Busoni had covered work that would normally take two years. The instruction, which Busoni wrote down word for word, was unmistakably conservative. In his home town of Prague, Mayer-Rémy was a member of the Davidsbündler-Kreise, along with Eduard Hanslick and the musical historian A. W. Ambros. His own composition was influenced by Schumann; his teaching of counterpoint was based on Cherubini and of orchestration on Berlioz; but he was firmly opposed to Wagner. Appointed director of the Styrian Musical Society in Graz in 1862, he resigned from the post in 1870 just to go on composing and teaching. Of his pupils, Richard Heuberger, Emil Nikolaus von Reznicek and Felix Weingartner were outstandingly successful.

The Graz Opera House, from time immemorial one of the leading theatres in Austria, had the same sort of formative influence on young Busoni as it had on Luigi Dallapiccola thirty-six years later. Ushered into Graz with a Stabat Mater of his own composition before beginning his training with Mayer-Rémy, he bade farewell with a concert in March 1881. Besides Schumann's piano concerto and Beethoven's Sonata, Opus 111, the programme included three of his own works: a string quartet, a piano prelude and fugue and a setting of the sixty-seventh psalm for choir and orchestra. Then the little family embarked once more on a restless nomadic way of life, occasionally calling a halt at the grandfather's house in Trieste. Ferruccio had reached the difficult years of puberty. He was composing more than ever, began to draw with enthusiasm, and at the same time became conscious of his manhood, an experience which he described later in a letter to his wife written shortly before visiting Trent: 'I have the impression that I ought to enjoy being in Trent. I was there in my thirteenth year when we left Vienna and were travelling about from place to place like a fair . . . I also believe that I felt the first stirrings of manhood there, because a chambermaid in the hotel with bright red hair and pitch black eyes once let me kiss her, whereupon my mother said *non è bello* and this served to bring it home to me.'

Whether this little incident really occurred before the Graz period, or whether Busoni's memory may have deceived him, the fact that he mentions it in 1906 shows how deep an impression it made on him.

In March 1882 Ferruccio, who was already considered a young

genius in Northern Italy, met up with his father in Bologna. He gave five concerts in that beautiful old city and one day a most unusual honour was conferred on the fifteen-year-old boy. He was made a member of the Accademia Filarmonica, who awarded him a diploma for composition and piano. The family spent the summer near Empoli where a brother of Ferdinando's was a successful wine-merchant. There was an exhibition of musical instruments being held in Arezzo and during September Ferruccio spent three weeks playing the various instruments. In spite of all his activities and social life he found time to compose his cantata for solo voices, choir and orchestra, *Il Sabato del Villaggio*, based on the poem by Giacomo Leopardi, which was performed for the first time on 2nd March 1883 with Luigi Mancinelli conducting. The work which was much admired by Arrigo Boito, composer of *Mefistofele* and librettist of Verdi's *Otello* and *Falstaff*, has never been published; the manuscript was recovered and became the property of the West Berlin National Library in 1965.

In the autumn of 1883 Ferruccio Busoni, now a young man, came to Vienna. There he made new artistic and social contacts. In November, with a monthly allowance from Baroness Todesco, Ferruccio gave a concert the programme for which included works by Beethoven, Bach, Schumann, Chopin and Liszt, as well as his own chamber music. On the recommendation of Hanslick he had submitted the score of one of his own orchestral suites to the director of the Philharmonic Concerts, Hans Richter. Richter accepted the piece. But it was not until a year later, in October 1884, that the orchestra after playing it through once made use of its prerogative to take a vote on whether it should be accepted. The result was negative. Busoni was deeply upset by this unfortunate affair, particularly as on hearing the piece played he had been satisfied and felt that his intentions had been realized.

During this visit to Vienna, when he was accompanied once again by his dyspeptic father confined almost permanently to his hotel room, his taste in music also underwent a considerable

23

change. Just at that time he lost a good friend, the pianist Luigi Cimoso from Trieste, who died in a mental home. Busoni dedicated to him a piano arrangement of the Funeral March from Wagner's *Götterdämmerung*, which was published in Lucca in 1883. It was his first tribute to a composer who appeared to have had no influence whatsoever on his music up till then. Possibly it was Wagner's death in February 1883 that drew Busoni's attention to the 'teutonic giant' whose orchestral strains he continued to find overpowering even in his later years, almost as if for him his music overstepped the barriers of mortal existence.

The disappointment with the Philharmonic had embittered his life in Vienna. He wanted to move on, to get to know other towns and countries. In February 1885 he arrived in Leipzig accompanied by Ferdinando. Through Mendelssohn and the Conservatory that flourished under his direction this middle-class Saxon town had become a rather conservative musical centre. The most important and influential personality there was Carl Reinecke. Ferruccio had been recommended to him through a letter from Johannes Brahms. Apart from this, Arthur Nikisch, a friend he had known in the early days in Vienna, had meanwhile been promoted to the position of leading conductor at the enterprising opera-house. This former violinist, one of Hellmesberger's pupils who had played with Busoni on his first appearance in Vienna, had exchanged his bow for the baton and was on his way to becoming one of the internationally famous stars of the conductor's rostrum.

Busoni got off to a good start in Leipzig. His String Quartet, composed between 1880 and 1881, was performed by Henri Petri and his Quartet, and he struck up a friendship with the Dutch violinist which was later transferred to his son Egon, Busoni's oldest and most distinguished piano pupil. He went on a trip to Berlin with his father. He played at the Singakademie, took an immediate liking to the city, but for the time being returned to Leipzig.

For many years the Busonis had spent their summer holidays in the Styrian health resort of Frohnleiten. It was there in 1885 that Ferruccio began work on his first opera. After rejecting various other plans Busoni decided on a libretto, *Sigune oder das stille Dorf* and spent several years on the composition. He stayed on in Frohnleiten until November. Then one day Ferruccio suddenly decided to travel to Vienna; he stayed there a couple of days and finally took himself to Leipzig. He was running away from the family. He took lodgings in Zentralstrasse opposite the Thomaskirche, rejoiced in his new-found freedom and set about making his living.

Publishers were beginning to take an interest in him. Kahnt, Peters and others were eager to get hold of this promising young artist. Eventually his work was put almost exclusively in the hands of Breitkopf & Härtel. He got to know famous contemporaries such as Eduard Grieg and Peter Tschaikowsky, others who were not yet famous such as Frederick Delius, Gustav Mahler and Christian Sinding. Only one thing depressed him and that was his domestic loneliness, accustomed as he was to living with his parents or at least with one or other of them. On top of this it was a struggle to make ends meet, as his Viennese friends had grown tired of paying his father's everlasting debts and conse-quently suspended Ferruccio's allowance as well. During these months of lonely poverty Ferruccio obviously remembered the little poodle that had been Ferdinando's companion in Trieste. Before long a large black labrador was permitted to share his loneliness, the famous 'Lesko', who caused as great a stir with his Finnish pupils as his successor, the St. Bernard 'Giotto', did in Zürich twenty-five years later. He missed the friends he had known previously in Leipzig. Luigi Cimoso had died; Mayer-Rémy's daughter Melanie, whom he had always liked, was living in Graz. They exchanged letters in which he complained that as a precocious young artist he was not satisfied with the com-pany of his contemporaries, yet the older generation would have nothing to do with him.

Apart from the overwhelming musical impressions to which he was constantly submitted in Leipzig in spite of the overall provincial atmosphere of the town, he was affected by other

25

incidents and experiences too. Like most people with progressive ideas he went through the inevitable period of socialist opposition to anything bourgeois, spent his time with politically radical Russian students, dressed like a worker and made speeches about socialism. His concert activities continued and led to sensational successes, particularly in Hamburg in 1887, in Trieste and Graz at the beginning of 1888, as well as in the smaller central German towns of Leipzig, Dresden and Halle. Leading men in the piano industry such as Julius Blüthner and Theodore Steinway took an interest in the twenty-one year old composer and virtuoso, gave him financial help and organized his concerts. It was only because of Steinway's death that a plan, by which Busoni was apparently to have been launched as a star pianist in America, come to nothing. In April 1888 Busoni received an unexpected proposition from Hugo Riemann. The thirty-eight year old musicologist had qualified for a lectureship at Leipzig University in 1878, and in addition was teaching piano and theory at the Hamburg Conservatory. He was in very close contact with the younger generation of composers, was one of the leading reformers in the study and theory of music, and liked Busoni's versatile rebellious mind. The offer, which Busoni accepted, was of a post teaching piano at the Conservatory in Helsinki.

Owing to the influence of some of the younger musicians, the Finnish capital was just beginning to become artistically aware at that time. In 1882 the Helsingfors-Orkesterförening had been set up by the conductor Robert Kajanus and the Helsingfors-Musikinstitut had been established by Martin Wegelius. With the help of his society Kajanus financed and organized the Philharmonic Orchestra and in 1885 he founded a practical school of orchestra for the new generation of Finnish musicians. With the support of the older Finnish choirs, Kajanus was responsible for the first performance in Finland of Beethoven's Ninth Symphony in 1888. Jean Sibelius, born in 1865, was one of the pupils trained by Wegelius at his academy.

After a stormy sea voyage from Lübeck to Helsinki which took three days and three nights, Busoni reached the Nordic capital

26

with his labrador, Lesko. Wegelius met him at the port, and the friendship which he showed towards the lonely young Italian from the very first day helped him to overcome many of the problems of a strange environment. He had hoped that his mother might come and live with him in Helsinki, but in this he was disappointed; Anna first of all said 'yes', then decided to stay in Italy. His post at the Conservatory consisted of four hours a day teaching moderately gifted students, mostly young girls, to play Clementi and Cramer. His personality had a particular fascination in this northern setting, with the result that he was also invited into Finnish homes as a private tutor. Among his pupils was a Swede three years older than himself called Adolf Paul; he later turned to literature, edited letters and memoirs by August Strindberg and achieved considerable success, particularly in Germany, with his comedies *Hille Bobbe* and *Der Triumph der Pompadour*. Paul, who for many years lived in Berlin and died there in 1943, described Busoni's first appearance as successor to a German professor who used to place a glass of water on the back of his pupils' hands and insist that they played like that without spilling a single drop. 'After him came Busoni. A small slim Italian with light brown beard and bright grey eyes, amusing and enthusiastic, dressed in a long grey tail-coat and a close-fitting travelling cap; always accompanied by a huge dog, Lesko, who used to lie on the rostrum next to the piano during lessons staring at us with big stern eyes, so that we were very careful not to play any wrong notes.'

Paul describes Busoni's Homeric laughter whenever he thought about his predecessor's glasses of water. He also speaks of his respect for the slightly younger professor who once outside the Conservatory joined in all sorts of crazy escapades.

In the middle of November Busoni, whose Italian origins had already roused considerable interest among the young Finnish girls of liberal upbringing, attended one of the popular concerts organized by Robert Kajanus. He was seen there by Gerda Sjöstrand, daughter of the Swedish sculptor Carl Aeneas Sjöstrand, a young pianist who did some teaching herself and would have liked to continue studying with Busoni. She was immediately impressed by the 'handsome young man with his short fair beard and mop of curly hair'. She met him again on various other occasions, such as just before Christmas at a concert given by Liszt's pupil Bernhard Stavenhagen, but did not have any opportunity of getting to know him better. Later she wrote : 'I can still see him running lightly down the stairs, as if he were on springs.' Then Busoni travelled back to Leipzig with Stavenhagen for the winter holidays. He had trouble with Petri who insisted against his wishes on introducing him to old Joseph Joachim and refused to share his interest in the compositions of young Richard Strauss. However the strained relations did not prevent his taking a piece of advice from Frau Kathi Petri. At an organ recital in the Thomaskirche she suggested to him that he should do a piano arrangement of Bach's Prelude and Fugue in D major. So began his lifelong interest in arranging and editing Bach's work.

He played the Prelude in D major and Fugue at a concert in Hamburg in January 1889. Soon after he returned to his post in Helsinki. On 18th March he attended a charity banquet where they were entertained with *tableaux vivants*. One of his students, Edvard Fazer, later a concert agent and then founder and director of the Finnish Opera in Helsinki, brought Gerda Sjöstrand over to Busoni's table where Fazer's sister Naema was already sitting. Later they were joined by Gerda's younger sister Helmi. The five of them spent the evening drinking champagne and on the way home Gerda was in such high spirits that she threw her galoshes into the air and sat down in the snow. Two days later Busoni called on father Sjöstrand and invited him and his two daughters to a recital. The performance which was an enormous success included works by Bach, Beethoven and Chopin and Liszt's *Venezia e Napoli*; Busoni never took his eyes off Gerda the whole time he was playing. In a couple of days' time Fazer and Busoni invited the young girl to dine in the best hotel in town. After the meal Fazer left the two of them alone for a short while and Busoni immediately rose to his feet and said : 'Will you be my wife?' and kissed Gerda. Next morning when Busoni asked father Sjöstrand for his daughter's hand in marriage, he gave his consent at once. There followed a period of blissful happiness; Busoni called on the Sjöstrands every day and Gerda usually picked him up from the Conservatory. One day a large box was delivered at the house. It was Busoni's engagement present: the big Brockhaus Encyclopaedia. This was Gerda's reaction: 'The nice thing about it was that Ferruccio very much wanted the encyclopaedia himself—he knew that I never wore jewellery.'

During that Finnish spring of 1889 a relationship remarkable for its closeness began to develop. Gerda was a woman of angelic disposition and there were no limits to the understanding she showed towards the man she loved who did not always make life easy for his companion.

After the end of term in June Busoni travelled to Weimar where Stavenhagen had a master-class. The only pupil from the Conservatory to follow him was Adolf Paul who has described this interlude in Weimar: 'The townspeople protected themselves as best they could against all this music and secured a police order which still holds good against playing the piano with the windows open, to which I immediately fell victim . . .' Busoni took lodgings in an outlying part of the town, in the house of Liszt's former cook in Schröterstrasse . . . During the course of the summer Busoni's parents arrived from Trieste. His mother, a slim gaunt lady with thick grey curly hair, was an exceptional pianist. From her Busoni not only inherited his beautiful hands but also received his basic training as an instrumentalist. His father . . . was a small jovial man with a Garibaldi beard, very temperamental. He could not stand German beer, German wine or German music. He protected himself against German beer by not drinking it. As a precaution against German wine, he carried round with him in a black leather bag a large supply of flat bottles filled with home-grown Italian red wine from which he obtained his daily quota of spiritual refreshment. His hostility to German music took the form of disputes with his son.

29

He would passionately maintain the superiority of Italian music over German, and in particular that of Verdi over Wagner, whom his son happened to admire intensely at the time. The issue was never resolved. Before a decisive battle could be fought, the Italian wine ran out. Old Busoni rushed back home to avoid dying of thirst and abandoned the field of battle, not of course conceding victory to his son and Wagner.'

From Weimar Busoni wrote daily to Gerda in Helsinki. At the beginning of August he travelled back just to be with her for five days. When he returned to his teaching post at the beginning of September he was accompanied by his mother. This was not easy for Gerda : 'His mother reminded me of one of the witches in *Macbeth*, with her grey hair, large nose and several warts. Although in fact there was nothing witch-like about her; she was a kind, distinguished and intelligent woman. She loved her son so much, that compared with this nothing else mattered. She simply could not bear the thought of having to lose this son through marriage.'

When Busoni asked her how she liked Gerda, his mother replied : 'Her hair is not as carefully styled as that of the girls at home.'

Ferruccio spent the Christmas holidays in Germany, and at a concert held at the Gewandhaus in Leipzig he was soloist in his own *Konzertstück* for piano and orchestra, Opus 31a. During this period Gerda visited her mother-in-law every day without managing to break the ice. 'When one has parents,' Anna told her, 'one should think of them and not about starting a family of one's own.' So Gerda tried to break off the engagement; whereupon Busoni, who by this time had returned, retorted : 'If you leave me, I shall lose all my strength.' Unfortunately he had inherited from his mother the jealousy that was so frequently and unjustly a source of torment to Gerda.

The Helsinki period was almost over. Busoni was recommended by Anton Rubinstein for a professorship at the Imperial Conservatory in Moscow. Before taking up his post there in September he was awarded the much sought-after Rubinstein prize for composition in St. Petersburg. Busoni did not feel comfortable in Russia; even later, in spite of his enormous admiration for men such as Dostoyevsky and Tolstoy, he always had tremendous reservations about all things Russian. The only Russian pieces that he played, and those very seldom, were the piano concerto by Sergius Liapunow; studies, variations, and two piano concertos by Rubinstein; and Tchaikowsky's Concerto in B flat minor. During a short trip which he made to Helsinki from St. Petersburg the wedding was arranged. The five thousand francs from the Rubinstein prize had removed a great burden from his shoulders. He could now pay off his father who was once again deep in debt and sending him pathetic letters from Görz, and rent an apartment for his parents in Trieste.

After spending two nights travelling Gerda arrived in Moscow on 27th September with her father, sister, and Busoni's dog. Ferruccio urged them to hurry, as the evangelical minister who had agreed to marry the young couple was going away on holiday that same morning. The wedding-dress stayed in the suitcase and Gerda became Frau Busoni wearing an old skirt and a red knitted jersey.

During their very first weeks Busoni realized that he would not be able to stay in Moscow long. He found the city alien, and apart from his friendship with Alexander Siloti he met with nothing but jealousy and ill-feeling at the Conservatory. So he accepted the Steinways' invitation to teach at the New England Conservatory in Boston. The young couple reached America at the beginning of September 1891. But the Boston post also proved disappointing, so after a year Busoni resigned. In May 1892 Gerda presented him with a son who was christened Benvenuto and today still lives a solitary life in Berlin.

Busoni's first contact with America had destroyed a number of illusions. He soon decided to return to Europe. Even New York where the little family had moved in the summer of 1892 and certainly felt happier than in the more conservative atmosphere of Boston could not hold him for long. It was only during later concert tours that he discovered another America whose ambivalence found expression in two distinct phenomena : Dr. Thaddäus Cahill's 'Dynamophone', a forerunner of the modern electronic organ; and the contrapuntal experimentation of Bernhard Ziehn and Wilhelm Middelschulte, the so-called 'Gothics of Chicago'.

Busoni was already in America when Bach's Inventions appeared in his edition. His transcriptions of works by Bach, such as the Organ Prelude with Fugue in D major which he had played frequently since 1888, and the Chaconne originally composed as a violin solo which appeared on the programme of a concert in Boston in 1893, were something quite different. His own compositions at this time included more than thirty numbered pieces, among them two string quartets, the *Konzertstück* for piano and orchestra, a symphonic orchestral suite, a sonata for violin and piano, and a work in variation form for cello and piano based on a Finnish folk-song *Kultaselle*.

The long concert tours in the United States undoubtedly brought him fame and material success, but so little artistic satisfaction that he became increasingly sceptical and self-critical until one day he rejected everything that he had accomplished so far. The crisis occurred in 1893, and seventeen years later he himself wrote of it : 'It was round about that time in my life when I had become so aware of imperfections and mistakes in my own playing that I firmly resolved to begin studying the piano all over again on an entirely new basis. I took the works of Liszt as my guide and from them I learnt a great deal about the finer points of his particular style. I based my "technique" on his "idiom". My gratitude and admiration for Liszt at that period made him my friend and master.'

It was Wegelius in Helsinki who had specifically drawn his attention to Liszt's music. True, Busoni was already playing the *Eroica* Study in 1881 and the complete *Venezia e Napoli* cycle in 1883, but without realizing the significance of Liszt. All this changed completely with the New York crisis. In 1900 Busoni wrote : 'Truly, in piano music, Bach is the Alpha and Liszt the Omega.'

1 Ferruccio Busoni, aged ten, at Gmunden

2 Busoni at the beginning of the century

Round about this period Busoni not only began to reconsider the fundamental basis of his piano playing and the artistic phenomenon of Franz Liszt; he re-examined his whole spiritual existence. He soon noticed that his external conditions also needed looking into. His escape from the family had on the face of it given him his freedom, but had done nothing to change the nomadic way of life to which his restless father had accustomed him. He was looking for a spiritual centre of gravity in order to settle down. He found it in the German Imperial capital.

When in 1894 the Busonis moved into their first home in Berlin, 153 Kantstrasse, the city was becoming increasingly important both economically and socially; not only as the residence of a young and ambitious Kaiser, but also because artists and intellectuals liked it for its fresh intellectual climate. With its theatres and concerts, its encouragement of the visual arts, it was beginning to compete more and more successfully with the older cultural centres of Germany. A number of representative buildings had sprung up in the Kaiser Wilhelm style, or were in the process of being built, such as the Reichstag building by Wallot, the Cathedral and the Kaiser Wilhelm memorial chapel. In 1889 Otto Brahm had founded the Freie Bühne together with its journal and in 1894 he opened the Deutsches Theater, where the modern dramatists Henrik Ibsen and Gerhart Hauptmann were given the opportunities so vital to their development. Young Max Liebermann was exhibiting his controversial paintings; and it was from among his followers that the Berlin Secession was to emerge a couple of years later. Arthur Nikisch had recently been engaged as chief conductor of the Philharmonic Orchestra at the Royal Opera House *Unter den Linden*, Felix Weingartner was conducting the symphony concerts, Dr. Carl Muck the operas, and Richard Strauss was just embarking on his activities as choirmaster. All these things must have attracted Busoni who always took a lively interest in the intellectual and artistic developments of the time. His own intellectual position was identical to that of the city itself, torn between old European traditions on the one hand and modern forward-looking ideas on the other. Berlin had fascinated him when he first went there in 1885; later when he paid it a brief visit on his way from Weimar to Helsinki in August 1889 he had admittedly been very disappointed. Once he had settled there he was spellbound by the cool charm of the city. He remained faithful to it until his death in 1924, which is to say a good thirty years, even though the war forced him to live in exile in Zürich for years. His first students in Berlin included the American, Augusta Cottlow, and the New York born Pole, Michael von Zadora.

In 1895 he embarked on an extensive series of concerts in Europe—Hermann Wolff, the concert agent, being largely responsible for their management. In June the Busonis moved from Kantstrasse into a larger apartment, 10a Tauentzienstrasse, where, incidentally, their second son Raffaello was born. Busoni had so arranged his life that he always began his long summer recess on 1st May; this was devoted to his own creative work and to teaching a large number of specially chosen pupils. The only way to appreciate the variety and richness of his output during those years is to consider the long list of major compositions dating from the same period : the Symphonic Tone Poem for Orchestra, the Four Ballet Sequences in the form of a concert waltz, the *Lustspiel* Overture, Opus 38, the Violin Concerto, the Second Sonata for Violin and Piano, the first part of the *Well-Tempered Clavier* in the Bach Edition, and a number of less important literary studies.

In 1900 and 1901, at the invitation of the Grandduke Carl Alexander, Busoni held master-classes for pianists in Weimar. Young Leo Kestenberg, whose artistic development had already been profoundly influenced by a concert of Busoni's in 1898, 'the turning-point in my life,' was one of those selected. The circle that assembled round the thirty-four year old Busoni included young people of all nationalities, Etelka Freund, Irene Schafsberg, Frieda Kindler, Selim Palmgren from Finland, Emil R. Blanchet from Switzerland, Theodor Szanto and Eduard van Doorn. They performed officially for the Master twice a week in the Tempelherrenhaus; besides this he used to meet his pupils almost every day. After they had played there would be a discussion between teacher and students, Busoni being mainly concerned with analysing the pieces. Incidentally, even then he refused to accept payment for private tuition. To him money was of such secondary importance that nobody was ever allowed to mention it. Kestenberg's description of this period is wonderfully enthusiastic : 'After our classes we would all go off with Busoni, singing and shouting . . . through the streets of the little town, and we usually ended up in one of the big public houses. On our way home late at night we would serenade each other, take turns in accompanying one another, and this naturally made a noise which was by no means popular in this quiet genteel town and occasionally even brought out the police. But we were all young, high-spirited and innocent, and Busoni took the lead in all our escapades. Before long I was getting on particularly well with Busoni and had the privilege of being allowed to visit him in the mornings—his classes were always held in the afternoon—and to help him with all the correspondence he was obliged to answer . . . During that time he was writing his Second Violin Sonata, still as vital and impressive even today, with its splendid well-known variations on Bach's Chorale, *Wie wohl ist mir, o Freund der Seelen, wenn ich in deiner Liebe ruh.*' In the summer of 1901 the Weimar course was repeated; among the new pupils were Egon Petri, the son of his Leipzig friend, and Maud Allan who later became a dancer; and from the previous group H. W. Draber from Switzerland, who has described the Weimar days with as much enthusiasm as Kestenberg : 'It was almost always the work of art as a whole, and subsequently its internal construction, that we discussed. Yet when Busoni sat down and played, every one of us realized how much he still had to learn in the way of technique, to be able to give a complete interpretation without making any slips . . . Strictly speaking, the teaching was virtually continuous because Busoni's hospitable house was open to his pupils at tea-time almost every afternoon.'

In 1902 Busoni embarked on a cycle of concerts with the Berlin Philharmonic Orchestra held in the Beethovensaal in Berlin, which was to continue until January 1909. He himself appeared as conductor, and occasionally as pianist too. However, the most significant aspect of the twelve evenings was the nature of the programmes. They contained almost exclusively contemporary music or else older pieces that were seldom performed. Thus in the first concert held on 8th November 1902 there were first performances of works by Edward Elgar, Guy Ropartz, Camille Saint-Saëns and Christian Sinding, together with violin pieces by Tartini and Corelli played by the Belgian violinist César Thomson. The second concert took place a week later, with Jean Sibelius conducting the first performance in Germany of his symphonic poem *En Saga*, the pianist and composer Théophile Ysaye (brother of the better known violinist Eugène) playing his own piano concerto, and Busoni conducting pieces by Eduard von Mihalovich and Frederick Delius, and Liszt's second *Mephisto Waltz*.

The programme for the only concert to be given in 1903 on 5th November (a second was cancelled) consisted of the first performances in Berlin of a number of French works. The symphonic overture to Vincent d'Indy's *L'Etranger* was followed by Claude Debussy's *Prélude à l'après-midi d'un Faune*, Berlioz' March from *The Trojans* and César Franck's *Les Djinns*, in which the piano part was played by Busoni's friend, the Portuguese pianist José Vianna da Motta, who was living in Berlin. New to Germany was Carl Nielsen's *The Four Temperaments*. The final item in the programme was a curiosity: the *Syrian Dances* by the Viennese musicologist and composer, Heinrich Schenker, orchestrated by Arnold Schoenberg.

Schoenberg had moved to Berlin in 1901 with his wife Mathilde, née von Zemlinsky, and was working as choral director at Ernst von Wolzogen's Buntes Theater. At that time Busoni had not yet met him. In July 1903 the Schoenbergs left Berlin again and it was not until September, which is to say two months before the concert in question, that Busoni got to know the already famous and controversial Viennese musician who was introduced to him by Schenker.

In 1904 Busoni visited America again. In March he embarked on a concert tour which began in Boston and finished up in Rochester, sending almost daily reports to his wife who had stayed behind in Berlin. He was less interested in the success and the laurels he gained in New York than in the works of art that filled the Gardners' house where he was staying as a guest, and which included Titian's *Rape of Europa*. In Chicago he went to *Die Walküre* and was disappointed by the music that had once captivated him, although he admired the performance of Felix Mottl. When the *Blücher* set sail in brilliant sunshine on 27th March, he was moved to tears by the sentimental German song that the band played and the view of New York with the Statue of Liberty. He had the feeling of turning his back on a period of his life, and at the same time anticipated the pleasure of rediscovering everything that was dear to him. During the voyage he read Stevenson's *Strange Case of Dr. Jekyll and Mr. Hyde*, also the score of Richard Strauss's *Symphonia Domestica* which he thought looked like the streets of New York. On 1st April he celebrated his thirty-eighth birthday on board and the following day disappointed his fellow passengers by refusing to play the piano. The voyage, which taxed his patience to breaking-point, ended in Cuxhaven.

On 10th November the cycle of concerts was resumed. The programme opened with the overture to Mozart's *Entführung* to which Busoni had added a concert ending, including a piece for strings by the Hungarian Ottokar Nováček who had died in his youth, and presented as its major work the first performance of Busoni's Concerto for piano, orchestra and male choir, Opus 39. Carl Muck conducted; the composer, who to the surprise of his audience was beardless, was at the piano. After his long silence, this major work proved that he had taken a fresh and closer look at artistic problems. It is composed symphonically in five parts, and at the first performance the audience were particularly confused by the last movement which Busoni calls 'Cantico'. Following the tradition of Beethoven's Ninth Symphony, the choir delivers the final word. Busoni uses a poem by the Dane,

Adam Gottlob Oehlenschläger, whose position in nineteenth-century Danish literature is that of a classical pantheist, harking back to Shakespeare, Goethe and Schiller. The predominantly negative reaction to this work, which he considered to be one of his most important pieces, made Busoni aware for the first time of what he called 'misunderstanding'. His performance as a pianist was praised, his creative effort despised. This did not prevent him from putting on a fifth concert on 1st December, in which he gave a now forgotten Czech composer, Rudolf Nováček, the opportunity to conduct a Sinfonietta for eight wind instruments; while he himself conducted César Franck's *Chasseur Maudit* and the first performance of Debussy's first and second Nocturnes (*Nuages* and *Fêtes*), and in conclusion presented the very first performance of his own *Geharnischte Suite* which although composed in 1895 was revised in 1903 and still bears the original dedication : 'To Lesko's four friends in Helsinki.' These were Jean Sibelius, Adolf Paul and the brothers Armas and Eero Jaernefeldt.

Among the people whom Busoni got to know outside the musical world was the author Jakob Wassermann whom he met in 1904. He was a friend of Hugo von Hofmannsthal, and in 1921 dedicated to his friend Busoni his tragically prophetic book, *Mein Weg als Deutscher und Jude*. In 1925, in his fine publication, *In memoriam Ferruccio Busoni*, he describes his first impression of the man : 'When I first met Busoni he was thirty-eight; an astonishingly good-looking man, very well-groomed, very spoilt, universally acclaimed, surrounded by an aura of adoring pupils, admirers and hangers-on, yet still unmistakably a virtuoso (even a typical virtuoso) with all the characteristics of hard-won skill; extremely energetic, nervous, intense, intellectually enthusiastic, but everything in embryo form still prior to the moment of self-awareness and the development of a specific personality.' During the course of the eighteen years that he knew Busoni, Wassermann maintains that he 'witnessed the most extraordinary inner growth . . . nothing short of a total transformation from which there emerged a valid and representative-type personality; a composite character; the final product of an era, and the first to represent a new one.'

Another witness from the literary world, Stefan Zweig, has described the change in Busoni's appearance once he shaved off his beard. From the numerous photographs of him that have been preserved from childhood onwards, we know that towards the end of the 'eighties he sported a closely trimmed beard, a symbol of the independence he had achieved in escaping from the watchful eye of his parents. During the Weimar piano course we see him surrounded by his many students, both young men and women, and by this time his beard is longer and well cared-for and he is wearing a nonchalant Lavallière cravat. 'For a long time,' writes Stefan Zweig, 'his actual face was hidden behind the dark cloud of his beard.' In 1904 the mask fell. From then on the noble European face, with its questioning eyes, powerful nose and sensual mouth, was unashamedly exposed.

The year 1905 began with rehearsals for the sixth orchestral concert of contemporary music. This time Busoni himself stepped into the background both as conductor and composer. He had simply prepared the Philharmonic Orchestra for the three guest artists who were to interpret their own work in Berlin on 12th January. The first item on the programme was Albéric Magnard's Third Symphony. The composer, about the same age as Busoni himself, was closely connected with the Vincent d'Indy group and musically under the influence of both Wagner and the archaistic Schola Cantorum in Paris. In 1914 he was killed by German soldiers while trying to prevent them from entering his house. The second person to take up the baton was Hans Pfitzner who conducted his Scherzo in C minor, a work dating from 1887. The programme ended with Jean Sibelius' Second Symphony, the most successful piece of the evening. There were fewer concerts than usual that year; no American tour, just the routine concerts in London, and in May a trip to Spain with Gerda, but not for professional reasons. Busoni was one of the greatest admirers of Cervantes, who was eventually represented in his own library by no less than 176 volumes in seven languages.

In May 1905 Madrid was celebrating the three-hundredth anniversary of the author of *Don Quixote* and the Busonis took an active part in the celebrations.

From the creative point of view it was the year of Gozzi's *Turandot* which Busoni wanted to use first as the basis of a concert work and then as an opera. The work went through various different stages, was taken up again in 1911 at the suggestion of Max Reinhardt as theatre music, and finally completed as a two act opera in 1917. The Busonis had moved into their third home in Berlin, 55 Augsburger Strasse, in 1902. From there Busoni wrote numerous letters to Gerda who was spending the summer of 1905 in Sweden, most of them telling her about his work on *Turandot*. He was in a good working frame of mind, was sleeping like a child, and every morning would set about enriching his 'charming Chinese tyrant'. He was enjoying the fine July weather, but found the apartment at the back of the house looking onto the courtyard rather gloomy. He was also alarmed by the thought of approaching forty. He was having some trouble with the Berlin Philharmonic who only wanted to give him two rehearsals for his seventh concert in October. He insisted on his rights and got them. On 21st October his own *Turandot* Suite was performed for the first time as the final item of a rather ill-assorted programme in the Philharmonic cycle. This included Gabriel Pierné's orchestral arrangement of the Prelude together with Chorale and Fugue of César Franck, a piano concerto by Otto Singer conducted by the composer with José Vianna da Motta as soloist, and the first performance in Germany of Berlioz' *Les Nuits d'Eté* sung by the Finnish singer Ida Ekman.

The year 1906 was also devoted to further work on *Turandot* and the libretto was completed in the summer. On 18th January he had directed the eighth of his concerts in the Singakademie. The programme included works by Rimsky-Korssakow, Vincent d'Indy, Eugène Ysaye, Eduard Böhm and Louis F. Delune, as well as Hans Hermann Wetzler's orchestration of Bach's E major Organ Sonata. At the beginning of February Gerda was summoned to her father's death-bed; Busoni wrote grief-stricken letters to her in Stockholm. At the beginning of March he had the pleasure of revisiting Trieste, which he found fascinating, the association with his parents reminding him of his childhood. He discovered in the publisher Schmiedl a courageous man who was prepared to print his revolutionary *Outline for a New Musical Aesthetics*. Gerda spent this summer too away from Berlin, first at Schloss Habrovan in Moravia which belonged to the singer Caroline Bettelheim, sister-in-law of Busoni's friend in Vienna, the fatherly Theodor Gomperz. Meanwhile a new operatic project was under way, based on a novella by another of Busoni's favourite writers, E. T. A. Hoffmann; this was *Die Brautwahl*. Gerda travelled to Alt-Aussee, Ferruccio to Trent where once again he read a lot of Italian, became very interested in Verdi's *A Masked Ball*, and was so delighted with Tirso de Molina's *Don Juan* that he proposed to write special music for it and offer the piece to Reinhardt. At the beginning of October he gave two concerts in Amsterdam, then hurried back to Berlin where the ninth orchestral concert was held on 8th November: the Symphony in B flat major and *Symphony on a French Mountain Air* by Vincent d'Indy, the first movement of Beethoven's Piano Concerto in C minor with Alkan's cadenza, and Gabriel Fauré's Orchestral Suite *Pelléas and Mélisande*. D'Indy conducted his own piano concerto; the soloist was not Busoni, but Rudolph Ganz.

Living in Berlin since 1905 was thirty-one year old Serge Koussevitzky who had just married Natalie Uschkowa, the daughter of a rich Moscow tea merchant. Koussevitzky had played the double-bass with the Moscow Imperial Orchestra; his virtuoso handling of this unusual concert instrument had been enthusiastically received in Germany in 1903, and he and his wife ran a large house in Berlin until 1909. Fedor Chaliapin, Fritz Kreisler, Arthur Nikisch, Leopold Godowsky and many other famous artists used to visit them. Soon the Busonis also joined these hospitable Russians' circle of friends. Koussevitzky's career as a conductor began when he conducted a programme of Russian music at one of the Philharmonic concerts on 23rd January 1908. In 1909, with a capital of one million marks he founded the Russian Music Publishers, and Alexander Skriabin was the first artist on their books.

During his visits to London Busoni had become very friendly with the Cambridge musicologist, Edward Dent. He soon became a regular guest in Berlin, enjoyed drinking his favourite Mosel wine in a public-house in Motzstrasse, and was later to become Busoni's biographer.

He also had an increasing number of pupils. Egon Petri, his keenest and most gifted performer, had arrived from Leipzig; in 1904 Leo Kestenberg settled permanently in the capital in order to work with Busoni.

After a short visit to Trieste and a stormy crossing, Busoni spent December 1906 in the British Isles, in Scotland in particular. He worked on a libretto *Der mächtige Zauberer* based on a novella by Gobineau; gave concerts with the violinist Sarasate; practised the 24 Chopin Preludes; and considered the invitation he had received to hold a master-class at the Conservatory in Vienna.

On 11th January 1907 the tenth orchestral concert was held; it opened with Busoni's *Lustspiel* Overture composed in 1904 and finished with Liszt's two *Episodes from Lenau's Faust*. In between these two pieces Hermann Behr and the Dutchman Johan Wagenaar conducted their own works, and Busoni conducted the first performance of a fantasia for violin and orchestra by Hugo Kaun with Michael Press as soloist.

A varied and productive year had begun. March brought concerts in Marseilles and Munich, and in between strenuous recording sessions for Welte-Mignon-Klavier in Freiburg. The *Brautwahl* was beginning to take shape. A series of articles were written for various Berlin periodicals : one on Strauss's *Salome*; one on playing from memory; another on the theme : 'How I compose.' Six pieces were ready to be published in the Bach Edition; among the Bach arrangements, the first volume of Chorale-Preludes for Organ and the Chaconne for violin, which was dedicated to Eugen d'Albert, all made their appearance that year. In Trieste, Schmiedl had followed up the publication of his *Outline for a New Musical Aesthetics* with *Der mächtige Zauberer*.

Busoni found it comparatively easy to work in his Berlin apartment, particularly as Gerda was often away. At the beginning of August he played in the elegant seaside resort of Norderney, then went straight on to Weimar where the complete Liszt edition was prepared. September brought him to England where he took part in a music festival at Cardiff, was enchanted by the city of Bath, and met Egon Petri and his wife in Manchester. He read with amusement and interest Thomas de Quincey's *On Murder as a Fine Art*.

Meanwhile the Viennese project had materialized. After a preliminary conference in September, he began work with the master-class a month later. Busoni was disappointed in the majority of the students taking part. But there was some real talent among them, such as Leo Sirota, Gregor Beklemishew, Vera Maurina-Press and the American girl, Georgine Nelson. Compared with Berlin Vienna seemed provincial. It was only in the Viennese studios, at literary gatherings, or in the company of Gustav Klimt that he felt really at ease. His apartment in the Schottenhof reminded him of Liszt, for whom he had played as a boy.

At the beginning of December he completed his Elegies for piano, and soon after began orchestrating the 104th Petrarch Sonnet by Liszt. The two versions of his cadenza to Mozart's D minor Concerto were also written in Vienna and dedicated to Richard Faltin.

'I think it is a good thing to have rounded off my present work with the sonnet, and I have sent you the finished manuscript just today,' he writes in a letter to Gerda dated 17th December. 'I am almost painfully exhausted—but also very pleased with the results of this most productive year, 1907 . . .'

Over and over again people tried to pin Busoni down to permanent academic teaching posts. The news of his master-class at the Vienna Conservatory was an encouragement because up till then Busoni had rebuffed any advances made in this direction. In the spring of 1907 Hans Huber, the director of the Allgemeine Musikschule in Basle, approached him about a master-class. Busoni greatly admired Huber both as a composer and teacher, and was in close contact with him during his years of exile in Switzerland. Nevertheless he refused; but he did at the same time suggest 'several splendid young men', including the 'distinguished and highly cultured' Waldemar Lütschg, the 'brilliant and audacious pianist' Michael von Zadora ('a "gentleman" too, but rather nervous with no real authority'), Theodor Szanto and Egon Petri ('the most genuine of all my pupils'). He also mentioned Bruno Mugellini, Alberto Fano, Johann Wijsman, Alfredo Casella (whom he could only recommend by hearsay) and finally Rudolph Ganz.

Immediately after New Year's Day 1908 he was preparing a concert in Berlin. The eleventh programme in the cycle of contemporary music was performed by the Philharmonic Orchestra on 3rd January. There were three pieces by Liszt including the Petrarch Sonnet *Pace non trovo* orchestrated by Busoni; the symphonic fantasia *Pohjola's Daughter* by Jean Sibelius; a bacchanal from the Harald Symphony by Paul Ertel, a former pupil of Liszt; besides Busoni's own Violin Concerto of 1899 with Emile Sauret. Shortly afterwards Busoni conducted an evening recital at the Singakademie where Leo Kestenberg played both Liszt's piano concertos and his *Dance of Death*.

But by the middle of January he had already resumed work in Vienna. Busoni writes to Gerda about it, but is continually digressing. He mentions the edition of Ibsen that she has just given him and maintains that *John Gabriel Borkmann* is Ibsen's greatest work. He is more interested in the successful flights of the Wright brothers in their flying machines than in his own concert held in the Grosser Musikvereinsaal. He is seeing a great deal of August Göllerich, Bruckner's biographer; and after the concert Franz Schalk, Dr. Hugo Botstiber (secretary to the Society for the Friends of Music), Heinrich Schenker and Gottfried Galston. He sends an article on Gerhart Hauptmann from the *Neue Wiener Tagblatt* to the poet.

But in private tensions were developing between him and the Conservatory. Busoni had a contract which tied him down not to specific days but to a total of 280 hours' teaching per annum. In February he informed them through his secretary that he would have to call off his second piano recital in Vienna as he had been taken ill in Paris; that he would not be able to teach regularly in Vienna until the period 21st April–July, and in the meantime could only make occasional visits. The result was that on 14th February he was dismissed for repeatedly failing to observe the timetable. His case was immediately taken up by the press, particularly in Berlin, where Busoni defended his position in the *Börsen-Courier*. On 3rd March he sent word from London that he wished to make his peace, at the same time protesting against the publication of a 'thoroughly premature decision' and the nomination of a successor. The telegram that he received from Vienna was negative.

The incident occupies very little space in his letters to Gerda. He was more concerned with his work on *Die Brautwahl*: 'I spent the week selecting notes for my betrothed : a good week!', he writes on 15th April. Even the Liszt edition was going ahead smoothly. In May he was working with greater ease than ever before; and after seeing a performance of *Rigoletto*, seriously considered the possibility of writing an Italian opera himself and abandoning his other projects based on material by Gustav Meyrink, Shaw and Gobineau. During a lightning visit to Leipzig he devoted six strenuous hours to a recording session with Phonola. In July he was once again up to his neck in *Die Brautwahl*, comparing Mozart's rapid rate of progress with the plodding pace of Flaubert whose *St. Antoine* he happened to be reading. He seldom mentions his male students, the girls not at all, even though Georgine Nelson had supported him most fervently in the master-class episode. His pupils included the American, L. T. Gruenberg, and Louis Closson, a Belgian.

In the autumn there were concert trips, one to Verona and

Milan where he made sarcastic observations about Italian women, another in November to England. In Manchester he met the elderly Hans Richter and the violinist, Jan Kubelik, and was delighted to hear from Cosima Wagner. He was interested in the possibility of using Leonardo da Vinci as the subject of an opera. He read the biographies by Vasari and Mereschkowsky, and for relaxation Anatole France's *Ile des Pingouins*.

Beside his operatic work, he also wrote his concert ending to Mozart's *Don Giovanni* Overture. On the literary side, a short scene entitled *From the classical Witches' Sabbath* appeared at the beginning of the year in the magazine *Die Musik*, written as a Shrovetide joke under the transparent pseudonym 'Ino-Sub-F'.

On 2nd January 1909 Busoni mounted the rostrum to conduct the Philharmonic Orchestra in the last of his twelve programmes of contemporary or rarely performed music. Apart from Liszt, César Franck, Mozart's *Don Giovanni* Overture (concert ending by Busoni) and an orchestrated Rondo for Violin by Schubert, the astonished Berliners also heard a scherzo from a Suite by the young Hungarian, Béla Bartók, who conducted his own piece. The twelve concerts had received predominantly hostile criticism, and the reaction to Bartók was also one of disgust. Busoni took sole responsibility for these concerts, both from the ethical and financial point of view. Kestenberg maintains that almost all the audience had free tickets. But one thing is certain, after a poor attendance in the early days the concerts did increasingly attract larger and enthusiastic audiences. Their public consisted not only of musicians but also of interested laymen, particularly writers such as Jakob Wassermann, Stefan Zweig and Alfred Kerr.

Restless winter months followed, with trips to Trieste, Vienna, Lyons, Milan, Genoa, Rome and Bologna. Everywhere he went Busoni was celebrated and admired as a pianist; everywhere he went he met important people, such as the composer Giovanni Sgambati in Bologna, Arrigo Boito in Milan, the piano builder Ludwig Bösendorfer in Vienna. As far as reading is concerned,

Busoni mentions Victor Hugo's poems, Plato and books on Leonardo da Vinci.

His father Ferdinando had been ill for many years. Busoni had visited him on 9th March before his concert in Trieste. His mother was not well either. Ferdinando died in May in his seventy-third year. Anna, a year older, followed him on 3rd October. Deeply moved by her death, Busoni wrote his *Berceuse Elégiaque* for Chamber Orchestra in a few days in London, harmonically one of his most adventurous works, a truly Utopian lullaby from the son at his mother's grave. He wrote to Gerda about his last visit to his parents : 'Although I don't much like old people, I must admit I was very relieved to find my mother up. Even though weak and obviously more frail than before, she was lucid and quick-thinking and so sweet! She gave me her blessing, saying, "Bless you for bringing your mother so much happiness and support." ' Busoni was less fond of his father. He had caused him anxiety and been a burden to him too often. Nevertheless he frequently thought of him during his travels when something happened to remind him of Ferdinando's cultural patriotism. When he was describing the Kremlin to Gerda he mentioned a church which was built on the plan of San Marco in Venice : 'My father would have been thrilled.'

Ferruccio spent the summer in Augsburger Strasse while Gerda took a rest cure in Varese and Gargnano on Lake Garda. The last concert trip that year took him to Vienna and Budapest. On the night-train to Vienna he met Emil Hertzka, director of Universal-Edition and promised him his arrangement of Schoenberg's piano piece Opus 11 no. 2 for publication. He was pleased by his success, and in Budapest even by his own playing. While he was there he was looked up by a young musician, Gisella Selden, who soon became his devoted disciple and later studied composition with him as well. He had met her through a fellow-student at a previous concert in Budapest and had taken one of her scores back to Berlin to read. During conversations with Boito in March Busoni had also produced the almost finished score of his *Brautwahl*, for which his old friend Augusto Anzoletti

47

had translated the text. It was another two years before the piece was given its first performance in Hamburg.

In 1910 Busoni went to America with Gerda for a concert tour lasting four months. He travelled mainly in the eastern part of the States, had enormous success as a pianist, but was much more interested in his own Bach studies. In Chicago he met two musicians of German origin who not only fascinated him but also inspired him with a new interest in counterpoint. He has described them in an article, *The Gothics of Chicago*, published in *Signale für die musikalische Welt*. The elder of the two, Bernhard Ziehn, came from Erfurt and had emigrated to America in 1868 at the age of twenty-three, where he taught music to private pupils. From Ziehn originates the theory of symmetrical inversion which was used mainly in composition technique, but was also applied to piano teaching. His pupil, Wilhelm Middelschulte, born 1863 in Werve (Westphalia), died 1943, had been living in Chicago since 1891. He enjoyed a high reputation as an organist and composer of organ music. As the result of conversations with these two musicians Busoni adopted a plan to complete Bach's *The Art of Fugue*. In a letter written 19th February 1910 from Cincinnati he mentions the title for the first time: *Fantasia contrappuntistica*. The many letters written to Gerda, who had stayed behind in New York, gradually build up a picture of this work. For the rest, the impressions were colourful, followed one upon another in rapid succession, and were recorded by Busoni in his own highly personal and witty manner. He celebrated his birthday on 1st April in Colorado Springs. But even in this Segantini landscape he kept thinking of Berlin, of the apartment at 11 Viktoria-Luise-Platz, where the Busonis were living by this time and which was to be his last home. 'I long to be with you at home, I long for peace and for my work,' he writes the evening before his birthday in a letter to Gerda who in the meantime had returned to Germany. Busoni did not believe in trying to account for lost time. It was against his nature to dwell on the past. But on this occasion, this lonely birthday spent at an altitude of two thousand metres, he did

48

try to assess the achievements of the past year. The list includes piano pieces *An die Jugend*, the Fantasia on Bach and the *Grosse Fuge*, the *Berceuse Elégiaque*, the outline for a new system of notation, the first volume of the Liszt edition, 180 pages of the *Brautwahl* score, plus concert tours in England, Switzerland, Austria and America where he played thirty-five times. The first of the six piano sonatinas, which is dedicated to Rudolph Ganz, also belongs with the other compositions dating from 1910. In Bach transcriptions there is the D major Organ Prelude with Fugue; on the literary side, an article on Galston's manual; another on the demands made on pianists; and towards the end of the year a very serious piece written on board ship near the Irish coast, 'How long can this go on?'

The Busonis spent the autumn in Switzerland where the master-class at the Allgemeine Musikschule in Basle now actually materialized. Busoni also gave a concert there, which was received with considerable scepticism by the leading critic, Karl Nef. He replied in a letter to Hans Huber : 'If only I understood the meaning of profundity in German music. I feel completely lost! In Beethoven I detect enormous humanity, freedom and originality; in Mozart enjoyment of life and beauty of form (which are actually Italian characteristics); in Bach, emotion, piety, greatness and skill.'

New Year's Day 1911 was also celebrated in America. Busoni was on the road from 13th February until 7th April, beginning his concert tour in Montreal, Canada. He was annoyed by the bigotry in New England, where elderly spinsters in glasses waited on him in the hotel, but he was pleased to see Boston again. Sitting in the orchestra pit, he listened as a specialist on the subject, to *Don Quixote* of Strauss whom he saw as 'a kind of Tiepolo'. He spent ten days in New York where he met Gustav Mahler, Arturo Toscanini and the sculptor, Prince Paul Trubetzkoj, with whom he could talk in Italian and spent one of his most enjoyable evenings in America. Then followed an incalculable number of recitals and symphony concerts in which he was the soloist. Four different programmes and three piano concertos were included

49

in the repertoire. In Los Angeles where he had a couple of free days in the middle of March he wrote a short article entitled: *The Future belongs to Melody*. He was enjoying reading *The New Machiavelli* by H. G. Wells. In San Francisco he made fun of the extreme nationalism of both the German and Italian emigrant musicians. 'Busoni won battle', said a review of the piano recital he gave there. He celebrated his birthday in Cincinnati, he was forty-five; a week later in New York he boarded the ship that was to take him home. He was homesick throughout the voyage. As early as 18th February he had written to Gerda from Boston saying: 'I cannot tell you how much I am looking forward to working this summer and autumn. The feeling of impatience and constraint with which I am continually having to battle here, has absorbed all my concentration. I'm like someone who has to lie in bed with a broken leg, but has nothing else wrong with him and is simply waiting to be able to walk and move about again. Once more I repeat: I must not waste the best years of my life.'

Soon after his return home, news reached Busoni of the death of Gustav Mahler with whom he had felt such a close affinity when in New York. Back in February the great conductor had had to postpone his American concert engagements. Busoni was disgusted by the reaction of the New Yorkers who took less interest in Mahler's illness than in the emergence of concert-master, Theodore Spiering, taking his place as conductor.

The spring was devoted to composition; alongside this, Busoni had to put in a lot of work on the piano in order to accomplish the enormous task that he had set himself for the autumn. The one hundredth anniversary of Liszt's birth was celebrated in October. Busoni gave six recitals of his work at the Beethovensaal. The Liszt celebrations at Basle on 22nd October were also distinguished by his presence.

During this same period Max Reinhardt produced with the Deutsches Theater a chamber presentation of Gozzi's *Turandot*, adapted by Karl Vollmoeller. Busoni had the pleasure of hearing his complete *Turandot* music of 1904, conducted by Oskar Fried.

The columns printed by the Deutsches Theater carried his article *Companion-piece to the Turandot Music*. But he was also concerned with other musical problems, such as the 'New Harmony', in connection with which he refers to Bernhard Ziehn's theory of symmetry, not however overlooking the connection with Schoenberg. In August a short article on the subject of routine appeared in Alfred Kerr's magazine, *Pan*; later in the year the famous review of a Schoenberg matinee : 'At the keyboards sit four young men with fine, distinctive features; it is almost touching to see with what fanaticism and zeal they apply their young minds to what is still an enigma. At the back of the small rostrum two eyes gleam anxiously, a baton is raised in short nervous movements. Only the head and hand of Schoenberg are visible as he prompts the four gallant lads, gradually infecting them with his own nervous agitation. An unusual scene, which together with the unusual sound, exerts a certain fascination.'

One of the 'four young men' was Eduard Steuermann who has also described the concert : 'I had only just begun studying with Schoenberg when he told me about a concert of his work to be held in the Choralionsaal, and asked me to play his newly composed Opus 19. I was also to accompany Frau Winternitz-Dorda, a very fine soprano from Hamburg, in the George songs. As she had perfect pitch this was not too difficult. We also played the first, second and fourth of the five orchestral pieces in an eight-handed arrangement for two pianos by Webern and Schoenberg. My partner was Louis Closson, one of Busoni's pupils from Belgium; the others were a very interesting pair : Webern and Louis Gruenberg. This "heresy" aroused violent opposition, but also some enthusiasm.' (From a conversation with Gunther Schuller, published in *Perspectives of New Music*. Copyright 1964, by Princeton University Press.)

As far as compositions were concerned, the year yielded two new *Turandot* pieces : *Despair and Resignation* and *Altoum's Warning*; as well as an arrangement of Bach's *chromatic fantasia and fugue*.

After a short trip to London at the beginning of 1912, when

he played Beethoven, Liszt, Chopin Ballades and the Brahms Paganini Variations, the next stop was Hamburg. Before leaving, he wrote to Gerda about a London exhibition of Futurists, and the fact that he preferred Umberto Boccioni's *Growing Town* and Carlo Carrà's *Leaving the Theatre* to the paintings of Gino Severini. Hamburg had undertaken the first performance of *Die Brautwahl* and Busoni was pleased with the first rehearsal on 25th March. He spent his birthday partly reading a book by Villiers de I'Isle Adam, partly at the opera house where once again he was surprised by the third act of *Die Walküre*. On 7th April Gerda arrived from Berlin. *Die Brautwahl* had its première on 12th and was warmly received. Gustav Brecher to whom the score is dedicated was responsible for the musical direction. The critics expressed reservations about the libretto.

Following this Busoni spent a busy summer in Berlin; Gerda was in Switzerland with the children. In August Ferrucio spent a couple of days in Paris where they had considered buying a house. He met Widor, talked with Gabriele d'Annunzio and Karl Vollmoeller, admired the architecture of the Garnier Opera House, and picked up a valuable book for his library. 'But in the evenings,' he wrote to Gerda, 'where are the lights, the flowers, the high spirits of Berlin?'

The autumn brought journeys further afield, one to England and in November one to Russia with Petersburg, Riga, Moscow and Warsaw as the main stopping-places. One concert was attended by the seventy-eight year old César Cui; in Moscow he was visited by Sergei Rachmaninoff and Josef Hofmann, and had a brief conversation with Alexander Skriabin. But the encouragement of 'competitiveness' among pianists was never to his liking, even though he himself had nothing to fear from it.

With his *Sonatina seconda* written in 1912 Busoni once again adopted the musical idiom that he had tried out in his *Berceuse Elégiaque* after his mother's death. The piece is rhythmically free and written without bar-lines. Harmonically it stands somewhere in the twilight of tonality and often comes close to the attonal music of Schoenberg. The sonatina is dedicated to the pianist Mark Hambourg. Meanwhile Busoni is making progress with his Bach and Liszt editions. The composition of his *Nocturne Symphonique* is completed in 1912, closely related in style to his *Berceuse* and 2nd Sonatina. In *Pan* Busoni writes a review of his own work in which he stresses the importance of his *Fantasia Contrappuntistica* and *Berceuse*. Of the *Berceuse* he says : 'With this piece . . . I succeeded for the first time in finding a personal sound and a form for my emotions.' He mentions the piano concerto using male choir of 1904 as the culmination of the first stage of manhood. Another literary piece, *Pianistic genius*, appeared in the *Allgemeine Musikzeitung*, criticizing the whole conception of genius.

Busoni does not mention the great musical events of 1912 and 1913. He appears to have heard Schoenberg's *Pierrot Lunaire* which had its first performance in Berlin in October 1912, but not Stravinsky's *The Rite of Spring*. The beginning of the year finds him travelling to London, Kassel and Mannheim where Arthur Bodanzky had undertaken a performance of *Die Brautwahl*.

In April and May 1913 Busoni was touring Milan, Bologna, Parma and other North Italian towns, with one of his famous cycles of piano recitals. There were eight different programmes representing the development of piano music from Bach to the present day. Busoni had already undertaken a similar project in Berlin; but for Italy it was something entirely new and out of the ordinary.

Towards the end of June he met d'Annunzio in Paris, and discussed with him plans for an opera about Leonardo da Vinci. He also met the leading Futurist, F. T. Marinetti, and visited an exhibition of Futurist sculpture by Boccioni. 'Compared with this art . . . Schoenberg's *Pierrot Lunaire* is like tepid lemonade !' He sat at the open window of the Hotel Foyot where Rilke was later to stay. He got to know Alfredo Casella. At the Théâtre du Châtelet he saw Ida Rubinstein as Pisanella in the text by d'Annunzio with music by Ildebrando Pizzetti, was appalled by

53

the effect of the French language on the stage and called the whole thing a mannered wildenbruch.

Gerda spent the holidays in Alt-Aussee, Busoni as usual composing in Berlin. He was working on a piece based on the music of the North American Indians, having seen something of their melodies through Natalie Curtis. He had already been corresponding with her on the subject of American folklore back in March 1911. The first piece to result from this was his *Indian Fantasia* for piano and orchestra, followed in 1915 by his *Indian Diary*. He also wrote to Gerda about his ideas on melody. September brought trips to Heidelberg, Geneva and Northern Italy, where Busoni was involved in recitals until the end of October. But it was not only concerts that took him there. After lengthy negotiations he had been persuaded to become director of the Liceo Musicale in Bologna. He took up the post on 1st October, but kept his apartment in Berlin. He planned to be there during the spring and autumn, to travel during the winter, and to spend Christmas and summer in Berlin. 'This is a pleasure which I find essential to me, and I should like to enjoy it before I am an old man. It keeps me young, otherwise I shall fall to pieces before my time.'

But in the long run he was dissatisfied with the work in Bologna. He had the same feeling of being constricted that he had so frequently experienced in Italy, and took his leave of the Liceo Musicale after the first trial year to return to Berlin. He spent the summer in his apartment, mainly busy with his edition of the Bach Keyboard Works. It was here that he lived through the beginning of the First World War, without realizing the magnitude of the disaster. He was convinced that Italy would remain neutral, while the rest of Europe seemed to him to be in an increasingly dangerous position. There were no more concert tours in 1914; nothing before an American tour to be prepared for January 1915. A Bach piano recital in aid of charity caused quite a stir in Berlin, but there was also a certain nationalistic reticence about the reviews.

Gerda accompanied him to America with their two sons;

Benvenuto, born in Boston, had the right to American citizenship. After completing his concert tour which ended in April, Busoni stayed on in New York with the family for a while. It was not until September that he set off for home with Gerda and Raffaelo, his younger son. They took an Italian boat, landed at Genoa, but did not travel to Bologna because the situation there had worsened. Important compositions written during the first years of the war include the Third Sonatina *ad usum infantis* and a certain number of the pieces inspired by Red Indian music. Among his literary work there is the *Doctor Faust* libretto, a commentary on the novella of E. T. A. Hoffmann, and a short piece : *On the Nature of Music*.

In October 1915, in view of the increasingly threatening international situation, Busoni made an important decision. He travelled to Zürich, looked up his old friend Dr. Volkmar Andreae and through him asked for political asylum in Switzerland. Andreae was not only a prolific composer but at that time director of the Zürich Conservatory and conductor with the Tonhalle-Gesellschaft. In 1926, when a memorial tablet was placed on Busoni's house in Zürich, he described this meeting : 'Previously I had known Busoni only as an artist and intellectual. Now he was a human being harried by the confusion of war, seeking help with tears in his eyes. I have seldom been so moved and at the same time so delighted; moved by the embarrassment of this great man, delighted by the fact that I could now call Busoni one of us.'

Although he was now an expatriate, the years in Switzerland brought Busoni plenty of work, friendship and intellectual stimulus. He soon found an apartment in Scheuchzer Strasse overlooking Zürich which became a meeting-place for artists and intellectuals from all over the world. When Andreae was called up in 1916, he handed over the direction of his subscription concerts in February, March and April to Ferruccio Busoni who had already made an appearance in January playing his own *Indian Fantasia* for piano and orchestra. Busoni devoted the February concert to works by Liszt, his favourite pupil Egon

Petri playing the A major concerto. In March he surprised his friends with a programme in which Sibelius' Second Symphony was followed by a Mozart concert aria and Tschaikowsky's Violin Concerto, ending with Wotan's Farewell and The Magic Fire Music from Wagner's *Walküre*. The third programme included his own *Rondeau harlequinesque*, framed by Mendelssohn, Mozart and Berlioz. The fourth programme ended with Beethoven's *Eroica*.

As a pianist Busoni also made his presence felt during the spring of 1916. Within a week or so four recitals were devoted exclusively to pieces by Bach, Beethoven, Chopin and Liszt. 'Busoni did not like the Romantics,' writes Robert Blum, later one of his composition students, who attended all the Zürich concerts, 'and yet in my opinion he played nothing but essentially Romantic music.'

His connections with Italy had not yet been severed. Busoni played in Rome with great success and spent June 1916 as a house guest of the Marchese Silvio Casanova in San Remigio. There he met Umberto Boccioni whose paintings he had already admired at a London exhibition in 1912 and who now painted Busoni's portrait. It was one of the last things he did. In July he joined the army and died in uniform after falling from his horse.

The years in Zürich were also rich in creative activity. The most important work, completed there in 1916, was his opera *Arlecchino*. As early as September 1913, in a letter written from Bergamo, Busoni mentioned showing a rough draft to his friend Emilio Anzoletti. The composition was begun in 1914 and virtually completed in Zürich in 1916. The Stadttheater in Zürich agreed to present the first performance, but were worried by the fact that it was not long enough to constitute a programme. So Busoni decided to resurrect his original idea of a *Turandot* opera. The work was completed in three months, so it was possible to produce the two operas together on 13th May 1917. The speaking part of Arlecchino was played by Alexander Moissi. Busoni conducted, the production was by Hans Rogorsch.

The first night was a great success; the theatre was attended by many who had shared the same fate as Busoni, and following his example found a peaceful exile in Zürich. After the première Busoni and his friends gathered in the Kronen-Halle where they were joined by members of the Max Reinhardt Theatre who were making a guest appearance in Zürich. Frank Wedekind sat in an adjoining room, lonely and embittered, refusing to take any part in the celebrations. Eventually Busoni joined him, and after talking for a long time succeeded in cheering him up. Wolfgang Hartmann has described the scene in a page of memoirs which also gives a list of all those who belonged to Busoni's circle in Zürich : the conductor Oskar Fried; the poets, Franz Werfel, René Schickele, Ludwig Rubiner, Leonhard Frank and Ivan Goll. Stefan Zweig, Fritz von Unruh, the Berlin publisher Paul Cassirer and his wife, and the actress Tilla Durieux were also living in Zürich at that time.

Busoni's group of pupils included Philipp Jarnach, Gisella Selden-Goth (later his biographer) and the composer Reinhold Laquai.

Through Jarnach Busoni also got to know the Irish writer, James Joyce, who had gone to Zürich in 1916. In January 1917 Joyce rented an apartment which he found himself sharing with Jarnach. As Joyce was in the habit of singing while he worked, a settlement had to be reached which would give Jarnach the peace he needed for composing. The two very different men became friends, even though Joyce—an admirer of Bellini and Donizetti and a sworn enemy of Wagner—disagreed with the younger musician in his ideas about music. In the Kronen-Halle Restaurant, Jarnach introduced his fellow-lodger to Busoni. When Joyce remarked that Shakespeare was more of a poet than a dramatist, Busoni replied somewhat heatedly that on the contrary it was the other way about. In April Joyce went to a Tonhalle concert where Busoni's *Gesang vom Reigen der Geister* was being performed. He was accompanied by Ottocaro Weiss, a Wagnerian and an admirer of Busoni, whom he reduced to helpless laughter with his remarks about the sexual symbolism of the musical instruments. Busoni, who happened to be watching, looked at them both disapprovingly.

Later Busoni spoke of Joyce as being greater than Jarnach. The Joyce Collection at Cornell University includes a letter written by Busoni to the author of *Ulysses*. Quite apart from this the two men had a common friend in the baritone Augustus Milner to whom Busoni dedicated two Goethe songs.

In spite of the friendship and the peace that Busoni and his family found in Switzerland he was not happy. The thought that Italy, his fatherland, and Germany, his spiritual home, were at war with one another was almost intolerable. He was aware of a lack of understanding, or at the very least a misunderstanding, on both sides and was divided between two loyalties neither of which could be expressed. Having to live without his Berlin library was a great sacrifice. He built up a smaller one in Zürich containing some of the books that he simply could not do without. Thus his fiftieth birthday, 'that fatal day', which he spent in Zürich on 1st April 1916, was not a day of celebration for him. His friends have described how he would often walk to the station, with only his huge St. Bernard, Giotto, for company, and sit in the restaurant drinking Neuchâtel wine, listening nostalgically for the trains travelling to Germany or Italy.

Busoni played his part in the artistic events of those years as a critical observer. He sat in the newly opened Cabaret Voltaire while Richard Hülsenbeck, Tristan Tzara, Ivan Goll, Hugo Ball, Hans Arp and Emmy Hennings read the first products of Dadaism, but did not enjoy 'this stuttering poetry'. He crossed swords intellectually with Igor Stravinsky, whom he did not yet know, but who sent word from Morges on Lake Geneva to the effect that he was surprised to find that Busoni liked the classical composers. He sent Stravinsky a message saying that if he bothered to get to know the German classical composers he too would appreciate them.

His concert commitments were not limited to Zürich. He was still in touch with old friends in Basle, in particular with Hans

Huber. Busoni admired him greatly, and his correspondence with him touched on musical and literary questions, a note of bitterness creeping in when Italy declared war on Germany in September 1916. Through Huber he gave four piano recitals with varied programmes in the new Concert Hall in Basle between 12th January and 2nd February 1917; during February and March 1918 he continued the cycle with another three engagements.

One of the anxieties of the war years was the fact that Benvenuto was called up by the American army. In 1917 he dedicated the fourth of his Piano Sonatinas to the son he had left behind in America. Christmas was a festival to which he attached more importance than most of his fellow countrymen. He had written a *Nuit de Noël* back in 1909. The sonatina, which was completed on 22nd December, is entitled *Sonatina in Diem nativitatis Christi 1917*. But most of his energy was devoted to his major work, *Doctor Faust*, which remained unfinished. Busoni himself comments: 'I wrote the first draft of *Doctor Faust* in a fever of excitement in six days, between the outbreak of war and preparing for an ocean voyage towards the end of 1914.' In the letters he wrote to Gerda from various towns in America during the course of his concert tour in 1915 he is continually talking about his Faust. But it was only in Switzerland that the composition really began to make progress. 'I have just this moment . . . written the last bar of the first scene of my fourth opera,' he says in a letter from Zürich on 29th September 1917. Then in January 1919 Volkmar Andreae received notice of the completion of the two orchestral pieces in *Doctor Faust* in the form of a wedding announcement:

Ferruccio Busoni and his Muse
have pleasure in announcing
the engagement of their daughter
Sarabande
with
Monsieur Cortège
Zürich—January 1919—Empoli

59

Finally in November 1918 the war ended. Busoni hesitated about returning to the political and economic upheavals of post-war Germany. Once again between February and April 1919 he set his stamp upon five popular concerts with the Tonhalle-Gesellschaft. With Doktor Volkmar Andreae conducting, he played a cycle of fourteen pieces under the heading *The Development of the Piano Concerto*, including work by Bach, Mozart, Hummel, Beethoven, Schumann, Mendelssohn, Weber, Saint-Saëns, Brahms, Liszt, Rubinstein, and finally his own Concerto for piano, orchestra and male choir.

Among the literary output of the Zürich period there was a dramatic sequence with mime, *Das Wandbild*, dedicated to Philipp Jarnach with music by Othmar Schoeck. As a counter-attack to Hans Pfitzner's pamphlet, *The Dangers of Futurism*, a spiteful reply to Busoni's *Outline for a New Musical Aesthetics* which appeared as an Insel Press publication in 1916, he wrote a letter which the *Vossische Zeitung* had the courage to print in 1917.

Soon after the war Busoni resumed his concert activities abroad. He was called to London and Paris, played with great success, met old friends once again, and in one of his many letters to Gerda described the afternoon when he received a visit from Bernard Shaw. They talked about Mozart, Wagner and Elgar.

In the autumn of 1919 an invitation arrived from Leo Kestenberg in Berlin. He offered Busoni a master-class at the Prussian Academy of Arts which would give him six months' leave annually for travelling. Busoni hesitated about leaving Switzerland. In July the University of Zürich had made him an Honorary Doctor of Philosophy, and he had responded by dedicating to them the libretto of his *Doctor Faust*. Nevertheless, he finally decided to return to Berlin where he had left behind a home, pianos and a library. In September 1920 he came back to Viktoria-Luise-Platz and found his apartment untouched. That same November he gave two concerts in a crowded Philharmonic Hall. He heard Eduard Erdmann play his piano concerto; he performed in Hamburg; and began to get used to the drab life of Berlin. In January 1921 three Philharmonic concerts organized by *Der Anbruch* were devoted to his compositions. He began working with his students. Busoni had taken on five : Luc Balmer, a Swiss; Robert Blum and Walter Geiser; Vladimir Vogel, a Russian; and the German Kurt Weill. The *Musikblätter des Anbruch*, the modernistic house magazine of Universal-Edition in Vienna, devoted their January double number to him. His Piano Toccata completed during his first weeks back in Berlin, was included in the number. On 13th May the State Opera House 'Unter den Linden', presented *Turandot* and *Arlecchino* under the musical direction of Leo Blech. A special number of *Blätter der Staatsoper* appeared with Busoni's 'tragic-comic folk drama', *Die Götterbraut*, a highly personal interpretation of the Indian story by Nala and Damayanti, written as a libretto for Louis T. Gruenberg who wrote the music for it in 1913.

Only in February he had been involved in concerts in London. In Rome, where as recently as 1919 Busoni had been dismissed as being pro-German, he was now made Commander of the Crown of Italy. Before the opening night of the State Opera House he gave two recitals in Berlin under Gustav Brecher, playing six Mozart piano concertos.

The spring and summer were spent as usual working in his Berlin apartment. 'The youngsters come on Mondays and Thursdays,' he wrote on 30th July 1921 to Gerda who was taking a holiday in Gross-Gmain near Salzburg. In actual fact he and his students met almost every day. Busoni was working mainly on *Doctor Faust* and finding it difficult to finish; but in his usual way he was also involved in other musical and literary projects at the same time.

A more serious bout of illness forced him very much against his will to consult a doctor in the autumn of 1921. The crisis passed, he was able to fulfil fresh concert commitments and make arrangements for a trip to London. His correspondence was growing all the time. Busoni had become something of a myth among modern musicians; whenever anyone wanted to

61

organize and encourage contemporary music, they sought his advice and collaboration. The two magazines, *Musikblätter des Anbruch* in Vienna and *Melos* in Berlin, managed to persuade him to contribute to their pages even though he had a somewhat sceptical opinion of them.

In 1920, at the suggestion of his musical director Heinrich Burkhard, Prince Max Egon zu Furstenberg undertook the organization of the first Chamber Music recitals to be held at Donaueschingen for the promotion of contemporary music. Richard Strauss was persuaded to be chairman of an advisory board, and among the other members were Busoni, Siegmund von Hausegger, Arthur Nikisch, Max Pauer, Hans Pfitzner and Franz Schreker. The first festival was held on 31st July and 1st August 1921. Busoni, who did not like to leave his Berlin apartment during the summer, was represented by Gerda. Besides Alois Hába's *Quarter-tone Quartet*, the programmes included works by Alban Berg, Paul Hindemith, Ernst Krenek and Busoni's pupil and friend, Philipp Jarnach. Busoni was by no means uncritical towards the movement that these musicians represented. In the numerous letters that he exchanged with Gisella Selden-Goth between 1920–22 he expressed doubts about atonality and musical expressionism. In another he played on the names Ernst Krenek and Felix Petyrek, writing 'Kschrennek's Nonen (ninths) und Chromosse, Petrifaxtaxen'. In principle, however, he considered the encouragement of new music more important than, let us say, the promotion of Wagner at the State Opera House in Berlin.

He visited London and Paris once more in January and February 1922. His last public appearance was on 29th May 1922 in the Philharmonic Hall in Berlin, when he played Beethoven's Concerto in E flat major. From then on his life was devoted exclusively to composition and teaching. He was obliged to give a lot of time to an edition of his collected writings published under the title : *On the Unity of Music.*

At the end of July the Donaueschingen Festival of Chamber Music was held for the second time, once again without Busoni.

His school was represented by the Clarinet Sonata by the Swiss composer, Reinhold Laquai, his friends by a String Quartet by the Dutch composer, Bernhard van Dieren. Then in no time at all there was the International Festival of Music at Salzburg, followed on 11th August by the inauguration of the International Society for New Music. The president, Edward Dent, asked Busoni for his support which in fact he promised them. But his health deteriorated. By the autumn of 1922 he had to be careful not to dissipate his energy. He cut down on his correspondence and concentrated mainly on his *Faust* score.

Jakob Wassermann, who had been one of Busoni's closest friends during the latter part of his stay in Zürich, has described visiting him : 'When I saw him for the last time in December 1922, he was fifty-six and looked an old man; his noble face ravaged by illness, his mouth noticeably pinched, his splendid brow crowned with snow-white hair, already showing signs of his fatal disease; one was struck not only by the obvious imminence of his physical collapse, but more particularly by his wonderful attitude to life which commanded respect even among those who had no personal involvement with him.' He was still full of ideas, and considered doing a new edition of the Mozart Piano Concertos with Egon Petri. In February 1923 Furtwängler conducted the Sarabande and Cortège from *Faust* but the pieces were not well received in Berlin. In Germany the political and economic situation was giving more and more cause for alarm due to the depreciation of the Mark. Busoni, who never thought about money and was not wealthy, suffered nonetheless during this difficult period. That year he sent his wife Gerda to Donaueschingen once again. His last letter to her, dated 28th June 1923, was sent there. It contains some sceptical remarks about Stravinsky's *The Soldier's Tale*. A few days later he followed up an invitation to Weimar where the Bauhaus was putting on a big Festival of Modern Art. He sat in a box in the Stadttheater, which he had once known so well, and for the first time actually heard *The Soldier's Tale* which he had previously known only from the score. Hermann Scherchen was

63

conducting, Carl Ebert spoke the commentator's part. Stravinsky was sitting in another box. Busoni was deeply moved by the piece.

There were tears in his eyes when Stravinsky was introduced to him and referring to the time they had crossed swords in Switzerland, said: 'Master, I have come to love the classical composers!'

In November 1923 Gisella Selden-Goth, whose book on Busoni had appeared barely a year previously, came to say goodbye to him: 'I found him exhausted and weary; illness and over-work had cast deep shadows over his noble, prematurely aged features.'

Moreover, he had just spent six weeks recuperating in Paris with Gerda. But once again his inexhaustible drive was greater than his strength. He was practising a lot, so as to be able to complete a concert tour he had planned in Finland; he had ideas which he discussed with his friend, Isidor Philipp, the great piano teacher. A specialist diagnosed his condition as incurable and tried to keep him away from alcohol and tobacco. Busoni returned unwillingly to the gloom of Berlin where Gisella Selden-Goth found him in the state she has described. Should he change his environment again? He discussed with his friend and biographer the possibility of renting a house in Tuscany, with a large room for his books and a shady garden. He even considered moving to London. But none of these plans materialized.

Busoni spent the last year of his life in the shadow of illness and poverty. Friends had to send him food from abroad. It was only after the stabilization of the German Reichsmark in Janaury 1924 that economic conditions in Germany very slowly began to improve. But Busoni did not live to see it. In May 1924 his condition became critical. He was suffering from a general sepsis, caused by a kidney infection many years previously which he had neglected. Busoni had prided himself on not having consulted a doctor for thirty years. Now it was too late. But his wonderful brain did not cease to function; on 8th June he was still capable of dictating an article *On the Nature of Music*, which was printed in the August edition of *Melos* that same

3 Busoni the pianist, Berlin 1906

4 Busoni the conductor, Berlin 1909

year. It ends with the words: 'Hail to the prophet!' During the last weeks a host of friends, and also many obtrusive acquaintances, gathered round the dying man. The periods of unconsciousness and semi-coma became more and more frequent. Day and night Gerda sat at the bedside of the dying man; and over and over again he expressed his gratitude to her, the gratitude that had constituted his evening-prayer ever since the early days of their marriage. Early on 27th July his heart stopped beating.

Busoni's personality has fascinated two generations of musicians and non-musicians too. There are a hundred descriptions of the man and no two are alike. The one thing that stands out in all these accounts is his unusual temperament, the sudden outbursts of Homeric laughter, or Dionysian anger which disappeared just as suddenly when he realized that he was wrong and someone else was right. Busoni was a Latin, very courteous and exceptionally gentlemanly. He would bow to a beautiful woman, he was polite to strangers and to his students, provided that they did not offend him by some thoughtless remark. Material things meant nothing to him when art was at stake. For him there was something very special about being an artist. He once wrote in a letter: 'I am quite convinced that there has to be a barrier between the public and a great work of art.' (1918, to Gisella Selden-Goth.) He ends the letter: 'In matters concerning art my feelings are those of an autocrat.' He lived like a *grand seigneur*, and it was not unknown for him to squander the money he so despised. He died in poverty, a kingly beggar, surrounded by beautiful objects among which his books were nearest to his heart. It was a great sacrifice for Gerda, who had been his companion for more than thirty years, to have to break up their home and library after his death. She was only able to keep the most personal of his possessions, letters, manuscripts and a few of his favourite books. She outlived him by thirty-two years, and when she was over eighty the Berlin apartment which she had left in 1943 was destroyed in an air-raid. Blind, looked after by her sister Helmi, she spent almost eleven years of her life in Sweden, dying in Lidingö at the age of ninety-four on 3rd

August 1956. Her younger son, Raffaelo, lived in New York as a successful designer until 1962. The elder, Benvenuto, still lives in Berlin.

Busoni's intellectual achievement has outlived him in various forms. His piano playing, his teaching, his articles about art and life, his music, his letters, and his example as a world citizen will continue to influence our cultural life.

The Reluctant Virtuoso

'My work on the operatic score has been interrupted again, and instead I have to labour at the Chopin pieces which I have expected to master for the last twenty-five years but find that I have to struggle with them afresh each time. This is now such a sterile experience that I am seriously thinking of giving up practising altogether . . . What is the future for piano playing? If there is to be any further development, we must have new literature and an enriched instrument.' This was what Busoni wrote to his Swiss friend Hans Huber on 17th September 1910, a few months after his triumphant tour of America and at the very height of his fame as a virtuoso performer. The idea of his 'giving up practising altogether' is monstrous, like so much else that this brilliant and eccentric man suggested as time and again in the course of his career he prepared to make a fresh start. It was certainly not prompted by a desire to opt out, as was the case with Liszt for example as he grew older; more likely by the fear of wasting his energies on something with no future, when they had to be kept in reserve for his creative work as a composer and writer.

Busoni's reputation as a pianist was legendary everywhere he performed. There is no other pianist of his generation who could match him in terms of prestige. Yet he was not a popular performer. He did not appeal to the ordinary people in the way that, let us say, Eugen d'Albert, Sergei Rachmaninoff or Ignaz Paderewski could pride themselves on doing. He held his audience spellbound almost like a hypnotist. But there was nothing about his performance to win the sympathy of the average listener. His art was on too high an intellectual level for that. At the piano he seemed remote, almost detached. His face showed no sign of the rigorous thought process, the vast amount of creative energy, that was clearly behind every detail of his playing. Like a beautiful marble statue—even his hands moved only minimally—he seemed to be merely the mouthpiece for the spirit that he evoked from the keys. Busoni hated his fame as a

67

pianist, and throughout his life was upset by the fact that people celebrated him for something that he himself considered inferior. Not that he despised the piano. All his compositions and arrangements show with what feeling and devotion he endeavoured to extract its maximum sonority, resonance, differentiation of volume levels and many-faceted sound. But artistically all this was nothing more than raw material to him, although admittedly he used it in a quite unprecedented manner. Busoni began as an infant prodigy, and when he gave his first concerts in Trieste and Vienna he played the conventional show-pieces popular at that time. One has only to read the programmes assembled by Dr. Friedrich Schnapp and published as an appendix to Edward Dent's biography, to see the way he developed.

In Trieste the seven-year old boy is playing one of Clementi's sonatinas, two of the easier Schumann pieces from his *Kinder-szenen* and the first movement of Mozart's Sonata in C major, the so-called *Kindersonate*. But only a a year later his Trieste programme includes two Handel fugues, Schumann's *Knight Rupert* and Johann Nepomuk Hummel's Variations, which is to say, difficult virtuoso music.

1875 is the year of Bach, and Busoni played his Preludes and Fugues in Trieste and Venice. The hardest task that Busoni faced during that period was Mozart's Concerto in C minor, K. 491, which he himself says that he played 'very precisely and with fine details'. Mendelssohn's Presto in E minor, Rameau's Gavotte with Variations in A minor, pieces by Hummel, Porpora and Scarlatti, Mozart's *Rondo alla Turca*, all these works lie outside the usual child-repertoire. In 1876 further pieces by Bach appear in programmes performed in Gmunden, Ischl and Baden bei Wien, which is when the Chromatic Fanatasia and Fugue is first mentioned. At this stage Busoni also includes works of his own in his programmes : in Vienna the Five Pieces, Opus 3, praised by Hanslick; in Baden a Fugue in C minor; in Vöslau a Gavotte in F major. Then suddenly the whole world of Romantic music is also available; and there is room for Chopin, Mendelssohn and Schubert. In Graz Busoni plays Schumann's Andante and Variations for Two Pianos with his mother, just as later he was to play whole programmes with Vianna da Motta, Lochbrunner or Egon Petri.

During the Graz period young Busoni concentrated mainly on his studies with Mayer-Rémy. The only concerts he gave were in small neighbouring towns such as Celje, Neuhaus, Bozen, Klagenfurt, and of course Graz itself; apart from pieces by Chopin such as the *Tarantelle, Berceuse* and A flat major Ballade, the programmes consist entirely of German music. Beethoven's C major Sonata, Opus 53, was instrumental in leading Busoni to the music of a master whom he himself later described as one of the most important composers in the development of piano music. In a piece written for the Zürich programmes in April 1916, he maintains that in the whole history of the instrument there is nothing comparable to the transformation from Haydn's and Mozart's sonatas to Beethoven's *Hammerklavier* : 'In his technique; in his use of high, low and widely spaced positions; in his treatment of the pedals; and through improving and enriching the quality of its sound, Beethoven created the modern grand piano.' Thus in 1880 the D minor Sonata, Opus 31, no. 2, was already appearing in the Graz programmes, and in 1881 the C minor Sonata, Opus 111, as well.

At this point the concert tours begin once more, those between 1881–83 taking him chiefly to towns in Italy. Milan, Trieste, Bologna, Bergamo, Modena and his home town of Empoli, all have the chance to hear the young virtuoso and his astonishing programmes. Apart from tributes to contemporary Italians such as Fumagalli and Golinelli, these include six Paganini Studies by Liszt, Beethoven's Thirty-two Variations [on an original theme] in C minor, besides the F minor Sonata, Opus 57, and in Graz the Schumann Piano Concerto. Not to mention numerous works of his own which, in the case of Bologna 1882, were selected in order to justify his honorary membership of the Academy there. It is significant of this period that the pieces of his own that Busoni played were mainly preludes and fugues, evidence of the strict training he had received with Mayer-Rémy.

His admiration for the music of Brahms at this time had increased through his personal contact with the master in Vienna. At his Vienna concerts in 1884 he not only played the F minor Sonata but also the technically and musically complex Handel Variations. A large number of his own pieces make their first appearance, including two different ballet sequences, various preludes, fugues and studies, one of them Opus 17 in variation form. In Trieste he played Chopin's Etudes in C sharp minor and A minor, the Polonaise in B flat and A flat, as well as the Sonata in B flat minor; and he also extended his Liszt repertoire.

A letter from his correspondence with the Viennese Philharmonic Society shows how remarkably confident the eighteen-year-old Busoni felt as an interpreter. He writes from Frohnleiten near Graz on 4th August 1884, offering himself as soloist for the 1884–85 season. This proud sentence is the culminating point of the letter : 'I am prepared to played any piece that the worshipful committee may care to choose, on the one condition that I am informed of their choice a few weeks beforehand.' Considering that it is a matter of playing piano concertos with orchestra, the offer is really astounding.

Both the Austrian and the Italians critics raved about Busoni's piano playing even in those early days. During his research on Busoni the English scholar, Ronald Stevenson, has discovered a number of early reviews among which that of *Don Quixote* in Bologna on 11th March 1882 is particularly revealing : 'As a composer Busoni deserves to be admired. His theme is always elegant, exquisite and select; the variations and development are charming, correct and classical. As a performer he is exceptional. In my opinion, the only criticism one could make is that his expression is too standardized. Otherwise, it is all very lively and accurate, his technique perfect.'

Busoni was disappointed in his hopes of playing with the Vienna Philharmonic, even though he repeated his offer with amazing determination in September and October 1884 and

70

again in the summer of 1885. The engagement that he wanted so much did not actually materialize until March 1899. In any case Busoni was world-famous by that time, following his success in Berlin and America. There were other piano recitals in Vienna and Trieste in the year 1885. Pieces new to his repertoire include Beethoven's F minor Sonata, Opus 2, no. 1; Chopin's B flat minor Sonata, F minor Ballade and Fantasie-Polonaise; the virtuoso pieces are the Pergolesi-Thalberg *Aria*, the Schubert-Liszt *Erlkönig* and the Donizetti-Liszt *Lucrezia Borgia*. At his concert in Trieste Busoni played Bach's Organ Toccata and Fugue in D minor in an arrangement by Tausig; his own dates from much later.

1886 was the year he escaped from the family. Busoni became independent, and in Leipzig came into contact with a series of people who were responsible for new departures. But the first year did not produce any additions to his repertoire. Instead, the programme of a concert given in Hamburg reflects the way Busoni has developed as a pianist. There again we find the purely virtuoso pieces such as Liszt's Tarantelle from *The Dumb Girl of Potici* (or *Masaniello*), Tausig's arrangements of Johann Strauss Waltzes and Weber's *Perpetuum mobile*, together with Chopin's D flat major Nocturne, the Variations from Haydn's D major Sonata, Mozart's *Rondo alla Turca*, and Liszt's transcription of Bach's Organ Fantasia with Fugue in D minor. It was also during the Leipzig period that Kathi Petri suggested that he should transcribe Bach's organ works himself. Busoni played the first of these arrangements, the Prelude with Fugue in D major, in Leipzig in 1888. That same year he began teaching in Helsinki, where his rendering of *The Well-Tempered Clavier* left a lasting impression. 'A heaven-born interpreter of Bach', says his former pupil, Adolf Paul, to whom Busoni dedicated in 1889 a volume of Preludes and Fugues with the inscription *Helsinki near Lapland*. In the Finnish concerts he played Beethoven's *Eroica* Variation and his own arrangement of the Ecossaises. Although he had been very friendly with Anton Rubinstein ever since they met in Vienna in 1876, he had not played anything of his other than an Etude in F major. It was in Helsinki in 1889 that he appeared as soloist in the Piano Concerto in D minor.

The letters that Busoni exchanged with his friends, the Petris, in Leipzig provide us with a record of the years he spent in Finland. On 14th October 1888 he writes: 'The day before yesterday I gave my Beethoven recital (Sonatas: Opus 31, Appassionata, and the final one, Opus 111; also: *Eroica* Variations and Fugue in E flat major, and the posthumous Ecossaises). People said that nothing comparable had been heard here since Bülow and Rubinstein. Anyway I have seldom played so well. It was an enormous success, the Ecossaises were encored, I am in a seventh heaven about the reviews. This Beethoven recital lasting two and a quarter hours was probably the *most important* thing I have done as a pianist so far. In any case my having to be here has its advantages for Ferruccio *the pianist*.'

We know that it was in Helsinki that Wegelius drew Busoni's attention to the significance of Liszt as a composer. Only gradually do the consequences of this appear in his concert programmes. But during the same period, since about 1890, the works of Beethoven assume an increasingly prominent place in his repertoire. Not only were there whole programmes devoted to his work, like the one described in the letter to Petri in 1888; Busoni now played the piano concertos as well, especially those in E flat and G, which from then on constitute an essential part of his programmes as soloist in Philharmonic concerts.

Ever since the years in Leipzig and increasingly in Helsinki Busoni's work as a pianist had become more and more closely linked with his work as a composer. He was fascinated by Bach, not only in relation to his teaching, and arranging organ and violin pieces for his own piano recitals; he had also begun work as editor of Bach's Keyboard Works. In Moscow in 1891 he was able to submit the Two-part Inventions as his first volume, and dedicated it to the Institute of Music in Helsinki. The preface contains certain basic ideas, such as when Busoni stresses the value of these pieces as compositions rather than as purely technical exercises, because it is this quality that is 'capable of developing the sheer musicality of a pupil and encouraging his critical faculties.' When a second edition was printed in 1914, Busoni produced another preface. He still agrees with the old edition on almost every point, but has this to say about his piano technique : 'Nowadays I seldom, if ever, change my fingering on repeated notes (the same goes for pralltrillers and mordents) and tend more and more to avoid thumb-crossing.' This is the logical consequence of the new technique that Busoni had developed during the major crisis of 1893–94. One should not underestimate the part played by the American tours in the transformation that took place. During these long trips when he frequently performed every day, Busoni experienced the 'shock' that he later expressed in the one word 'misunderstanding'. His creative needs came into conflict with the image that the world had of him, which was based exclusively on his activity as a virtuoso.

As a pianist he was always enthusiastically received by the public, but the attitude of the critics was often more sceptical. He was living in Berlin and had already revised his technique when the following review of a concert held in Milan in 1895 appeared in the Corriere della Sera and is quoted by Stevenson : 'His appearance particularly intrigued the ladies who were obviously delighted by his Christ-like features, his long flowing hair and fervent eyes, which immediately earned him the title of the "Lohengrin with the white cravat". However when he played, even the ladies' enthusiasm was . . . restrained. Remarkable though his performance was, I heard them remark : it appeals to the intellect, but not to the emotions. Whether or not we agree with the opinion expressed by the fairer section of the audience, we do openly admit that Busoni astonished us but failed to move us.'

This basic criticism stubbornly pursued Busoni throughout his career as a virtuoso, in Italy as well as in Germany. What then was the particular quality responsible for the magic of his playing? Among the Berlin critics there was one who had heard

c*   73

Busoni while still a student at Harvard University between 1891–94 and who met him again in Germany : Hugo Leichtentritt. In a short treatise written in 1916 he defines what in his opinion are the basic elements of Busoni's incomparable style of playing : the architectonic and the painterly. By architectonic Leichtentritt means 'his feeling for the monumental nature of Gothic architecture, for the subtle combination of linear rhythms . . . within the structure . . . from the massive buttresses down to the most delicate and fanciful decorative carving'. By painterly, the 'sensitive modern Impressionist's feeling for the delicate blend of colours in one another chosen from a palette unbelievably rich in subtle shades'.

By tracing Busoni's terminology through his compositions and Bach editions, one can form a clear picture of his development and objective. He is working towards assembling the various techniques of fingering, touch, dynamics and phrasing, and subordinating them to one fundamental idea. This idea is also his objective : to elucidate polyphony. While each voice within the fabric is clearly defined and can easily be picked out by the listener even in complex chord sequences, the spirit of western music is ultimately an interweaving of horizontal and vertical thinking, of hearing and shaping. With Busoni this combination becomes a perfect synthesis, originating from what he has repeatedly described as the unity of music. I myself have only twice heard Busoni play. First in Berlin in 1921 when he was playing a concerto for two pianos with Egon Petri. I shall never forget it. His very appearance outshone all the pictures one had ever seen of him. As he sat at his instrument, his face was pale and motionless as marble, the almost ethereal features a combination of intelligence and extreme sensitivity. He might have been a *grand seigneur*. With him playing the piano seemed to be merely a means to a more important end : which was to shed maximum light on a work of art. I clearly remember the tempo of the Sonata in D major, K. 448, particularly the naturally paced Andante in the second minuet-like movement. His rendering of the fast-moving outer movements was a unique and fascinating display of virtuosity, apparently effortless; exceptional in the constant variety of colour and quality of touch, in the economic treatment of the pedal, and the skilful use of phrasing to make a melody appear fresh and new. I also remember how in his own *Duettino Concertante* (after the finale of the Concerto in F, K. 459) Busoni took a step back behind his partner Egon Petri, even though he was still a *primus inter pares*. The other time I heard him was also in Berlin, when he was playing Beethoven's E flat major Concerto in the Philharmonic Hall.

It has often been said, that as a pianist Busoni followed in the path of Franz Liszt. The reforms instigated by Liszt reach far beyond his own epoch. His extending the octave range beyond seven octaves; making more subtle use of the pedals and touch; deepening orchestral polyphony by means of the singing tenor-register; mixing extreme colour effects with high treble and low bass; all of which can be traced in the work of Debussy, Ravel and Messiaen, Bartók, Skriabin and Reger.

During the 1890s Busoni also began to write about the problems of piano playing. The preface to the first volume of *The Well-Tempered Clavier* in the Bach edition, written in New York in January 1894, marks the beginning of the major crisis in Busoni's development as a pianist and composer. There we read of Bach: 'The point of departure for modern piano playing corresponds with the foundations he laid for present-day compositional trends.' Busoni then goes on to defend the modernizing of Bach's work by Liszt, Tausig and others; of himself he says that his aim is to show how the branches of modern piano technique can be traced back 'to the main stem, as it were', which is to say, *The Well-Tempered Clavier*. In a postscript which appears to have been added in 1897 he deals with the problems of transferring from organ to piano. Here he is in favour of using the pedals: 'No one should take any notice of the legendary tradition whereby Bach is supposed to be played without pedals.' He also disassociates himself from 'people . . . who furthermore insist that Bach should only be performed on the spinet or clavichord,' saying that these are the same people who oppose the playing of Liszt, the later Beethoven and valve trumpets.

For sustained organ notes he uses the third pedal, or sustaining pedal, introduced in Steinway's grand pianos, which is cleaner than the old damper-pedal as the rest of the strings cannot sound at the same time. He goes on to compare the function of touch on the piano with the organist's choice of register : 'With the organ the performer has to know how to choose his stops; with the piano, it is up to the fingers to create this effect.' As a prototype for Bach transcription, he quotes Liszt's Variations on *Weinen, Klagen*.

In a letter written to Gerda Busoni on 20th July 1898 he gives an account of the technique he uses for practising; he says : 'Practise the passage with the most difficult fingering; once you have mastered it, then enjoy yourself with the easiest fingering.' Again : 'Don't make a point of trying to master pieces that you have previously practised badly and therefore been unable to play; it is generally a complete waste of time. But if in the meantime you have totally changed your technique, begin at the beginning as if you had never seen the piece before.'

This kind of radical thinking was fundamental to his attitude to life. Busoni despised mediocrity because he valued only the best. In this he is a forerunner of the modern perfectionist. Even the cycle-form which his programmes had tended to follow since the Berlin days is the product of this same attitude to life and to art. At the Conservatory in Helsinki he was already fascinating his pupils with his 'historical evenings'; and according to Adolf Paul, he knew almost all the literature written on the subject of the piano. In Berlin he played six Mozart piano concertos with the Philharmonic Orchestra in two evenings; and in 1911, on the occasion of Liszt's hundredth anniversary, he gave six recitals including a total of forty-six works by Liszt.

All those who have heard him agree that he transformed even familiar music. Bruno Götz, who admired him long before he came into personal contact with him in Zürich in 1917, gives this account of his playing : '. . . what I heard were no longer the same pieces; through the music emerged fleeting aural visions, such as the masters who created them may have inwardly perceived before writing them down . . . From the technical and musical point of view his performance was faultless. Without paying the slightest attention to the usual traditions, he returned to the original source, as it were, and recreated them—so that they sounded new and unfamiliar as if they were being played for the first time.'

Nevertheless in a letter to the Belgian critic, Marcel Remy, he defends himself against the accusation that he intended to modernize the works in his performance. He maintains that his intention was rather to rejuvenate them by shaking off the dust of tradition. (Similar feelings were expressed about this time by Gustav Mahler—Busoni's letter dates from 1902—when he said that tradition was the equivalent of slovenliness.) By visualizing the character of Beethoven as a person, he formed an image of his music that was not 'modern' but alive. Apparently he did the same thing with Liszt and César Franck. He also says that from Chopin and Liszt he learned that a passage orchestrated 'fortissimo' can be played softly, but that a 'pianissimo' can never be rendered loudly.

One of Busoni's later pupils, Heinrich Kosnick, writing on the master's piano playing, has pointed out a passage in a letter written to Gerda in 1906 where Busoni says : 'I hardly play with my hands any more. This way of playing is equally effective whatever the piece.' Kosnick then speaks of a 'creative transposition in organ terms' which he goes on to describe : 'He seemed to produce his slurs almost by magic now, by anticipating even creating the resistance, the counter-pressure of the keys or the base of the keys, as if he were playing an organ . . . As a result of this spiritual-cum-physical contact his passage-work had an almost glissando-like foundation, was to some extent anchored to the bed of the stream.' The point he is making here is important, because it shows that with Busoni the spiritual-intellectual element is inseparable from the physical. As one of the instigators of the annual Busoni Contest held at Bozen,

Kosnick has constantly insisted on this inter-relationship when criticizing the young pianists competing. He thus endorses the theory, that a phenomenal talent such as Busoni's can only be understood as a unity. Body, mind and soul are totally integrated in his art.

In an article on playing from memory, written for a journal in 1907, Busoni became involved in the enigmatic relationship between mental memory and 'finger memory'. The Fugue from Beethoven's Sonata Opus 106 is one of the few pieces that impress themselves more quickly on the fingers than on the mind. Stage-fright can easily cloud the mind and cause a lapse of memory; but this can also happen when playing from music at a public concert, and the result is inaccuracy, lack of rhythm and an increase in tempo.

Unfortunately, his contemporaries' accounts of his playing generally give an overall impression, and only very seldom go into technicalities. This even applies to such a well-informed musician and author as Hugo Leichtentritt. Gisella Selden-Goth was the first of Busoni's biographers to offer concrete examples and analyses of his piano technique. Her book was written 1921–22; her view was quite comprehensive for that time. Her first point is, that Busoni realized that the slurred note, the legato, is not an organic part of piano playing. This is why he chisels out each note separately and only arrives at a legato cantilena through constant use of the pedal. This technique has been named 'non-legato playing', borrowing one of Busoni's own favourite terms. He was also helped by his extraordinary reach, his hands though not large being flexible and highly trained. He could reach five-voiced chords within the span of a tenth, without having to resort to the arpeggio which he considered as taboo. Gisella Selden-Goth describes a typical performance as a 'disembodied wave of mixed notes gliding past and blending in all sorts of subtle and ethereal ways'. By using his thumb, Busoni apparently made the bass notes peal like bells.

Walter Niemann, himself a pianist and composer of piano music, calls Busoni's playing 'quite incomprehensible, this modern way of playing octaves, light as a feather, all the strain taken by the back muscles'; but at the same time he infers that he could not make the piano sing like Thalberg or Chopin.

The French musicologist, Jean Philippe Chantavoine, a friend of Busoni's, speaks of a degree of perfection and transcendent virtuosity that goes far beyond mere keyboard acrobatics. He also mentions the phenomenal flexibility of the fingers, the supple elasticity of the wrist, all of which would be quite meaningless without an exceptional and subtle brain to direct them. Edward Dent goes a step further and says that it is the passionate desire to know the truth that turns the modern musician into an interpretive artist. He also emphasizes that one had to be thoroughly familiar with the pieces Busoni played, and that his rendering of the last Beethoven Sonatas required a constant mental effort on the part of the listener. Referring to Busoni's Bach performance, he draws attention to his firm metallic touch which rang out loud and clear like a trumpet, drowning the pedal vibrato of the strings.

The pianist, Mark Hambourg, who had known Busoni since his visit to London in 1906, is quoted by Harold C. Schonberg as witness to the fact that he had very slim hands and had to practise a lot to keep in form. He is said to have played from the shoulder rather than the wrist, with powerful results. The critic, Rita Boetticher, a rather quaint hunchback creature who was friendly with Busoni during the last years of his life (she used to write under the pseudonym Thurneiser), state categorically that he transformed the 'piano into an impressive substitute for the orchestra'. She goes on to say that the secret of his playing rested essentially on 'conscious polyphony of sounds', plus a phrasing that was carefully anticipated and prepared, laying bare the very bones of the piece. In her opinion his rendering of compositions involved their total exposure and produced some surprising sounds. Polyphonic listening was as natural to him as breathing. Besides which he, as it were, orchestrated every piano piece he played. In her essay *Busoni's Music and the Microphone* which appeared in 1934, she goes on to draw parallels between his ability to exchange one sound effect for another and modern attempts to track down new or imitative sounds with electrical devices. There are better grounds for this comparison than may at first appear. Because in 1906 in America Busoni had been introduced to the electric dynamophone invented by Dr. Thaddäus Cahill; the possibilities it offered of producing synthetic sound fascinated him and inspired a vivid description of the instrument in his *Outline for a New Musical Aesthetics*. The pianist, Theophil Demetriescu, who also knew Busoni well during his last years in Berlin, praises 'the rhythmical richness, the chiselled, chased, quality of his technique; the pianola-like (in the best sense of the word) precision of his touch; the inimitable skill in phrasing; the lightness, economy, spontaneity...' of his performance. Because of his feeling of responsibility towards his audience and pupils, he felt it his duty to give of his best at every performance. Which is why virtually no one ever heard him play badly. It appears that he spoke of other pianists with respect but seldom with admiration. He did not like being able to detect the tears and sweat that had gone into the performance of a great technician. Apparently he once stayed in London at the same hotel as a famous virtuoso who practised the same passage from Liszt's A major Concerto for hours at a time. Busoni ended this story with the question : 'Is that talent?'

Although Busoni spiritually followed in the footsteps of Franz Liszt, he was not directly influenced by him as a pianist. His meeting with him in Vienna as a child was too brief, and later Abbé Liszt retired from public life and Busoni never heard him play again. Whereas Anton Rubinstein, of whom he always spoke with unreserved admiration even when he himself was a mature musician, was unquestionably his model. He had known the Russian well ever since the five piano recitals he gave in Vienna in 1884. It was then that he played him his Sonata in F minor which is dedicated to Rubinstein. After Busoni's death Dr. Friedrich Schnapp published a piece on Rubinstein written by Busoni in 1885, in which he says that his rendering of Chopin's

C minor Nocturne 'was more valuable than a whole course of lessons'. Rubinstein liked him in return, and encouraged the young student in every possible way. During the winter of 1890–91 Busoni heard him play the Schubert-Liszt *Erlkönig* on an old clapped-out grand piano, an experience that brought tears to his eyes.

Philipp Jarnach has mentioned the fact, that Busoni had no time for the intermediate levels of ability in his concept of art and forced all technical questions into the realm of creativity. This is confirmed by many of Busoni's own comments on piano playing. Most of these were written down in 1910. 'One should respect the piano,' he says in a footnote to Gottfried Galston's manual; and as for the pedal : 'People treat it as if they were trying to force air and water into geometrical forms... The pedal has a bad name. The senseless liberties that people have taken with it are entirely to blame. Let them try taking significant liberties with it . . .' As to the requirements of a pianist, Busoni writes that a great pianist must first and foremost be a great technician. But, he says, technique does not depend solely on fingers and wrists, strength and persistence. It is seated in the brain and consists of the ability to judge distances and organize well; but even this is only a beginning because touch and pedal treatment also have a contribution to make. From the great artist Busoni demands not only intelligence, culture and a comprehensive training in music, literature and human nature, but character and a whole list of other qualities besides.

In connection with Galston he observes, that the pianist only finds himself faced with a new task when he is presented with a new musical dimension, such as the harmony of César Franck. Thinking about Balzac, who with four thousand characters in his *Comédie Humaine* must have been able to identify everyone he met, Busoni relegates all pianists with a limited repertoire into a secondary category. Let Galston prove that his aspirations went beyond the level of a repertory performer and a virtuoso : 'In order to get beyond the virtuoso level, one must first be a virtuoso : one arrives at something more, not something different.'

Ultimately Busoni comes down quite definitely in favour of musical arrangements such as Liszt's version of Schubert's *Wanderer* Fantasy and countless other pieces. Quite rightly, he names Johann Sebastian Bach as one of the most prolific arrangers of his own and other people's work. After all, he maintains, every performance of a work is a transcription, in fact the very process of writing down an idea inevitably changes it from its original form : 'The idea becomes a sonata or a concerto : that is already an arrangement of the original.' On the question of 'pianistic genius' Busoni says in 1912, that it is the ability to do something unprecedented in a totally new territory, something which requires a certain distance in time before it can be appreciated. In his opinion Beethoven, Chopin and Liszt did just this. Only someone who initially stands alone and is later imitated, only someone who forces innovations in the very structure of the piano and writes music that demands something more than a routine performance, can be called a pianistic genius.

Without any doubt Busoni had widely conflicting feelings about his own playing. He found it exasperating having to practise the same pieces at fifty as at fifteen. When in 1919 he held a reception at his apartment in Zürich for the university professors who were awarding him an honorary doctorate, he was deeply moved by the honour and the laudation, but simply could not bring himself to do what was expected of him : sit down at the piano and play. He entrusted a number of his most important works to the instrument he had served even as a child, particularly those in which he moved furthest away from conventional composition, such as the *Sonatina seconda*. But there were times when he hated the piano because he felt that it stood in the way of the only thing that was really important to him : communicating with kindred spirits through his creative ability.

Busoni's Bach transcriptions have received a lot of criticism; for musical purists they represented an inadmissible interference with the essential character of Bach's music. The same went for his Bach Edition, which in fact does not contain any actual transcriptions, only rearrangements of Bach piano pieces for modern performance. One of the most objective and painstaking reviewers of Busoni's work with Bach was the composer and teacher, August Halm, who wrote a very comprehensive article on the subject in *Melos* in 1921. In this he warns against indiscriminately adopting certain of Busoni's methods, such as octave-doublings or octave displacements in the bass. As an example he quotes the C minor Fugue from the second book of *The Well-Tempered Clavier*. But even when Halm feels obliged to criticize what Busoni has done, as for example in his transcription of the Violin Chaconne to the piano, he does so with the greatest respect and is always careful to point out where the arrangement in question has succeeded. Finally he considers Busoni's *Experiment in Organic Piano Notation* which is included in the seventh volume of the Bach Edition and appeared in 1910. Here Busoni is trying to dispense with transposition signs, which is to say sharps, flats and naturals, in order to eliminate mistakes in sight-reading. It is a form of notation which, unlike our traditional one, is not derived from tonal relationships but from the keyboard itself. Although it was never established, this form of notation could have been used for atonal music and twelve-tone compositions for keyboard instruments—in 1920 Joseph Matthias Hauer produced a rival method that was closely related. It is significant that Busoni devised this scheme during the years when his own compositions were moving steadily away from the principles of tonality, that is to say after 1909.

During the critical period 1893–94 a number of important works by Liszt make their first appearance in Busoni's programmes : The Fantasia and Fugue B-A-C-H, the two St. Francis Legends, the A major Concerto and the Spanish Rhapsody, together with the Fantasias on Bellini's *Norma* and on Verdi's *Rigoletto*. By that time he was living in Berlin where his first recitals met with somewhat incredulous admiration. In 1895 he played Beethoven's Diabelli Variations, Chopin's Scherzo in B flat minor, and a number of lesser known pieces by Liszt such as the Variations on Bach's *Weinen, Klagen*, the Ballades, the

Hexameron, but also the popular 12th Hungarian Rhapsody and the *Tannhäuser* Overture.

In the years that followed, 1896–1900, Beethoven was increasingly in evidence; in Düsseldorf Busoni played his *Choral Fantasia*, in Trieste and London the Sonatas in E flat Opus 81a, and in F sharp, Opus 78, the late Bagatelles, Opus 126, and the Sonata in C sharp minor from Opus 27. In addition to these in Berlin we find the twelve Chopin Etudes, Weber's C major Sonata, Chopin's B flat minor Sonata, Brahms' Paganini Variations, and Rubinstein's Variations in G major. His Liszt repertoire has been considerably extended. Busoni is now playing *Après une lecture de Dante* from the *Années de Pélérinage* in Berlin, all twelve *Etudes d'exécution transcendante*, transcriptions of Schubert's *Soirées de Vienne*, *Lindenbaum*, *Auf dem Wasser zu singen*, and *Wanderer* (with orchestra), Donizetti's *Lucia* and *Parisina (Valse à capriccio)*, Meyerbeer's *Robert le Diable*, and the C major Polonaise and the B flat minor Sonata. During these five years Busoni was soloist in Grieg's A minor Concerto in Copenhagen; Rubinstein's E flat major Concerto and Brahms' D minor Concerto in Vienna; and Tschaikowsky's B flat minor Concerto in London. During 1898 Berlin heard him play five concertos with orchestra : Chopin's E minor, Henselt's F minor, Hummel's B flat minor, Mendelssohn's G minor and Mozart's A major. In Vienna he partnered José Vianna da Motta in Liszt's *Faust Symphony* for two pianos and in his arrangement of Beethoven's Ninth Symphony.

During this period there occurs too a change in Busoni's attitude to Romantic composers such as Chopin, Henselt and Mendelssohn; for a short time Bach faded into the background, at any rate as far as his concert work was concerned. In Helsinki Busoni played his D minor Concerto, in Manchester his arrangement of the Organ Toccata, Adagio and Fugue in C major.

Busoni met the conductor, Henry Wood during his first concert trip to London. In his memoirs, *My Life of Music*, Wood speaks of the extraordinarily strong impression that the great Italian musician made on him both as an artist and as a man. At the same time there were things that puzzled him, such as the fact that each time they passed the Royal Academy of Music, Busoni raised his hat in mock respect. There were critical moments when it seemed he would forget everything, including his own concert engagements. This was regularly the case whenever he met his friend Jean Sibelius in London; the two musicians would go from one restaurant to another, absorbed in conversation and quite unaware how late it was, often not even conscious which day of the week was drawing to a close.

Only once did Henry Wood succeed in overcoming Busoni's aversion to Tschaikowsky's B flat minor Concerto and persuade him to play the work in one of his concerts, and that was in 1900. Busoni himself wrote the following day: 'The Tschaikowsky Concerto is over and went extremely well; but, as the English say, "once and never again"; I felt as if I were wearing a new pair of boots; they looked elegant, but I was glad to take them off . . .'

The conductor was surprised by the unusually wide piano stool that Busoni used during his performance, a kind of organ bench. He asked why and was told, that while playing Busoni often moved his body to the right or left in order to reach the highest or lowest octaves. This physical mobility was also something that he taught his pupils; it was to some extent responsible for his much-praised accuracy when playing at the extremities of the keyboard.

After 1901 Alkan's Etudes, Opus 35, and other less important pieces appeared together with works by French and Belgian musicians, such as the F major Concerto by Saint-Saëns and César Franck's Prelude, Chorale and Fugue. Pablo Casals, who admired Busoni so much as an artist that he even respected his views on art although he could not agree with them, had doubts about his 'determination to distort what he felt'. In Franck's Triptych Busoni replaced his emotion with '. . . something diabolical . . . a distortion which he had to force out of himself.'

Busoni's wide range of achievement in piano playing included

85

Chopin's twelve *Etudes* in Berlin in 1902, the twenty-four Preludes in Zürich in 1906. Between these dates, apart from Liszt's Transcendental *Etudes*, his *Années de Pélérinage*, *Totentanz*, *Apparitions*, *Valse Mélancolique*, and the *Concerto Pathétique* for two pianos (with Egon Petri). Beethoven is represented in his programmes by the *Pathétique*, the Sonata Opus 110 and the C minor Concerto. His most recent struggle with Brahms, who was becoming increasingly alien to him, was a book of four chorale-preludes, transferred from the organ to the piano.

The most ambitious product of his own creative work at this time was the all-embracing Piano Concerto with Male Choir. This piece, which was first performed in Berlin in 1904, represents in piano composition alone a compendium of all the experience Busoni has derived from earlier works. In his *Outline for a New Musical Aesthetics*, which was written in Berlin in 1905–6, Busoni sets down his own views on interpretation : 'Musical performance is born in those same sublime regions from which music itself has descended. Whenever the music is in danger of becoming earthbound, the performance must elevate it and help it to regain its original ethereal quality . . . It is the duty of the performer to liberate it from the deadness of the printed page and bring it to life again', and he disputes the 'lawgivers' for whom the printed notes are more important than music itself.

There are no additions to his repertoire during the year 1907. He is busy with his master-class in Vienna, and particularly with work on compositions such as *Die Brautwahl*, the Elegies and the Liszt Sonnet *Pace non trovo*.

'I find piano practising a great effort, yet one dare not ignore it,' he writes to Gerda in July; 'It's like an animal whose heads are continually growing again, however many one cuts off.' Then from Vienna, where he has heard Gottfried Galston's concerts : 'As far as Galston's rendering of Liszt is concerned, I am delighted by his success. Once one has really absorbed Liszt's style, his pieces always sound better than any others . . .'

In 1906 Busoni had worked up some of the pieces in his repertoire for Welte-Mignon in Freiburg. These recordings of the *Campanella* and other pieces by Liszt give some indication of his superhuman technical facility, the singing quality of his non-legato, his supremely skilful phrasing, and the force and brilliance of his trill.

After 1908 his own compositions appear with greater regularity in his programmes. In Berlin he played the Six Elegies, in London in 1909 Bach-studies and transcriptions such as the *Fuga figurata* based on *The Well-Tempered Clavier* and, influenced by the death of his father Ferdinando, the Fantasia on *Christ, du bist der helle Tag*. Pieces selected from Mozart and Paganini are re-shaped and given a new interpretation. In 1910 his *Fantasia Contrappuntistica* and first Sonatina are given their first hearing in Basle.

Apart from Liszt (the complete *Années de Pélérinage* performed by him for the first time in Berlin) and Mozart, the programmes reveal very few innovations; in 1909 and 1910 nothing besides his arrangements. It was during this period that Busoni was introduced to the first atonal compositions of Arnold Schoenberg. The piano pieces, Opus 11, fascinated him so much that he undertook a 'concerto-like interpretation' of the second. Comparing his arrangement with the original, it immediately becomes clear that Busoni's prime concern is the harmonic problem posed by this music. He examines the unfamiliar chord progressions, charges them with even greater resonance, doubling the bass in octaves. He repeats characteristic combinations, carrying them into higher and lower octaves. He even adds notes or intervals, in order to emphasize the relevant overtones. But above all he changes the basic form of the piano composition by breaking up simple quaver passages into repeated semi-quavers, transferring certain passages from the right hand to the left and vice versa. Various extensions are introduced, continuing the thought process by which Schoenberg himself follows through his themes. In Busoni's version the piece is extended from sixty-six bars to seventy-eight. Schoenberg's polyphony is particularly difficult for him to grasp. In bars 50 and 51 of his interpretation he leaves out altogether the canonic lower voice that Schoenberg has introduced in bars 43 and 44. In bar 56 (bar 49 with Schoenberg) he breaks up the even rhythms of the ascending bass notes and descending upper voice with hiccupping quaver grace-notes. The first 'pianissimo' theme Busoni plays 'sotto voce'; the second 'piano' theme he indicates as 'ritenuto', and on its return as 'espressivo'. Schoenberg's indication 'fliessender' at the third theme (bar 16, 18 in Busoni's version) becomes 'lebendiger'. The extreme softness of bars 26 and 27 : pppp-pp-ppp-ppsf-ppp is simplified by Busoni (bars 29 and 30) into ppp-p-pp. These sort of radical changes can only be justified by his desire to make it easier for the listener to approach a new style, a startling musical language. Basically, Busoni uses the same methods as Liszt in his transcriptions. Only he uses them to promote a language frequently cried down and dismissed as revolutionary, which he himself supports without thoroughly having understood it. Busoni never actually performed his 'concerto-like interpretation' himself. But the work he did on it was later reflected in his *Sonatina seconda* which appeared with the *Berceuse* and the fourth Ballet Sequence on a Milan concert programme in 1913.

Although as a thinker and composer Busoni sympathized with the most modern development in music, in fact even anticipated it in many parts of his *Outline for a New Musical Aesthetics* and in pieces such as the *Berceuse Elégiaque*, he never played any contemporary music in concerts. The most modern pieces in his programme, apart from his own, were Grieg's Concerto in A minor and Saint-Saëns' Scherzo for Two Pianos. There is a whole era in the history of piano music, which Busoni certainly witnessed and to some extent supported, but as an interpretive artist totally ignored. Neither Strauss' Burleske nor Reger's Piano Concerto were ever performed by him. Skriabin's Sonatas and small pieces, Bartók's Bagatelles, Debussy's two books of Preludes, his *Estampes* and *Images*, Ravel's *Miroirs*, his *Sonatine* and *Gaspard de la Nuit*, Schoenberg's piano pieces, Opus 11 and

19, Alban Berg's Sonata, Albéniz's Spanish minature-painting, Turina and Granados—all these were banished from Busoni's concert repertoire. This is all the more puzzling, since in his orchestral concerts held between 1902 and 1909 he emphatically supported Debussy and Bartók, as well as Sibelius and Carl Nielsen. For a while he was very friendly with Reger. He considered Strauss to be the most intelligent musician of his time. He met Debussy in Paris and played Liszt's *Jeux d'eau de la Villa d'Este* for him. About the same time he got to know and admire Casella, and probably through him the music of Stravinsky too.

Clearly Busoni had a totally different relationship with musical phenomena as a pianist. He could come to terms with things, to the point of identifying with them, as his 'concerto-like interpretation' of the Schoenberg piece proves. But he was not prepared to find room for it in the hierarchy of his piano recitals.

For the Liszt celebrations held in Berlin in 1911, he included in his cycle pieces that he had not touched for years : the first *Valse oubliée, Zelle in Nonnenwerth,* and the Fantasias on Schubert's *Trout,* Verdi's *Trovatore* and (in his own version) Mozart's *Figaro.*

During the years preceding the First World War Busoni developed an increasingly subjective approach to his rendering which would have been artistically damaging in any other pianist. But the unique combination of intellect, taste and complete technical mastery raised his playing to the level of the creative. Busoni said of Liszt, that he had raised the status of the piano to that of a prince in order to make it worthy of him; he himself transformed piano playing into something that the best of his contemporaries considered as brilliant, a superlative artistic feat. Leichtentritt has spoken of the glittering audiences that attended Busoni's later recitals in Berlin. Apart from the pianists, all the most influential supporters of music were present, educated people of all nationalities, the most cultivated and beautiful women. It would seem that Busoni made no concessions to this cosmopolitan audience and offered them the most difficult programmes. Even his stereotype opening, one of his own transcriptions of a Bach organ piece, left no doubts on this score. Among the Bach transcriptions to appear in his programmes between 1913 and 1914 were Adagio and Fugue in C major, the Capriccio of the Departure of a Beloved Brother, the *Goldberg Variations*, and transcribed from the harpsichord, Prelude Fugue and Allegro in E flat major. Works of his own composition, apart from those played in Milan in 1913, were not performed in Berlin before 1914 : his *Indian Fantasia* with orchestra, and two dance pieces Opus 30 a dating from a much earlier period, the titles of which *Waffentanz* (Dance of Weapons) and *Friedentanz* (Dance of Peace) are strangely topical in this first year of the War.

1915, his most critical year from a personal point of view, produced nothing new in Busoni's programmes. It was not until he settled in Zürich in the autumn that he resumed his activity as a thinking pianist, dedicated to the highest tasks of comparing musical epochs. In January 1916 he played three piano concertos in one evening at a concert given at the Tonhalle with Volkmar Andreae conducting : Beethoven's Concerto in E flat major, his own *Indian Fantasia* and Liszt's *Totentanz*. The four piano recitals held in March and April were devoted to Bach, Beethoven, Chopin and Liszt. As for the programmes ! The Beethoven recital alone, with the Sonata Opus 111, Bagatelles Opus 126 and the *Hammerklavier* Sonata, presented both players and audience with an unusual challenge; the same was true a week later of his combination of twelve *Etudes*, twenty-four Preludes, the F minor Ballade, C sharp minor Scherzo and A flat major Polonaise by Chopin. Seldom has any man been more generous to his contemporaries on his fiftieth birthday !

In Basle people more or less expected this sort of thing from Busoni; he had already given this Chopin recital there, with a couple of minor variations, back in 1910. Then in January 1916 the Basle audience was able to enjoy a foretaste of the four

Zürich programmes, the Beethoven recital, introduced once more by the *Eroica* Variation and continuing with Opus 109 instead of 111. To round off his achievements as an interpreter that year, Busoni presented another three enormous programmes in Zürich in November and December, including as 'innovations' six preludes from *The Well-Tempered Clavier*, books I and II, and his transcription of the organ prelude *Komm Gott Schöpfer*. The climax was reached in the second programme with Franck's Prelude, Chorale and Fugue, Chopin's B flat minor Sonata, and Brahms' Handel and Paganini Variations.

A short article written in 1917 on Mozart's *Don Giovanni* and Liszt's *Don Juan Fantasia* introduces fresh ideas on piano playing and piano transcriptions. Busoni points out that what may appear as unnecessary exuberance in reading or playing, was 'for someone like Liszt an effortless game that he casually mastered and performed'. He therefore advises a musician to strive for the lucidity and lightness of Mozart's language. Of himself, as editor of the Liszt transcriptions, Busoni says, that throughout his lifelong study of the piano he has always aimed at 'simplifying the mechanics of piano playing and reducing it to the least possible movement and physical effort'. Technique is acquired, he says, by adapting a problem to suit one's own abilities; an intellectual grasp of the issue is more important than physical practise. 'It is not by tackling a difficulty repeatedly, but by analysing the problem, that one may possibly succeed in solving it.'

In Zürich in 1917 Busoni presented the first performance of his *Sonatina ad usum infantis* composed the previous year, and his even earlier *Indian Diary*, on the same evening. At the end of December, at a recital for two pianos with Ernst Lochbrunner as his partner, he played his improvisation based on the Bach Chorale *Wie wohl ist mir*, together with pieces by Mozart, Liszt, Schumann and Saint-Saëns.

His correspondence with his friend Hans Huber, particularly during the years 1917 and 1918, shows how distressed he was by the frequently harsh criticism of his playing and his Bach

91

editions. So he was all the more delighted by the view expressed by Albert Schweitzer in his *Bach*, where he describes the Busoni edition of the Chromatic Fantasia as 'one of the finest achievements in this field'. The Basle, St. Gall and Zürich concert programmes of 1919 reveal a series of concertos with orchestra, including his own arrangement of Bach's D minor Concerto, the first version of Liszt's *Totentanz*, Mozart's Concertos in A major and C minor, and Beethoven's C major Concerto.

In 1920 the world was once again at the feet of a man already tired and ill. He had new works to offer : in Zürich the fourth *Sonatina In diem nativitatis Christi*, in London his brilliant *Sonatina super Carmen*, in Berlin the most mature product of his last creative years : the three-part Toccata. For another two years this incomparable pianist was able to bewitch audiences in Berlin, London, Liverpool and Paris. Apart from his own three *Album-leaves*, the programmes include mainly works by Mozart or Mozart transcriptions, such as that of the Fantasia in F minor for a mechanical organ, which he played in Berlin with Egon Petri on two pianos; also the two Concertos in E flat major, K. 271 and 482.

'He seems to be secretly listening to himself whilst playing,' Stefan Zweig remarked of the mature Busoni. Jakob Wassermann, another of his writer friends, describes how 'all the Latin superficiality and the worldly element in his character disappeared as soon as he sat down at the piano. Suddenly the Nordic element emerged, the restraint, the discipline and violence, that were a part of him.'

Busoni himself provides the key to an understanding of the driving force behind his activity as a pianist when he says, that the piano provides the individual with the possibility of mastering something complete. He saw the instrument as some kind of super-orchestra. One has only to compare his transcriptions with the originals, no matter whether these are organ pieces or orchestral scores, in order to have the clearest possible picture of the spiritual path that he followed in his music. The idea of unity was of prime importance to Busoni. It embraces more than just the worldly and spiritual spheres; it is projected into the creative and post-creative aspects of music-making. His was a strictly ordered world; yet he was so completely in control of it, that he could present it as an improvisation. In Busoni's art inspiration and realization have become one.

The Composer

'First there has to be the *idea*, then *inspiration* follows, or if it does not one goes in search of it, and finally there is the *realization* . . . In my case, I usually make my musical discoveries while out walking in the street, preferably in a lively part of the town and in the evening. The realization happens at home, when I have a free morning.' This was how Busoni replied to a questionnaire circulated in May 1907 by the Berlin magazine, *Der Konzertsaal*.

From early childhood he had been used to expressing himself in musical terms, making shapes in sound. Even in the early days people had been impressed by the spontaneity of his creative work, particularly Eduard Hanslick, who remarked on it in his reviews. From the very beginning Busoni had a facility for composing. Music was his element, the very air he breathed. As opposed to Stravinsky, for whom writing begins at the table, an act of will dependent on hours of concentration, this Tuscan finds his inspiration 'while out walking'. He is even more precise about it, and adds : 'in a lively part of the town.' Busoni was a townsman, and relatively unaffected by landscape. To be at his most creative, he needed company, excitement, and other people around him. He liked the evening, it fired his imagination. Yet the realization of his ideas, the real work, was reserved for the bright morning light. It is as well to bear in mind the dual aspect of his creative act, the way it is divided into the processes of discovery and elaboration. It provides at least one key to the many mysteries contained in his music.

One of these mysteries is its apparent timelessness. Admittedly, there is not a bar that could have been written at any time other than the twentieth century, or during the last decades of the nineteenth century. Yet many of the characteristics of the post-Wagnerian period are conspicuously absent from Busoni's music. He himself realized this, and disassociated himself from almost all his musical contemporaries. But at the same time he was by no means what one would call an outsider; he took a serious interest in, and frequently admired the work of other great composers, such as Richard Strauss, Gustav Mahler, Claude Debussy and Béla Bartók. But even in his admiration, he remained critical; his appreciation was always qualified.

On many occasions Busoni has looked back on his own work and expressed misgivings. One of his most important observations, also quoted by Edward Dent, appears in a letter written to Gerda Busoni from Norderney on 2nd August 1907 : 'This summer I have definitely taken a step forward in my development. As you know, the first stage in the formation of my musical taste was to get Schumann and Mendelssohn out of my system; Liszt, I misunderstood, then worshipped, and eventually admired more calmly; Wagner, I regarded with hostility, then awe, and subsequently being a Latin rejected him again; Berlioz took me by surprise. One of the most difficult things of all, was learning to distinguish between the good and bad in Beethoven. Recently I discovered the latest French composers, and when I found myself falling for them too readily, promptly dropped them again. Finally, I have drawn spiritually closer to the older Italian theatre music. These metamorphoses cover a span of twenty years. Throughout that time my admiration for the Figaro score remained constant, like a beacon in a restless sea. But when I looked at it again a week ago, for the first time I detected human weaknesses in it. I was delighted to discover that I was no longer so completely under its spell, although on the other hand it is a real loss and shows the transience of all human activity (particularly my own !) . . .'

Four months later he wrote a short article on the misleading nature of his Opus numbers, in which he says : 'As a child, I wrote a great deal and published a lot prematurely. Being wrongly advised and totally inexperienced myself, I numbered the things that were published in order of composition rather than of publication . . . I was about seventeen by the time Opus nos. 1–14 and 30–40 had been published . . . the real juvenilia appeared when I was eighteen . . . properly speaking, I only found my feet as a composer with the second Violin

95

Sonata, Opus 36a (which among friends I call my Opus 1), followed by the Concerto and *Turandot* (the real nos. 2 and 3). But I did not really have a personal idiom before the Elegies.'

The predominant influences that Dent mentions and examines in detail are Liszt, Verdi, Bach and Mozart. The tendency is for each of these composers to influence a specific type of composition, although admittedly they do overlap and cross one another's paths. It is clear that Liszt has left his imprint more particularly on the piano compositions, and not merely on their instrumental style. Verdi, on the other hand, is more apparent in the dramatic works, from the *Brautwahl* to the operatic version of the *Turandot* music. Busoni became aware of Verdi relatively late. Admittedly, even as a grown man, he never forgot the production of *Rigoletto* that he had seen in Trieste as a child. Nevertheless, his discovery of Verdi dates from a Berlin production of *Falstaff* on 22nd April 1894, with Franz Betz in the title role. At the time he wrote to his mother in amazement, saying how incredible it was, that a man of eighty should be able to write things that he could never have written earlier, things, in fact, that no one before him had done. About the same period he drafted a letter to the old master, which reflects more clearly than ever before the inner conflicts of a man torn between different nations and different cultures. In it he says: 'My youth was devoted to studies . . . based on German art and scholarship. But I had scarcely completed my theoretical studies . . . when I began to grasp, understand, even approach the spirit and essence of art. So my admiration for your masterpieces . . . came relatively too late . . . eventually, however, *Falstaff* provoked such a complete spiritual and emotional upheaval, that I can honestly say it marked the beginning of a new era in my life as an artist.' Busoni intended to enclose with this letter, which was never actually sent, the score of his *Symphonic Tone-Poem*, written about the same time. Admittedly, this piece was not entirely new. It had first appeared in 1888–89 in the form of a Concert Fantasy for piano and orchestra. Then four years later Busoni re-wrote it as a purely orchestral work, and dedicated it to Arthur Nikisch who gave it

5 Busoni in Zurich during the First World War

6 Giotto, Busoni's St. Bernard dog, Zurich 1918

its first performance with the Boston Symphony Orchestra. The actual piece has virtually nothing to do with Verdi. On the contrary, the influence of Richard Strauss, whose *Don Juan*, *Macbeth* and *Death and Transfiguration* Busoni knew well, is more apparent here than in any other piece. Back in 1888 there had been a violent quarrel between Busoni and his older friend, Henri Petri, on the subject of Strauss whom Busoni emphatically supported. What is particularly typical of Strauss in the *Symphonic Tone-Poem* is the harmonic language, the chromaticism which goes far beyond the Tristan influence, and the implication of a programme even though the content remains hidden. The thing that distinguishes the style of this score from Strauss is the recurrence of a ruthlessly linear polyphonic language. Even the imitative opening, a free canon with a profusion of entrances, has the feeling of Bach polyphony, which Hanslick had already noticed in Busoni's childhood work. It is characteristic of Busoni, that he preferred the gay and lively passages of Verdi and incorporated them in his own style. In *Rigoletto* it was the whispered Abduction Chorus that held him spellbound; while *Falstaff* consists mainly of statements made in this dry, bright and lively style. What obviously appealed to him much less was the sentimental side of Verdi's music, particularly the sort of arias, duets and ensembles inspired by passion. Busoni's philosophy of art is definitely opposed to eroticism. He considered that love was not a fitting subject for art. Love arias and lovers' duets were, so to speak, on his index— a fact that is clearly connected with an inborn aversion to giving musical expression to private and intimate experience. Admittedly, the impact of such emotions is all the stronger when, refuting all his theories and aesthetic convictions, they do manage to infiltrate his work. Busoni's operas contain very few arias and lovers' duets, such as the one in *Die Brautwahl*; consequently, they are all the more effective.

Leafing through a catalogue of his early work, compositions dating from the 'seventies and 'eighties, one is struck not only by the preponderance of material for the piano, but also by the number of songs. His choice of texts is not without interest; poets such as Lord Byron, Theodor Fontane, Victor Blüthgen. Rudolf Baumbach, and the Minnesänger poets, Neidhard von Reuenthal and Walther von der Vogelweide, appear alongside Arrigo Boito and his father, Ferdinando Busoni. *Des Sängers Fluch* by Ludwig Uhland is also one of the German texts set to music. (Emotion and all the excesses of Romantic love, after all! . . . one might say, on looking at these settings.) But they are not characteristic of Busoni as a person, typical rather of the period that produced them. Busoni was a precocious child and with him puberty, which always fosters emotionalism and erotic sensibility, began earlier than with other children and finished later than average. The vocal compositions, including a major choral work, *Il Sabato del Villaggio*, based on the famous poem by Giacomo Leopardi, almost all date from this period of extended puberty. After that Busoni wrote no more songs at all for many years. It was not until 1919 that he began work on a new series of songs, based entirely on poems by Goethe, which admittedly rank among the finest musical statements that Busoni has made. The *Sabato del Villaggio*, a cantata for solo voices, choir and orchestra, appeared in 1882, which means that Busoni wrote it in his sixteenth year; at the time of its first performance in the Civic Theatre in Bologna, it was much admired by the old master, Arrigo Boito, who a quarter of a century later reproached Busoni for not having devoted himself exclusively to composition. The three hundred page score remained unpublished; but in 1965, through a stroke of good fortune, it became the property of the Stiftung Preussischer Kulturbesitz and so returned to Berlin. Considering the age of the composer, it shows remarkable assurance in the technique of instrumental and vocal writing, as well as in the handling of harmonic language and polyphony. It tells us nothing about Busoni himself.

By this time Busoni had also begun composing chamber music. But neither the String Quartets of 1881 and 1889, nor the first Sonata for Violin and Piano which won the Rubinstein prize for composition in 1890, are really typical of Busoni. The influence of Johannes Brahms is unmistakable, obviously a result of the encouragement that the old master had given the boy in Vienna. It seems as though Busoni continued to follow his lead up to the composition of the *Lustspiel* Overture in 1897. There for the first time, it is possible to detect the influence of Mozart. But his Second Sonata in E minor for Violin and Piano, the one which among friends he called his Opus 1, is a chamber work written in his own personal style. Hugo Leichtentritt, a friend and admirer from the Boston period, speaking of this piece, mentions 'the expressive world of Bach organ compositions and the last Beethoven Sonatas'. He is quite right, and furthermore Busoni evokes the figure of Bach himself for the first time in his work, with a quotation which serves as a theme for variations in the last of the three movements : *Wie wohl ist mir, o Freund der Seelen.*

The Second Sonata belongs to the Berlin period. It dates from a time when Busoni was tormented by grave doubts about his artistic life. He was busy revising the very foundations of his already world-famous piano playing. He was working on the most important pieces in the huge Bach Edition, and on the first Liszt editions, which preceded the large complete edition (1907–1936). Also composed in Berlin was the vast Concerto for Piano and Orchestra with closing chorus, which received such a controversial reception when first performed in Berlin. Busoni had prepared the way for this piece in 1890 with a virtuoso concert piece, a preliminary attempt to come to terms with the dialogue between piano and orchestra. The Concerto, written between 1903–4, is in five movements and ends with a chorus of male voices based on verses by the Danish poet, Adam Gottlob Oehlenschläger, taken from his autobiographical fairy-play *Aladdin*, naturally in the German translation. Busoni himself designed a title-page for the score, strongly influenced by the period and his own youthful style, illustrating the mystic-symbolical nature of the five movements. A doric temple represents the first movement, interspersed with choral themes; half a pyramid with a sphinx stretched out in front of it, the wide-ranging middle movement, an adagio entitled *Pezzo Serioso*; a sort of tomb in front of a belching volcano, the final movement with the chorus for male voices. The first movement and the Finale are thematically related, the latter being a continuation of the former with symphonic additions. A *Pezzo Giocoso* and a more light-hearted episode *All' italiana* provide the second and fourth movements. The piano writing of the solo part is full of unusual innovations and difficulties. The full symphonic range of the orchestra is brought into play and becomes quite a challenge to the solo instrument. There is no doubt as to the brilliance of the individual details, they are effective even today. Yet the unity of the style is jeopardized by the desire to combine altogether too many different forms, styles and artistic attitudes, and to build them into something monumental. There is a hint of gigantomania in this score, an almost Kaiser Wilhelm-like, modern German tendency towards overstatement. Busoni has admittedly escaped the threat of Wagner in his musical language, but a Wagnerian love of the 'outsize' makes any listener, who has trained his ear and taken his bearings from the late Busoni and his 'new Classicism', stop and wonder. At the time when this 'super-concerto' appeared, Gustav Mahler had just progressed from his vocal symphonies to the C charp minor Symphony, the fifth, which is also in five movements. Busoni, who knew and admired Mahler, seems to have fallen for the symphonic style that he borrowed from Beethoven. Yet the emotional urgency, that is so convincing with Mahler, is totally absent from the vocal element of Busoni's final movement. The obvious musical and spiritual relationship between the light-hearted intermezzi in this concerto and Oehlenschläger's Hymnus, sung by bass voices, is missing. Falstaff's gaiety is incompatible with the presence of the sphinx and the strange bird-man, whom Busoni has drawn on his title-page to represent Oehlenschläger's natural mysticism.

In 1904, close on the heels of the Piano Concerto, came the Orchestral Suite based on Gozzi's *Turandot*. To begin with,

Busoni wrote it purely as a concert piece, without any idea of turning it into theatre music or indeed into an opera. Every line of this music unmistakably expresses his personality, and for the first time there are no obvious signs of the influence of other composers. The very first piece, *Hinrichtung, Stadttor, Abschied* based on the first act of Gozzi's fairy-tale, gives us a clear idea of the essential Busoni. There, in the *cor anglais* and the bassoons, we find the chromatic surrounding of a central tone; the intervals gradually becoming larger and then smaller again, moving away from the traditional concept of a key, although the ostinato figure of the drums on E flat and G flat hammers in the tonic of E flat for fifty-four bars, and after considerable modulations the composition returns to this key. Yet neither the passages in a specific key nor the bold modulations follow the traditional cadence that predominates in the work of, say, Mahler and Richard Strauss, in spite of all their freedom of movement. In this respect, the *Turandot Suite*, and Busoni's music in general, has more in common with the modern French composers, than with any German, or any Italian before Malipiero and Casella. The subsequent March of the eunuch Truffaldino, with its chuckling staccato introduction in which bass strings alternate with brass and bassoons, is a virtuoso piece in the 'buffo' style, which grew out of Busoni's knowledge of Verdi's *Falstaff* and the work of Mozart. The rapid and frequent changes from major to minor key are also typical of Busoni, and correspond with his theory, that the latter is merely a sort of psychological variant of the former, 'they are really two versions of the same thing'; 'one more light-hearted, the other more serious; a light stroke of the brush is enough to transform one into the other,' he says in his *Outline for a New Musical Aesthetics*. In the great March of the Princess Turandot, Busoni ingeniously manages to combine this feeling of unity between major and minor with a discreet use of the Chinese pentatonic scale, which can be detected in almost all movements of the *Turandot* music. On the other hand, in the sixth movement *Tanz and Gesang*, an oriental scale predominates, reminiscent of the gypsy scales with its two

101

augmented seconds: A flat–B, and F sharp–E flat. Obviously, this is supposed to suggest the presence of middle-eastern figures, perhaps even the origins of Prince Kalaf. This exoticism, together with Busoni's tendency to chromatically surround a central tone, reappears in the *Nächtlicher Walzer*, one of the climaxes of the entire *Turandot* music. Busoni later arranged this brilliant piece for the piano and incorporated it in the six Elegies, which in his opinion represent the final stage in acquiring his own personal style. Even *Turandots Frauengemach*, the most conventional piece in the Suite, was assimilated in the Elegies as a virtuoso intermezzo, dedicated to the star-pianist, Michael von Zadora. At almost every stage in his creative career, Busoni borrowed from earlier works in this way; but in so doing, he introduced large or small variations which often throw more light on his development than the pieces themselves.

The Elegies, written while he was teaching his master-class at the Vienna Conservatory, are Janus-faced, looking back to the past and forward to the future. In a letter to Gerda, written from Vienna on 1st December 1907, he mentions in passing: 'Have just finished the five piano pieces . . . The last (to appear) is certainly the most interesting.'

The *Elegies* volume contains six pieces, and the piano version of the *Berceuse* was also added later. Busoni placed the first piece in front of the original five, its very title testifying like a kind of motto to the position it occupies in his work. He calls this prelude *Nach der Wendung*, and its first three bars anticipate with variations the last bars of the closing piece, the *Erscheinung*. He even adds a subtitle, *Recueillement* which means, composure or self-communion, perhaps even meditation. In actual fact, it is the only one of the Elegies that is not recognizably an arrangement of an earlier work or the starting-point of a later piece. The second, *All' Italia! In modo napolitano* is taken from the Concerto, where as *Tarantella* it constitutes the fourth movement. The third, the choral prelude *Meine Seele bangt und hofft zu Dir*, reappears in the *Fantasia Contrappuntistica*. No. 4, *Turandots Frauengemach, Intermezzo*, is an extended arrangement of the fifth piece in the Orchestral Suite, brought in there as an introduction to the third act.

In some cases, the variations concerned are formal extensions, introductory bars, for example, or short passages inserted between bars. Busoni frequently resorts to the practice of repeating phrases, perhaps with slight variations, so as to increase their impact. To some extent, however, he does introduce harmonic enrichments, which show that he was concerned with consonance, although not entirely indifferent to 'dissonance'. Here the inundation of tonal triads and four-part chords—and in the melodic realm, of diatonic steps—by chromaticism, plays an important part.

When Busoni himself maintains that the *Erscheinung* is the most interesting piece in the collection, he is judging it on the basis of his stylistic achievements at the time of its composition. In retrospect, the situation appears slightly different; a piece such as the *Nächtliche*, the fifth of the Elegies and a variation on the *Nächtlicher Walzer* from the *Turandot Suite*, is very similar to the *Erscheinung*, from the point of view of harmonic language and tonality.

Edgar Varèse, who went to Berlin in 1907 and knew Busoni well, has drawn attention to the remarkable discrepancy between Busoni's theories and aesthetic speculations and his actual compositions. Having been impressed by the revolutionary ideas of the *Outline for a New Musical Aesthetics*, he was surprised by the orthodoxy of Busoni's taste and music. *'Tu te prives d'une belle chose,'* replied the elder of the two friends, when Varèse told him that he was no longer interested in tonality. In the Elegies, as in most of Busoni's work, tonality is respected. His endings are triadic. Yet in the *Nächtlicher Walzer* from *Turandot*, there are scales that have no connection with the traditional, such as the sequence right at the beginning, after the sustained A minor chord: E–D sharp–E–F–G sharp–A–B flat–C sharp–D–E flat–F sharp–G. This is formed entirely of semitones and augmented seconds (diminished thirds), and has nothing to do with tonality. In order to continue the progression, A flat–B–C

103

should follow. Busoni leaves out the A flat, but adds B and C, so completing the twelve semitones. E and E flat are the only notes to appear twice. Strangely enough, the actual themes are excluded from this chromatic deluge. Nonetheless, Busoni makes use of the complete range of semitones more and more often in his music. Whenever there are two versions of a piece, separated by a period of several years, it is always possible to trace the development towards a chromatic harmonic language that is not always tonally one-dimensional. This is particularly true of *Die Nächtlichen*. We must bear this in mind, in order to understand Busoni's opinion of his final Elegy. For here again, the harmonic language is frequently at odds with tonal function. The chords themselves often depart from the traditional form, based on thirds. Instead, the intervals are fourths, and they now play a leading role in the melodic writing as well. Thus the main theme in the *Erscheinung*, which emerges unaccompanied *dolcissimo e sostenuto*, is built up quite differently from the vocal themes that we find in Busoni's earlier work. From this melodic idea, which appears in various keys, and as the main theme dominates the entire piece, Busoni develops an upbeat quaver-figure, which also announces itself unaccompanied and represents a complete twelve-tone row with only three notes repeated. The paradoxical thing about this piece is, that all its harmonic and tonal extravaganza are clad in the form of a Liszt-type virtuoso piece. Busoni cannot resist the pianistic effect of drumming chords in rapid demi-quaver sequences, full-blown tremoli, and runs gliding 'leggierissimo' up and down the keyboard. The harmonization of these runs is to some extent bitonal, that is to say, the key of the melodious treble is totally different from that of the accompanying chords. The chords themselves change without traditional cadences, without in fact abiding by any of the rules of modulation. They supersede one another on the principle of fluctuation between chromatically contiguous steps. In the last bars, for example, D flat major follows E major, A minor follows D flat major, while the runs in the right hand cover the very intervals that are not accounted for in the accompanying chords. So even here he is moving towards the total chromatic. Tacked on to the final A minor chord, like a tiny codetta, is the same musical idea that we find at the beginning of the first piece *Nach der Wendung*. Yet even here the principle of variation holds good; both the accompanying chords and the melodic line are dissimilar. The piece ends with a C major chord, the third, E, prefacing an F sharp as a suspension.

Busoni dedicated the Elegies to six pianists, all friends of his, and some of them pupils as well : Gottfried Galston, Egon Petri, Gregor Beklemishev, Michael von Zadora, O'Neil Philips and Leo Kestenberg.

When his mother, Anna Busoni, died in 1909, Busoni wrote in London one of his most original pieces : the *Berceuse Elégiaque*, with its subtitle *Des Mannes Wiegenlied am Sarge seiner Mutter*. The piece is written for a small chamber orchestra of twenty-four strings 'con sordino', plus three flutes, an oboe, three clarinets, four horns, gong, harp and celeste. Busoni also prepared a piano version which, although it does not retain the extraordinary magic of the chamber orchestra rendering, manages nevertheless to convey the striking dematerialization of this strange music. The harmonic premise is bitonal; the following pairs of keys appear one after another : F major–A flat minor, E flat major–F sharp minor, D flat major–E minor, C major–E flat minor, D major–F minor, E major–G minor, etc. In the sequence of these pairs of keys, repetition of tones is often avoided, so that indirectly the effect is totally chromatic. But the piano version goes even further than the chamber orchestra piece, in so far as both pedals are held constantly throughout the chord passages of the bitonal middle section, with the result that all the chords ultimately merge into one another. The date of this piece, 1909, is important, because about this time Schoenberg and his pupils in Vienna forged ahead to achieve very similar harmonic effects on the extreme frontiers of tonality and beyond.

Moreover, the third Elegy, the chorale-prelude *Meine Seele bangt and hofft zu Dir*, also indulges in sorties into a tonal no-man's-land. The same freedom of movement prevails in the use of unrelated chords. There are bars in which four keys appear side by side, others in which two keys are consistently merged. Even the great arpeggios in intervals of thirds, related to various different keys, are characteristic of this sphere of music. The chorale-prelude is the vital seed from which the *Fantasia Contrappuntistica* developed three years later. In the course of an American tour, Busoni wrote from Denver to Berlin on 18th April 1910: 'Yesterday in the train . . . a splendid idea: make the *Great Fugue* into an orchestral work, re-arrange the chorale-prelude . . . as an introduction, also for orchestra, and refer back to it again before the stretto in the Fugue. A major undertaking! Who will give me another lifetime?'

A major undertaking indeed! This mention of the *Great Fugue* refers to Busoni's attempt to complete Bach's final work. He must have conceived the plan in 1909; because when in Chicago, Wilhelm Middelschulte brought him an article written by Bernhard Ziehn on Bach's unfinished Fugue, Busoni commented: 'Appeared just at the right moment.' In the Berlin periodical *Signale für die musikalische Welt* he wrote an article entitled *The Gothics of Chicago, Ill.*, introducing the two German musicians living in America. He completed the composition in New Orleans on 1st March, after exactly two months' work; and shortly afterwards the first version appeared with Schirmer of New York, entitled: *Grosse Fuge, contrapuntal fantasia on Johann Sebastian Bach's last unfinished work*, dedicated to 'Wilhelm Middelschulte, master of counterpoint'.

Bach's last work, *The Art of Fugue*, is a progressive application of complex fugue forms. The thematic material consists of the main theme and its seven variants, as well as seven counter-subjects, of which three also appear in inversion. The seventh counter-subject begins with the notes 'B–A–C–H'. There has been much speculation as to how the nineteenth, and final Fugue, was meant to end. Each had made use of three themes. His composition, dictated by the master, when he was already blind, to his son-in-law, Altnikol, breaks off at the point where the B–A–C–H

106

theme appears. It is fairly safe to assume that Bach, who until then had only made use of counter-subjects, intended to introduce the B–A–C–H theme as a main theme. Gustav Nottebohm had already published a possible ending along these lines in the magazine *Musikwelt* in 1880.

Busoni's *Grosse Fuge* adopts Middelschulte's solution to the problem. But in the footnote to the twenty-seventh bar of the fourth Fugue, he writes: 'It is to the studies of Herr Bernhard Ziehn in Chicago, that I am indebted, for this combination of the main theme from *The Art of Fugue* with the three previous subjects.' In his article *The Gothics of Chicago*, he calls Middelschulte 'an underestimated master', praises his ability to construct and 'polish', as well as his sense of rhythm; Ziehn, on the other hand, he calls a theorist, 'who points out the possible existence of undiscovered territory and trains potential Columbuses'. His idea of 'Gothicism', which he compares with the 'styleless period' of the 'eighties, the Vienna of Makart, the novels of Felix Dahn and the Teutonism of Wagner, is explained in musical terms. Busoni says, that the essence of it is: a feeling, a mood and an idea, that is expressed through counterpoint. He speaks of 'fine, uninterrupted lines', of the 'rejuvenating colours of a great new harmonic language which, through the uncompromisingly logical working-out of intervals in the individual voices, makes these independent of one another; and at the specific points where they do meet, creates unusual chord formations'. In 1917 the theorist, Ernst Kurth, evolved his *Principles of Linear Counterpoint* and Bach's 'melodic polyphony' along similar lines. Busoni dreams of 'canonic answers at the tenth and in inversion', which open up the possibility of new interval regions and these in turn are conceived as independent keys. But he is particularly concerned about 'inevitable chord combinations' which result from imitative activity. Among contemporary composers, he considers César Franck to be the exponent of this type of Gothicism.

In the *Grosse Fuge* there is merely a hint of this logical process, possibly in the stretto after the quadruple fugue, where chords are strung together as the harmonizations of melodic tones regardless of the primary key. This practice had already been adopted by Mussorgsky and the younger Russians; in the case of Busoni, it is subordinated to a complex thought process.

Meanwhile, Busoni was far from satisfied with this version. Shortly afterwards an eleven page introduction appeared, in which he makes use of the third Elegy, with the Chorale *Allein Gott in der Höh' sei Ehr'* in A major above the pedal-point E flat. There is a short new transitional passage leading to the first fugue. Whereas the first three fugues and the intermezzo with three variations and cadenza are hardly re-arranged at all, the Quadruple Fugue takes on a somewhat different form. The texture is more complex, the number of voices and themes increased. Busoni re-introduces the Chorale, *Allein Gott in der Höh' sei Ehr'*, this time in E major above a pedal-point B flat, before the stretto, which in itself is considerably changed. In this way, the principle of bitonality, which was so important in the Elegies, also prevails in his confrontation with Bach. It unites with the polyphonic approach, which also produces polytonal chords and chord progressions verging on the borders of tonality.

In this extended, definitive form, Busoni now calls the *Grosse Fuge, Fantasia Contrappuntistica*. The notation is for the piano, but presupposes a number of imaginary players. Observations such as 'quasi trombe dolci' or 'quasi flauto' or 'quasi arpa' or 'fuori' go to show that an orchestral presentation would be consistent with its conception. In fact, Busoni later authorized an orchestrated version by Frederick Stock and himself wrote a version for two pianos. The *Fantasia Contrappuntistica* not only requires a pianist of the highest order, but also an interpreter capable of understanding and then rendering its rich polyphonic structure. It is because it is exceptionally difficult, that this brilliant piece has not become more widely known; only in the middle of the twentieth century have pianists such as Pietro Scarpini, Gunnar Johannson, John Ogdon and Alfred Brendel, devoted their talents to this delightful completion of Bach's final work.

The *An die Jugend* cycle dates from the year 1909. The four pieces are dedicated to pianists who were Busoni's students, Gruenberg, Sirota, Closson and Blanchet. Characteristic of these pieces, as of *Nuit de Noël* (also written in 1909), is the way in which the harmonic language and melodic writing gravitate away from the home key, frequently using the whole-tone scale favoured by the modern French composers. This applies, for example, to parts of the first piece *Preludio, fughetta ed esercizio*, which like the last *Introduzione, capriccio, epilogo*, reappears in the first Sonatina.

The Sonatinas, which give such a clear picture of Busoni's intellectual approach and temperament, were also conceived in 1909—in a letter written to Gerda on 1st April 1910, his forty-fourth birthday, Busoni gives a list, incomplete though it is, of work produced that year : The *An die Jugend* pieces, *Berceuse*, Bach-Fantasia, *Berceuse Elégiaque* for orchestra, the *Grosse Fuge*, *A New Musical Notation*, the first volume of the Liszt edition 3, one hundred and eighty pages of the *Brautwahl* score, *Frau Potiphar*, various articles for periodicals, countless letters, competitions for the *Signale*.

Die Brautwahl, the score of which has just been mentioned, was the first of Busoni's operas to appear as a finished work. Busoni himself wrote the libretto, based on a novella of the same name by E. T. A. Hoffmann. The greatest visionary among the early German Romantic poets, he had been Busoni's favourite author since childhood. Indeed, Busoni and his circle of friends emanated something akin to the bizarre atmosphere of a Hoffmann story, without being in the least frightening. There is no doubt that Busoni, who visited Berlin for the first time at the age of nineteen, was familiar with the city from Hoffmann's descriptions of it. Even later, he always saw it in a strange Hoffmannesque twilight, a mixture of prosaic Prussian industry and the slightly intoxicating world of the supernatural. The setting of *Die Brautwahl* is also Berlin. As early as February 1906, Busoni refers to the libretto in a letter to Gerda as a 'completed draft'. In June of the same year, he writes, that it is finished up

109

to the last scene with the third casket. A year later, on 17th July 1907, he is able to announce the completion of the first act; six days later the first section of the second act is ready; a year after he writes from Vienna to say that he is working on the 'little love duet'.

The project is continually being interrupted by other activities; nevertheless, it continues to obsess Busoni, dragging on over the years from 1906 until the eventual first performance in Hamburg in 1911, frequently splitting up into sketches and full score, stimulating fresh ideas all the time on the problems of musical drama, rousing all kinds of hopes in its creator, none of which were to be fully realized.

The action takes place on two levels, one realistic, the other supernatural. On the one hand, it is the middle-class idyll of the 'nouveau riche' Kommissionsrat Voswinkel, who promises his beautiful, intelligent and musical daughter, Albertine, to his old school friend, Geheimrat Thusman, a bachelor who has the mid-summer urge to abandon the world of books. But a man of quite a different sort, a young painter named Edmund Lehsen, has fallen in love with Albertine, 'Tinchen'. Lehsen is an anagram of Hensel, the painter whom Mendelssohn's sister Fanny married, and Busoni reproduces his likeness in the libretto. We are in the simple, homely environment of early nineteenth century Berlin. The date is 1820. The first meeting between Voswinkel and Lehsen takes place in the pavilions on the edge of the Tiergarten. These were outdoor public-houses, where in summer people used to drink Berlin 'Weissbier', and on Sundays listen to music; they continued to exist right up to the time of the Second World War. Busoni has been amazingly successful in conveying the familiar atmosphere of this milieu, the brass bands and the tobacco smoke. The first scene captures more brilliantly than anything else in the theatre the essence of life in Berlin at that time. The essential outlines are all there, and yet there is the same tender feeling for detail that we find in the Parisian milieu of Auguste Renoir's *Moulin de la Galette* thirty years earlier.

Busoni puts his operatic theories into practise when it becomes apparent that aside from the supernatural, dance-music and marches are what is principally required. The brass band, an essential element of the 'pavilions', plays good popular music. First the march from Rossini's *Moses*, then a short medley from Mozart's F major, D major, and A major German dances, K. 600 and 602, during which the Kommissionsrat helps himself from the painter's well-stocked cigar case, observing as he does so, that Albertine knows a lot about painting and he himself is fond of art. Meanwhile the inevitable has happened, the painter has fallen desperately in love; and as soon as the old man begins to talk to some acquaintances, the young couple sing a duet, in which a poem by Friedrich de la Motte Fouqué is accompanied in a 'lazy, dreamy, slightly languid' fashion by a barcarole of strangely iridescent tonality. This song, so Busoni wrote to his wife Gerda, is the focal point of the scene. The march and dance music provide the framework; shortly after comes the *Kleeblatt*, and the Kommissionsrat, his daughter and the young painter return home to the strains of the Rossini march.

This then is the realistic plane, the middle-class milieu in which part of the closely-knit plot is enacted. Suddenly, as if by magic, a handsome noble-looking man appears on the stage, who seems to have stepped from some bygone age. He is the goldsmith, Leonhard, who cannot die and has been alive for the last three hundred years, a kindly genius and patron of the arts, the painter's guardian spirit, who as it were represents the art of white magic, the benevolence of supernatural powers. After a short time, he is sitting in the wine-shop, facing the man who represents the very opposite, old Manasse, who as the court money-lender, Lippold, was at one time executed in Berlin and has haunted the place ever since. Two spirits, eternally opposed, beings who have the power to do more than merely work and drink wine. They are immortals, no different from Heine's and Wagner's *Flying Dutchman*, Shaw's Methuselah, and Karel Čapek's Elina Makropulos, who at the age of 327 continues her existence as Emilia Marty.

Beside the two spirits sits a third man, Privy Counsellor

Thusman, none other than the school friend of Albertine's father. Leonhard has decided, that he cannot have the girl because Edmund is to have her. The two spirits begin to exercise their magic powers. Leonhard's face assumes the features of a fox, Manasse turns slices of radish into ducats, which once in Leonhard's hands disappear in the twinkling of an eye. But Albertine has yet a third suitor, the young millionaire Benjamin, who, as the nephew of Manasse, has appealed to the Austrian Baron Bensch. While Manasse is pleading his nephew's case, Albertine sits at the spinet and accompanies herself in the Fouqué song, until the painter appears and joins her in this romantic piece. As they are embracing Thusman comes in, and claims that he has prior rights. The angry Edmund paints the old man's face with green oil paint and pushes him towards the door, where the Kommissionsrat is standing. Leonhard also appears unexpectedly, and the five of them join in a quintet, which is interrupted by the sudden arrival of Manasse with Baron Bensch. The young millionaire asks Albertine for a kiss, and everyone is up in arms. Leonhard intervenes with a piece of magic, and the scene ends with a curse from old Manasse. From a musical point of view, the finale of this eerie scene reveals imaginative qualities worthy of the poet who inspired it.

The overture to the third act is a posthorn solo played behind the curtain, and it is suggested that it should be played 'in the German manner, somewhat langorously, otherwise freely'. The night scene is set beside the frog pond in the Tiergarten. Thusman is in a suicidal mood because of his green face. The omnipresent Leonhard removes the tiresome paint, but warns him against continuing to pursue Albertine, unless he wants to turn into a frog. The final scene is the episode with the caskets. Leonhard proposes, that the suitors choose from three caskets, one of which contains a picture of Albertine. *Die Brautwahl* ends with this ordeal, obviously modelled after Shakespeare's *Merchant of Venice*. Naturally, Leonhard has made sure that the painter wins.

The Jewish element is such an integral part of the early nine-

112

teenth century Berlin, which provides the setting for *Die Brautwahl*, that Busoni could hardly dispense with it. A city and a period, in which the Mendelssohns and the Meyerbeers were essential to the survival of the German Romantic tradition in music, in which Rachel Varnhagen ran a literary salon, Heine lived, and Kommissionsrat Friedrich Cerf established the first private opera-house with royal permission to compete seriously with the Hofbühne—Berlin had succeeded in integrating the Jew as completely as she had integrated the Huguenot in the past.

For Busoni, the Jewish element also provided a sort of exotic local colour. There is evidence of this throughout the second part of the first act, beginning with the orchestral intermezzo entitled *Manasse*, that is to be played *andante sostenuto in modo giudaico*, and increasingly in Leonhard's story of Lippold, the money-lender. In this, Busoni not only uses oriental Hebraic idioms and scales with augmented seconds, plaintive and chromatically drawn out idioms, and shrill screeches from the orchestra in the manner of the quarrelling Jews in Mussorgsky's *Pictures at an Exhibition*, he even quotes liturgical melodies, including a variation on the Kol Nidre.

Quite apart from this, there is plenty of unusual local colour in this exceptionally colourful score. The Kommissionsrat, with his world-wide business connections, is familiar with all kinds of foreign cultures. He sings of 'negroes, toiling in plantations, to the strains of exotic allegros', and imitates a banjo-player, shouting joyfully the words 'Hiawatha, Manahatta, Appalacco and Tobacco', to the accompaniment of a pentatonic melody in variation form.

Busoni's major-minor theory ('two versions of the same thing, one more light-hearted, the other more serious'), is convincingly illustrated in the *Brautwahl* duet. In the first phase of the melody, ascending in uneven steps, to which Edmund sings the words:

'Säng' ich es nach, was leise solch stilles Leben spricht'
(Were I to repeat what is whispered softly by so calm a life . . .)

113

we find two rising major sixths, through which minor becomes major; and then immediately afterwards, in the second phrase, the minor sixths through which it returns to the minor key. But at the same time the tonal pillars also shift in intervals of minor thirds, so that the impression created is of fourfold tonality. We are already familiar with this kind of tonally ambiguous complex in early Bartók and late Skriabin. We find their systematic exploitation, and classification into the so-called 'modes that can only be transposed a certain number of times', in the work of Olivier Messiaen forty years later.

Nevertheless, the *Brautwahl* music is traditional rather than contemporary. Its starting-point is the triad and cadence, and in both melody and form it favours simple periods. Yet time and again, the familiar contours appear in a strange half-light, that lends a new, often fantastic radiance, to the slightest change. Even the overture, which begins in a light Mozartian vein with rapidly arpeggiated triadic basses, passes almost imperceptibly into alien harmonies and triad progressions. Whenever Busoni wants to present the supernatural, he sooner or later finds himself in the realms of atonality. This is what happens when Leonhard is threatening Thusman: 'Otherwise, woe betide you, on this night of the equinox . . .' accompanied by a whole-tone counter-movement in treble chords and deep basses. A climax of erotic ecstasy, such as the lovers' embrace, is accompanied by a non-functional series of fourths. This progression reappears at the end, when Edmund has chosen the right casket and the betrothed couple finally fall into one another's arms. Busoni introduces a particularly ingenious idea in the night scene beside the pond in the Tiergarten, when the frog-spawn is represented by repeated seconds, a technique that Henry Cowell later called 'tone-clusters', and which we, in German, call '*Tontrauben*'.

Paradoxically, the originality of the work consists of returning to the operatic style of the past. Busoni underlines his hostility to Wagner's theory of through-composition, by specifically dividing his work into numbers, separate pieces of music, frequently differentiated by titles as well. In this respect, *Die*

114

Brautwahl anticipates the later *Doctor Faust*; in fact, it exploits at a much earlier date the structural ideas embodied in Alban Berg's *Wozzeck* and the formal concept of Hindemith's *Cardillac*.

Individual forms of this type include the overtures, the allegro at the beginning, the whirlwind waltz of the spirits before the first act, the short viola solo before the second scene of this act, the posthorn solo before the third act, the stormy introduction to the last scene, and the short dry prelude to the epilogue; all symphonic pieces, entirely different in character and range. Also the bizarre transformation music after the pavilion scene, and the great Manasse Intermezzo. Furthermore, the ballad-like numbers, the stories, the duet, and finally the controversial church scene for which Busoni developed a new passacaglia-type form. Then the continually recurring dances, waltzes of all kinds, a minuet, the 'tempo di polacca' at the frog-pond, the gallop in the magic scene when Bensch and Thusman glide across the stage. Finally, the purely vocal forms, often parts of climactic finale : duets, quintets, and the concluding four-part scherzo.

The weaknesses, for which the score has been criticized time and again, lie in a certain hypertrophy in the orchestral treatment and too many ideas crowded in together. Without any doubt, the German predilection for counterpoint, which Richard Strauss mentions in the preface to his *Intermezzo*, is also apparent in *Die Brautwahl*.

The musical difficulties, which prevented the work from being properly understood in 1911, no longer constitute any problem for contemporary ears. Instead, the music has retained its peculiar freshness. Its most striking characteristic is a remarkably dry warmth, a breath of southern climes and Latin attitudes, which never for one moment conceal its romantic undertones. Busoni's staggering talent for all aspects of composition and orchestral treatment has never been questioned. But how much did he know about the human voice? By far the major part of his work is instrumental. Not one of his many articles on music deals with vocal problems.

Nevertheless, Busoni's ability to think in vocal terms can only

115

be compared with that of Rossini, Verdi or Mozart. Thus each of his operatic roles is conceived as an extension of song. Indeed, they always unmistakably represent the range to which they belong, whether this is 'basso buffo' or 'heldentenor', lyric soprano or coloratura soprano. You need to have heard Dietrich Fischer-Dieskau singing Busoni's *Faust*, in order to realize to what extent this character embodies the essence of dramatic vocal delivery.

Many of Busoni's operatic characters have obvious affinities with those of Mozart. It has already been suggested that the Moor, Monostatos, in *The Magic Flute*, provided the prototype for Thusman; and similarities have been pointed out between Albertine and Pamina. But there are also points that tie up with Wagner; and Thusman has features in common with Beckmesser as well as Monostatos, just as Leonhard on the other hand bears a slight family resemblance to Hans Sachs in the *Meistersinger*.

But the most unmistakably personal element in this work is Busoni's rendering of the supernatural, the atmosphere of magic and enchantment, which he has conveyed more convincingly than Offenbach himself in the closely related scenes of his *Tales of Hoffmann*. There is nothing crude, rough or vulgar about Busoni's art. Even when he is representing the realities of every-day life, which is the case in many scenes in the *Brautwahl*, he does so in a language that is carefully chosen, cultivated and refined, where anything banal is inadmissible. The concept of a 'new classicism' did not yet exist in contemporary music when *Die Brautwahl* was written. Busoni himself coined the term in 1920. But in this respect too, the score is ahead of its time. Owing to the qualities, which he later defined so clearly, and which were already apparent in his earlier music, Busoni had a forma-tive influence on stylistic developments. In a short piece entitled *An die Jugend*, he expressed the love, respect and gratitude, that he felt towards the younger generation. Even in *Die Brautwahl*, the youngsters are eventually proved right; Edmund wins Albertine. But we must not forget, that it is the guardian spirit, Leonhard, the age-old and yet ageless goldsmith, who has

116

dealt the cards of destiny and made sure that youth is granted its rights. Since he represents the creative artist, the message of this work is perfectly clear : the guardian spirit always sides with youth, even when the young use their talents in the wrong way, like Edmund pointlessly obliterating his rival's face with a brushful of green paint.

Of the six Sonatinas, the first harks back to the *An die Jugend* cycle. The second, with its Latin title *Sonatina seconda*, did not appear before 1912, which is to say three years later. There is something unusual and revolutionary about the very appearance of the music, which reminds one of the *Berceuse* and one or two other pieces by Busoni. There are no bar lines, and no indication as to key or metre. The accidentals only apply to the note immediately following (as in the piano pieces of Josef Matthias Hauer). Neither the beginning nor the end give any indication of a key. The two movements, which are separated by a pause, do not follow any familiar form. Melodies for one voice, encompassed by tonally irregular passages, alternate with full-blown chordal textures. In the *Andante tranquillo* of the second movement, there is a three-part canon, in which the twelve semitones follow in rapid succession, and shortly before the end this reappears, *Piuttosto Adagio*, in inversion. Polytonal passages are created by the counter-movement of various six-four chords. The principle of tonality is exploded more convincingly in this piece than in any other work by Busoni. The influences behind it, if one is to insist on looking for them, are obviously those of Johann Sebastian Bach in the uncompromising nature of the vocal writing, and of Arnold Schoenberg in the lack of functional harmony. Although in the *Berceuse* it was not difficult to detect the blurred outlines of contemporary French music, here the outlines are basically sharp and clearly defined.

Busoni had long had a revolutionary attitude to the orchestra. He certainly knew how to handle it in a virtuoso fasion, but he was never satisfied with purely virtuoso instrumentation. Time and again, the idea of perfecting the orchestra and even the instruments themselves, crops up in his letters and articles.

117

He continued his search for new sounds, which in the case of the *Berceuse Elégiaque* were extracted from a Chamber Ensemble, in his *Nocturne symphonique* of 1912. Busoni dedicated the piece to the Berlin conductor, Oscar Fried, who was one of the champions of modern music, and from time to time one of his regular visitors in Berlin and Zürich. Here the musical apparatus is much larger than in the *Berceuse*. Woodwinds in twos or threes and horns combine with a large orchestra of strings, plus harp and celeste. Apart from the second Sonatina, this Nocturne is Busoni's most radical work, as far as the use of polytonal dissonances is concerned. It ends with the chord : E flat–B flat–G flat–D–G–B flat–C–E flat–G, which is to say, E flat minor, plus G minor, plus C minor.

Busoni's interest in exotic music, which had to some extent borne fruit in the scores of *Turandot* and *Die Brautwahl*, was reawakened for a time in America through the research work of his former pupil, Natalie Curtis. She had steeped herself in Red Indian folk music, and subsequently showed him some of the melodies she had collected, which he very much liked. Three pieces appeared, as the direct result of this interest : the *Indian Fantasia* for piano and orchestra of 1913, the *Indian Diary* for piano of 1915, and the second volume of this, the *Gesang vom Reigen der Geister*, for a small orchestra. In his correspondence with Natalie Curtis, Busoni had already criticized certain bastardizations attempted by Dvořák and other composers. His own interest in this exotic material did not take him much further. The only real merit of the three Indian pieces lies in their value as studies in piano and orchestral composition, having something of the spirit of Liszt and a freer, modern harmonic language.

At about this time Busoni began work on a light-hearted theatrical piece; and in September 1913, in Bergamo, he read the first draft aloud to his friend, Emilio Anzoletti. This one-act play he called *Arlecchino*, and later added the subtitle 'The windows, a theatrical capriccio'. Busoni wrote the music between 1914 and 1916, first in Berlin, then as from 1916 in Zürich where it was first performed in 1917. The basic idea of the piece, with its pacifist and anti-bourgeois tendencies, was to combine a major speaking role with singers and an orchestra, in the manner of the 'opera buffa'. Busoni was aiming at an operatic play in the style of the Italian Commedia dell' Arte. Certain specific types and characters were to appear on the stage, who must inevitably antagonize one another. It is clear that the music is intended as a parody, from the way it burlesques operatic forms : a revenge-aria, a piece in praise of wine, and various other witty details. The hero of the title runs off with the young wife of the tailor, Matteo, as he reads his Dante. Arlecchino reappears as a bogus barbarian captain, as a husband duelling with the noble-born suitor Leandro, and as victor, announcing the moral of the piece in an epilogue : never to bow one's head, even when wearing rags and tatters, and thereby retain one's rights. The piece enters the realm of the absurd when, in the presence of the knight Leandro who is believed to be dead, the Abbate strikes up a choral-type song in praise of the donkey of destiny who comes trotting in. This is where the most ingenious number, musically speaking, begins—the quartet, in which the love aria sung by Leandro and his duet with Colombina parody the style of Italian opera from Scarlatti to Verdi. Although the musical idiom of the entire work has a dance-like, joyful and transparent quality, reminiscent of the 'buffo' style, this apparent light-heartedness is a cloak for bold harmonic effects. The orchestration is unsurpassed in brilliance and elegant flexibility. The quotations from Mozart's *Don Giovanni* and Donizetti's *Bergamasco* are exactly right. One of the most charming inventions, apart from the introductory twelve-tone Fanfare, is Colombina's Minuet, which reappears in 1916 as a Polonaise in the third Sonatina.

Arlecchino has been called inhuman and immoral. Nothing could be further from the truth. The excellent libretto appears more naïve than it really is; here we have a plea for freedom and honesty, a protest against the lies and taboos of modern society. The *Rondo arlecchinesco* has achieved independent status as a by-product of the score.

119

As this piece lasts only fifty-five minutes, a programme filler was required when it was first performed in Zürich. Busoni went back to his original idea of a *Turandot* opera, and used the material of the 1906 Orchestral Suite as well as the theatre music for Max Reinhardt's production of *Turandot* in 1911, in Carl Vollmoeller's adaptation, for a two act play. The libretto, based on Gozzi's original version, gives more scope to the comic figures than Puccini's somewhat later opera. The eunuch Truffaldino becomes a major character; the two ministers, Pantalone and Tartaglia, accompany their imperial master Altoum, wherever he goes. The three riddles, that Prince Kalaf has to solve and in fact does, are concerned in typical Busoni fashion with the interpretation of intellect, morality and art. Busoni is as terse in describing the Chinese princess as he is in describing her fortunate suitor.

The scenes that are the most personal and stylistically original are those in which the comic and serious elements are perfectly blended, where Commedia dell' Arte characters intervene in the dangerous game of riddles, where Truffaldino boasts of his eunuch virtues. There are little jewels, such as the passage for bassoons when the hangman appears, the flute cadence when Kalaf refuses to tell the Emperor his name, and the previously mentioned Nocturnal Waltz interlude. But as a whole, *Turandot* is slightly inferior stylistically to *Arlecchino*.

Two Sonatinas also belong to the same period as the two one-act operas: the third, with its Latin dedication to a little American girl, closely related to *Arlecchino* quite apart from the Polonaise, a charming piece in four movements, far from easy to play, modulating in labyrinthine fashion from A minor to F major; and the fourth, dedicated to Busoni's son, Benvenuto. Busoni wrote it in Zürich, finishing it on 22nd December 1917, and giving it the title *Sonatina in Diem Nativitatis Christi MCMXVII*. Like all the Sonatinas, this piece also reflects the creative work that preceded it. In the polyphony, which towards the end condenses into a four-part fugato, there is an echo of his preoccupation with the Bach Edition. In the free association

120

of keys, which mingle bitonally, with dissonances in five or six voices, it is reminiscent of the expressionist passages in *Doctor Faust*. The Christmas Pastoral is also included. A scherzo-type middle section presents a lively siciliano in six-eight time, the bass figure turning into a peal of bells, five in number, which keep being repeated against the beat, then grow slower and eventually fade away. The original theme of the piece seems to have grown in stature towards the end, *quasi transfigurato*. In addition, a tender middle voice lingers about the first notes of the Chorale, *Von Himmel hoch da komm' ich her*, and in a strange, almost melancholy modulation, moves towards a plagal cadence, which is followed by the fifth without third, A–E, as the final chord. So this was how Busoni spent the Advent of 1917 in Zürich, sending greetings to his son, living far away in America. In all these years, the Sonatina has not lost the crystalline splendour of its form or the magic of its mood.

The major work of this period, however, is the unfinished *Doctor Faust*. As potential material for a composition, this inexhaustible character had fascinated Busoni for a long time. He felt, and not without justification, that he himself had affinities with Faust; furthermore, he was familiar with many of the adaptations, which in the course of centuries had treated the theme of the strange life of the German magician. In 1908, while reading Mereschkowsky's book on Leonardo da Vinci, whom he had considered as a possible hero for an Italian opera, he was reminded of the Faust puppet-play. Leonardo's role as 'maître de plaisir' at the court of Sforza in Milan was for him reminiscent of Faust's post with the Duke of Parma; and oddly enough, these comparisons lead him to draw further parallels with the character of Hans Sachs in the *Meistersinger*. In 1912 Frank Wedekind approached Busoni about writing a score for his new play *Franziska*, a Faust-parody. He was tempted by the proposition, but he still had reservations, partly because of the inferior role that the music was intended to play, merely linking the acts: 'What do these theatre people, artists and those associated with them, really think music is? Just another thing,

121

like subdued lighting, a kind of padding,' he wrote in a letter to Gerda. And again, a few days later on 24th July : 'Would destroy my own ideas about Faust . . .' Wedekind's offer was declined.

In 1913 he was obsessed by the Faust project once again. He very much liked an edition of *Faust*, published by the Insel-Verlag with illustrations by Eugène Delacroix; in September he read Goethe's *Urfaust*, and like a philologist, compared it with details from the definitive version. But as to writing music for Goethe's *Faust*, it was, as he admitted in 1922 in an article 'On the score of *Doctor Faust*', the 'enormity of the task' that held him back. The turning-point in this conflict was reached in 1914. Busoni decided on a version of the Faust puppet-play, and 'almost in a fever', wrote the first draft of his *Doctor Faust* libretto in six days. This was in Berlin, where he was living when the First World War broke out; he left there at the beginning of January 1915 for an American tour.

Busoni is strangely slow in getting to the main point of the plot. First there is a prologue in which the poet addresses the spectators, then there is the first introductory scene where Faust appears with Wagner and the three ghostly students from Cracow, whom only he can see and who hand him the book of magic. In the second scene six spirits apply to be Faust's assistant. He chooses the last, Mephistopheles, because he prides himself on being as swift as thought. In spite of the warning bells and Easter choirs, the pact with the Devil is signed and sealed with blood : Mephisto kills the beadles that knock at Faust's door. The following scene takes place in the chapel in the cathedral. Gretchen's brother is also the victim of Mephistophelian intrigue. Faust's adversaries are eliminated.

All these scenes are a traditional part of the Faust legend, and can be traced back to the puppet-play, and to some extent to Goethe. 'My own drama,' Busoni writes, 'begins with the scene at the court of Parma.' Faust appears during the wedding celebrations. He sets out to win the Duke's bride, dazzling her with a phantasmagoria of Biblical figures, such as Solomon, Samson and Salome. She gives herself to him, follows the

122

adventurer, and bears him a child, whose dead body Mephisto-pheles presents to Faust in a Wittenberg students' tavern. The corpse turns into a straw doll which goes up in flames, and from these flames rises the vision of Helen. The final scene is also set in Wittenberg. Faust has gone to pieces. The three students from Cracow, who in the tavern asked him to give back the book of magic, but to no purpose, have announced the end of his allotted span of life. In the dark snow-clad street he meets his former famulus, Wagner, whom students are now honouring with the title of Rector Magnificus. A beggar-woman with the features of the Duchess, standing before a house, offers him the child once more. He takes up the little corpse and carries it to the church, where Gretchen's brother stands in his way. He tries to pray, and the crucified figure assumes the features of Helen, the face of eternal youth and eternal love. For the last time Faust makes use of his magic powers. With the child in his arms, he steps inside the magic circle. Faust dies. A young boy rises up in his place. This resurrection carries with it the promise of eternal life. 'I, Faust, an eternal will', are the last words of the dying man, who has finally arrived at self-knowledge. Busoni had reached the point, where he was convinced that the child represented the survival of the individual.

Busoni has ascertained two important facts about this piece of music, both of them established in the article previously men-tioned on the score of *Doctor Faust*. The *Nocturne symphonique* and *Sonatina seconda* are preliminary studies for the composition, in other words, pieces dating from 1912 and 1913. With regard to form, he mentions the variation sequence for the six voices of the demons in the second scene of the introduction; the rondo of the scenic intermezzo in the Romanesque chapel; the ballet suite for the garden-party at the court of the Duke of Parma; the three 'premises' of the peal of bells, which form a sinfonia before the beginning of the first scene, and are joined in their instrumental rendering by the 'Pax'-calls of the mixed choir, swelling into six voices. Apart from these, focal points in the score are provided by two pieces, that date from 1918 to 1919, and according to Busoni 'are separated from the main body of the work, and yet an inherent part of it': Sarabande and Cortège. The one, a *symphonic intermezzo*, serves as a transition from the Parma scene to the Wittenberg tavern; the other precedes the Parma scene like an overture. When one considers that the score was written between 1916 and 1924, it sounds amazingly modern, with its polytonal counterpoint, its series of chords of fourths (which admittedly stem from the musical domain of the second Sonatina and the Symphonic Night-piece), and even its glittering sequences of seconds that are reminiscent of Alban Berg's *Wozzeck*, written at more or less the same time. Many of the things, that later helped to form the style of Hindemith in his early and middle years, and reappeared in the work of Benjamin Britten and Luigi Dallapiccola, are established in this piece.

If, however, this mature and highly intellectualized music sometimes appears inaccessible, it is not so much because of its frequently complex combinations, but because it contains too many ideas and distinctive features. Ideas come so readily to Busoni, that he often fails to work out even the finest and most significant of them. In this respect, his music has spiritual affinities with that of Schoenberg, at least with the pieces Schoenberg wrote before 1921, and particularly with those he wrote before 1908. On the other hand, Busoni differs from Schoenberg in a certain aristocratic aloofness, which is sometimes mistaken for lack of warmth. The Classic in Busoni has always seen to it, that this emotional reserve retains the upper hand, in spite of the Romantic exuberance which was also a vital part of his character. Yet in numerous scenes in *Doctor Faust*, such as the evocation of the spirits, with its system of mounting variation in which the voices ascend from basso profondo to the brilliant tenor of Mephistopheles, and perhaps even more in the Wittenberg tavern, with the double chorus of Catholic and Protestant students reaching a climax in the Chorale: *Ein' feste Burg ist unser Gott*, it is the dramatic impact that triumphs over all aesthetic speculation.

124

Characteristic of Busoni's musical language is his predilection for note-groups that chromatically surround a central tone. This process can be observed clearly in the Spirit Variations, where the motif C–D flat–B–C, in many forms and permutations, is the basis of a theme. At the same time Busoni also makes use of the alternative so popular with the Schoenberg school, which consists of replacing an interval with its octave complement. When Faust addresses the first spirit, the words he uses are *Du Erster, du tiefster*, accompanied by the semitone progression, C–D flat–B–C, which is immediately followed by the words *Gib deinen Namen*, with a descending major seventh, C–D flat, an ascending augmented sixth, D flat–B, and another descending major seventh, B–C. For the rest, Busoni is equally deliberate in his use of well-tried polyphonic techniques, such as the organum at the fourth and fifth at the beginning of the orchestral symphony, classical symphonic practice, modern chord combinations, and linear polyphony.

The Suite, the form which Busoni has given to the park scene at Parma, is introduced by the Cortège, the metre of which, a mixture of three-four and two-four time, clearly suggests a Polonaise or Polacca. This is followed by the short pastoral movement with the peasants, where we hear the sound of bagpipes and pedal-points on shifting tonics, G, F, and back to G. It ties up with the hunting-scene, with horns on the stage, and similar ostinato repetitions of basic-tones. Boys duelling move to a *Tempo di Valzer vivace*, and this is followed by the magnificent minuet that accompanies the entrance of the master of ceremonies and the Duke and his wife. After the short Mephistopheles Intermezzo, a march heralds the appearance of Faust with his fantastic retinue. An uncanny Chorale introduces the scene in which the Duchess is bewitched, a new waltz tempo the sequence in which Faust conjures forth the Biblical figures, which in themselves form a sort of independent suite. The hymnal aria sung by the Duchess, a number conceived and carried out in the grand dramatic style, marks the end of this portentous night. When day breaks, the Duke finds that he has been abandoned

125

by his young wife. Mephisto, disguised as court chaplain, fosters his ambition in the form of a stretto.

The basic attitude to form of the Suite is retained even in the subsequent symphonic intermezzo, which resembles a sustained and heavy Sarabande, with plucked strings as an accompaniment, muted trombones for the sustained pianissimo chords. Even here, the idea of a central tone with double chromatic decoration keeps cropping up, in a melodic or harmonic context.

Although Busoni saw the Faust music as his spiritual legacy, and was still working on it during the last months of his life, the piece remained fragmentary. It was completed by his friend and pupil, Philipp Jarnach, who mentioned this work in a letter he wrote to me : 'After Busoni's death, the score of *Doctor Faust* turned up, in a splendid fair copy. As for the missing parts, however, there was no sign of even a rough outline. These included : *(a)* In the scene set in Auerbach's Cellar—the whole of the vision of Helen. I myself composed this intermediate passage, from the final notes of the choir in the distance until after the words : *"Der Mensch ist dem Vollkommenen nicht gewachsen"* (Man is unable to live up to perfection). (Piano arrangement, pages 265–68.) From then on, and up to the end of this scene, the music is Busoni's again. *(b)* The entire ending of the opera, from the beginning of the long monologue and the words *"Wo die Worte finden"* (Where to find the words). (Piano arrangement, page 310.) As there was no indication as to how Busoni had intended this conclusion to be, I have followed as closely as possible the themes, which in the course of the opera assume to a greater or lesser extent the characteristics of a leitmotiv. The only liberty that I have taken, is in shortening the text in the final monologue, which even so lasts almost twenty minutes.'

The first performance of *Doctor Faust* was held in the Dresden Staatstheater on 21st May 1925. It was conducted by Fritz Busch, and produced by Alfred Reucker. The work had a certain 'succès d'estime', nothing more. The performance happened to coincide with a period in which new and revolutionary ideas

126

were to be found in every sphere of art. To the traditionalists, Busoni represented the revolutionary ideas reflected in his *Outline for a New Musical Aesthetics*. To the young, particularly those who belonged to the school of Franz Schreker or Arnold Schoenberg, he represented the ideas of the new classicism, which were considered to be reactionary. So his last work was equally unacceptable to both camps. The magazine *Melos*, to which Busoni was a regular contributor and which as recently as August 1924 had published his last article *On the Nature of Music*, ignored the première. Even the first performance in Berlin, on 27th October 1927, did not really provide the requisite break-through. Nevertheless, the piece remained in the repertoire until 1929, conducted by Leo Blech, with Friedrich Schorr as Faust, Fritz Soot as Mephisto and Frida Leider as the Duchess; but there were only eleven performances. The real stature of *Doctor Faust*, and its influence on the future, were not recognized until after the Second World War. It was fundamentally Dietrich Fischer-Dieskau, who assured the lasting success of this work, by singing the title role, first in Berlin in 1954 and later in England as well.

Busoni worked on the score of *Doctor Faust* for more than eight years. During that time there were numerous occasions when the work was interrupted, frequently for long periods. It sometimes seemed as if he had given it up altogether. But this fascinating score, Busoni's last and most mature work, always reasserted its almost magical hold on him. All the same, other large and important pieces appeared in the meantime, not least among them the Bach Edition and the comic opera *Arlecchino*. Many of these pieces were connected in some way with the major work, *Doctor Faust*. These include, in order of composition : the improvisation on Bach's Chorale *Wie wohl ist mir, o Freund der Seele* (1916), the same piece that had already provided the theme for variations in the Finale of the Second Violin Sonata of 1898; also Mephistopheles' song from Goethe's *Faust*, '*Es war einmal ein König*' (once upon a time there was a king . . .), for baritone and small orchestra (1918), the fifth and

127

sixth Sonatinas, the Concertino for clarinet and orchestra, the *Duettino concertante* after Mozart, the large-scale Toccata for Piano, the Flute Divertimento, the Romance with Scherzoso for piano and orchestra, the arrangement of the *Fantasia contrappuntistica* for two pianos, six short pieces intended to encourage polyphonic playing, and the last splendid Goethe songs.

With regard to the fifth Sonatina, subtitled *Sonatina Brevis in signo Joannis Sebastiani Magni*, Busoni says, in a letter written from Zürich on 20th August 1918 : 'Yesterday and the day before I spent writing a short sonatina, based on three bars from Bach, and I am very pleased with it.' The piece, which has only one movement and is dedicated to Philipp Jarnach, is a free imitation of Bach's short D minor Fantasia and Fugue. In the co-existence of various different keys and in its strongly chromatic melodic writing, it is directly related to the *Faust* music. More than any of the other Sonatinas, particularly the sixth which is also called *Kammerfantasie über Bizets Carmen*, it is based on a contrapuntal and fugal premise.

With the Clarinet Concertino, Busoni returns for a moment to the world of his childhood, the image of his father. This virtuoso piece is written in one movement, but divides into four contrasting sections. The first, almost like an overture, is an Allegretto sostenuto in B flat major, alla breve. The second, an Andantino in a pastoral six-eight time, in a strangely varying key. The third is a brilliant Allegro introduced by a sort of recitative, dominated by semiquaver arpeggios for the solo instrument, mainly in B flat major. The final section, a minuet in the same key, restrained and slightly pompous in character, following the current Italian style of clarinet playing, ends with a rocket-like upward-rushing chromatic run, the kind of thing that Busoni's father liked to play at the end of a concert number.

One of the longest and most important pieces written during the last years of Busoni's life is the powerful A flat minor Toccata, with its ironical epigraph borrowed from Frescobaldi *'Non è senza difficoltá che si arriva al fine'*. This work, which makes tremendous demands on any pianist, and which Busoni dedicated

128

7 Busoni the author during the Zurich years

8 Busoni with his pupils: Kurt Weill, Walther Geiser, Luc Balmer, Wladimir Vogel, Berlin 1922

to the pianist and teacher, Isidor Philipp, a Hungarian living in Paris, consists of three parts: Preludio, Fantasia and Ciaccona. It differs in form from the traditional toccata, in that it contains no fugal sections. Busoni returns to the original concept, developed on the organ, a sort of technical exercise for the consummate virtuoso, out of which a form gradually emerges, becoming more and more apparent until it eventually ends up as the Ciaccona, a real ostinato piece. The Fantasia contains one of the finest and most characteristic of Busoni's melodic inventions. It begins in the spirit of the free Bach Fantasias, where even the counterpoint is not bound by any strict rules, and the melodic theme develops from the bass into a finished product in E flat major, *un poco animando con calora*, exhausted almost before it has made its appearance. It reappears towards the end of the Fantasia as a simple repetition transposed into the key of D flat major, but surrounded by semiquaver arpeggios from the piano, not unlike those written into the Allegretto of the little Clarinet Concerto. Its affinity with the *Faust* music is most apparent in the Ciaccona, where the theme develops out of a simple chromatically-rising octave passage. The piece ends with a lapidary final cadence, jumping straight from D major to A flat minor.

Busoni had written from Berlin on 16th September 1920, announcing that the work was completed; but not without a sigh of relief, 'at last!', indicating how long the composition had been on his mind. Three days later he wrote to Gerda, saying that he was very pleased with the Toccata, although in another two days he had 're-touched' it. At the same time, 'just for fun', he was working on a waltz after Johann Strauss, the instrumentation of which was to preoccupy him a while longer. (In December 1920, Maurice Ravel's *La Valse* was given its first performance.)

The six short pieces, written to encourage polyphonic playing, appeared in 1923 as part of the larger *Exercises for the Piano*, which Busoni had begun in 1917 for the Musikschule and Conservatory in Basle, and later continued, completing the work with the Etudes after Paganini-Liszt. They contain fully-

E

realized pieces in the spirit of Bach, such as a short *Spielfuge*, side by side with chromatic chord progressions, purely pianistic exercises in fingering, passages written round slow chorale-type melodies, four-voice textures of rhythmic complexity, and finally a transcription from the scene with the two armed men in Mozart's *Magic Flute*.

The Goethe songs, written between 1919 and 1924, are closely connected with the *Faust* project. One of them, *Die Bekehrte*, is written for a female voice with piano accompaniment and dedicated to the soprano, Lola Artôt de Padilla, of the Berlin Staatsoper; the other five are for baritone. The words for Mephistopheles' song and the *Lied des Brander* are taken from Goethe's *Faust*; the *Lied des Unmuts* from the *Westöstlicher Divan*; the *Zigeunerlied* and *Schlechter Trost* from other works by Goethe. The *Zigeunerlied* of 1923 is somewhat puzzlingly numbered Opus 55, no. 2. Busoni's biographer Dent, has remarked on the fact that : 'there is no Opus 55, no. 1.' Perhaps the *Lied des Brander*, which has no date and seems to have considerable spiritual affinities with the *Zigeunerlied*, is supposed to be this Opus 55, no. 1? The music is not obviously similar in any way to the music of *Doctor Faust*, at any rate, no more so than that of the other Goethe songs of the same period.

In all these songs, Busoni is aiming at something rather different from most of the Goethe composers after Schubert. His songs are vocal scenes, not altogether intimate in nature but not altogether directed towards public performance, belonging somewhere half-way between the atelier and the theatre. Each one of them is based on a single, simple musical idea. The two earliest, the Mephistopheles' Song and the *Lied des Unmuts*, are based on staccato figures on the piano, which are sometimes developed in growing rhythmical movement, and sometimes alternate with a kind of recitative. *Die Bekehrte* of 1921, a musical setting of one of Busoni's favourite poems, which he also gave to his students to work on, is basically a lullaby rhythm in six-eight time, which in the final lament livens up into a semiquaver figure. The accompaniment of *Das Lied des Brander* is a more or less consistent staccato invention from beginning to end, interspersed with ostinato chord progressions; the *Zigeunerlied* is equally ostinato in character, with its persistent semiquavers and the almost uncanny progression of gliding semitones in the bass. In *Schlechter Trost*, two consecutive crotchets, repeated monotonously on the piano, accompany a vocal line, which is taken direct from the *Doctor Faust* music— from the conjuring-up of the spirits in the second scene of the introduction, to be more precise.

Busoni's vocal treatment in these six songs is not only ingenious and original, but shows considerable understanding of vocal problems. The most obvious comparison is with Schubert's writing in the great vocal passages of something like the *Erlkönig*. Verdi also attempted something similar on one occasion, in one of his few songs, *Gretchen am Spinnrad*, which is equally remote from the 'bel canto' style.

Although the effect is not actually operatic, the dramatic and emotional impact of these late songs of Busoni's is occasionally alarmingly direct. In fact, they are among the most mature and original products of a musical idiom that has its roots in dramatic composition. This is most apparent in the brilliant *Zigeunerlied*, which effectively suggests the nocturnal atmosphere of the snow-clad woods, with owls hooting and wolves howling. One needs to have heard this song sung by Fischer-Dieskau, in order to appreciate the depth of its musical content. Another thing worth noticing in this piece, as in many others that Busoni wrote late in life, is the way he returns to the early influence of Brahms, referring back to one of his Haydn-Variations in the accompaniment figure. *Schlechter Trost* is Busoni's last composition, completed in the year of his death, a deeply moving swan-song, which ends with a vision of ghosts gliding past the sleepless man, refusing him any kind of comfort.

Even though pessimism and melancholy are the prevailing mood in these Goethe songs, there is also sufficient evidence of Busoni's wit. It is most apparent in *Das Lied des Brander* and Mephistopheles' Song, but it also sets the tone in the *Zigeunerlied*,

131

when the witches' language is parodied in natural sounds : 'Willi wau wau wau willi wo wo wo wi-to witto hu.'

And so the final product of this extremely flexible and versatile mind is a combination of all the characteristics that were peculiar to his music from the beginning. These include the qualities of dramatic art and virtuosity, a feeling for the supernatural and a gift for critical rationalism, an ability to think in terms of several voices and on various levels, and unlimited imagination and invention with regard to harmony and colour. The erotic element, so strongly developed in Busoni as a person, plays a very secondary role in his art; whereas the metaphysical side of his nature comes increasingly to the fore, constantly trying to solve the riddles of life. Even today, restricting oneself to the pieces that Busoni himself approved, it is difficult to trace the unifying element in his music. But the one thing they all have in common is an extraordinary clarity in composition, harmonic language, scoring and form. This transparency is retained and is still apparent, even when Busoni ventures beyond the limits of traditional music, in pieces such as the *Berceuse Elégiaque*, the *Nocturne*, the Second Sonatina, and the masterpiece of his declining years, the *Faust* opera.

The Poet

'I find writing far less of an effort than composing *(sans comparaison!)*; probably because I have less ability for it . . .' Busoni wrote to Gisella Selden-Goth from Zürich in 1920. There is something almost coquettish about this gross understatement; Busoni knew perfectly well that he could write, that he had in fact shown remarkable skill in mastering the art of literary expression in several languages. The following lines from his poetic work, *Der mächtige Zauberer*, which he wrote before the *Outline for a New Musical Aesthetics*, reveal a totally different attitude to language : 'I want to attain the unknown !' he says, 'what I already know is boundless. But I want to go even further. The final word still eludes me.' We know, that even as a child Busoni had tried his hand as a writer; and there were times in his life, when his interest in literature was stronger than his interest in music. In Trieste, back in 1884, the newspaper *L'Independente* had printed reviews, which he sent in from Vienna under the pseudonym, Bruno Fierosucci, a anagram of his real name; these included one on piano recitals by Anton Rubinstein, and another on Hans von Bülow. In the same year, an article appeared in the *Grazer Tagespost* on the musical situation in Italy. In 1887, Busoni wrote a very detailed treatise for the jubilee aniversary of Mozart's *Don Juan*, which was published in the *Neue Zeitschrift für Musik* along with pieces on Sgambati and Verdi's *Otello*. In 1898, *Die allgemeine Musikzeitung* carried Busoni's obituary on his teacher, Dr. Wilhelm Mayer (W. A. Rémy).

In addition to the journalistic articles and essays, from 1894 onwards there are also the prefaces to the Bach editions, occasionally epilogues as well, beginning with the introduction to the *Well-Tempered Clavier*. A bibliographical-cum-critical study, *The Editions of Liszt's Piano Compositions*, has also been preserved, in which Busoni set out the fundamental principles of the complete Liszt edition that he was planning. The articles on Mozart's *Don Juan* and Liszt, which amount to some twenty

133

or thirty printed pages, reveal Busoni's natural bent for work of an orderly, scholarly nature, together with the ability of a mind trained in various directions and interested in a hundred different styles and periods. 'I know, you are a philologist,' said the Italian poet, Gabriele d'Annunzio, when they met in Paris in 1912. The philologist in Busoni investigated, among other things, various German translations of the *Don Juan* libretto comparing them syllable by syllable with the Italian original, and examining them for any rhythmical discrepancy from Mozart's music. In the process of so doing, his inquiry often reaches far beyond the specific details of his subject and touches on aesthetic problems, and the point of view of the artist in general. It is typical of Busoni as a young man, that he chooses to measure Mozart's greatness in terms of versatility. His own versatility as a creative person certainly extended far beyond the world of music, and brought him in contact with spheres of activity that inevitably remained inaccessible to Mozart himself. The Liszt article is much more academic, more concerned with its subject than with associated ideas of a general nature, and therefore quite rightly described as a 'study', whereas the Mozart article is called 'a critical commentary'.

The written texts in the Bach editions reveal the extraordinary range of Busoni's imagination, which increases as the years go by. Although the piece in question always remains the focal point of his studies, the number of other famous works involved increases, until we have a little cosmos of comparative criticism. If Busoni is dealing with the subject of Bach's toccatas, he will not forget to mention an analogous example in Schumann's Opus 7. If he is talking about the fugal technique of *The Well-Tempered Clavier*, the crowning point in his inquiry is an analysis of the fugue from Beethoven's *Hammerklavier* Sonata, Opus 106. The texts linking the various pieces in the individual volumes of the Bach Edition are frequently concentrated statements drawn from every conceivable branch of musical and instrumental pedagogy. The brilliant way in which they are set out, can only be compared with Hans von Bülow's commentaries in his Beethoven edition. Busoni later included some of these texts in the omnibus volume, *On the Unity of Music*, which he assembled for the Berlin publisher, Max Hesse, in 1922 and dedicated to the author Jakob Wassermann.

But Busoni did not limit himself to writing about music. Ever since 1905, he had been working almost constantly on dramatizations. The first of these, *Der mächtige Zauberer*, is based on a novella by Comte Joseph Arthur de Gobineau. The choice of material is typical, indicative of Busoni's taste for magic and his desire to rise above ordinary, day-to-day causality. In his librettos, there are almost inevitably characters endowed with magic powers. Objects are constantly being changed into something else, in this case a brazier turns into a 'magnificent golden statue of the Buddha'. The first draft of the *Brautwahl* libretto also dates from the year 1905, using characters, scenes and plot motivation, borrowed from the novellas of E. T. A. Hoffmann. In 1909, Busoni was once again obsessed with *Der mächtige Zauberer*, and in a letter to Gerda we find him speculating on how, for example, one might represent a journey through the desert in terms of the stage : 'first perhaps an empty stage with appropriate scenery, then the wandering Kassem, exhausted; the voices of the invisible spirits of the magician and the young woman, alternately enticing and warning him. The brazier of the first scene must be there from *the very beginning*; instead of the magician drawing gold from it (which would not make a sufficient impact on the audience), the whole brazier is transformed . . .' Meanwhile, work on *Die Brautwahl* continued, in spite of being constantly interrupted by other compositions, concert tours, and various literary and domestic distractions.

1906 was a relatively settled year. Busoni was not involved in any major concert tours overseas. He played in Switzerland, in his native Trieste and Bologna, in England, Holland and Scotland. He spent a holiday in Northern Italy. In London, he appeared together with the elderly but famous singer, Adelina Patti. In a letter to his wife Gerda, he describes the scurrilous concert in the following terms :

'Patti—age 63
Santley—age 72
A female violinist—age 11
Ben Davies—weight 100 kilos.
And as for the Albert Hall . . . All very well for a bull-fight, maybe !
But for piano playing? And as for the programme—and the music . . . !'

In other letters, he frequently mentions characters from the *Brautwahl* libretto, which he was still working on, Thusman, Leonhard, the Kommissionsrat and Manasse; but also Tirso de Molina's *Don Juan Tenorio*, for which he would have liked to write a stage score for Max Reinhardt. Also during the same year, he had to cope with the preparations and rehearsals for one of the famous orchestral concerts with first performances, which he conducted in the Berlin Beethovensaal. And apart from all this, he was writing notes, which quite unintentionally assumed the form of a short book. This was his *Outline for a New Musical Aesthetics*, a truly brilliant product of the feeling of rebellion that Busoni experienced at the age of forty. This little book, respectfully and affectionately dedicated to Rainer Maria Rilke, presents a kind of Utopia. Its prophetic qualities, in looking forward into the future of music, are constantly being confirmed even today. All the ideas formulated in perhaps forty pages of writing spring from his basic dissatisfaction with tradition. Yet Busoni manages to express his qualms in a bright and cheerfully optimistic tone, that is reminiscent of the words spoken at a later date by his *Doctor Faust* : 'the only person to look cheerful, is one who looks continually towards the future.' The influence of Nietzsche is unmistakable, in the first place in the aphoristic style of writing, but equally in the absence of all partiality and the revaluation of all accepted musical values. Only a man as widely cultured as Busoni could have written this joyful pamphlet, in which quotations from Hugo von Hofmannsthal, Edgar Allan Poe, Nietzsche and Leo Tolstoy, appear alongside others from his two favourite poets, Goethe and E. T. A. Hoffman. Among the great composers that he mentions are Bach, Mozart, Beethoven, Berlioz, Schubert, Schumann, Liszt, Wagner, Offenbach and Vincent d'Indy (two works by d'Indy appear on the programme of Busoni's orchestral concert of 8th November 1906); musicologists include Andreas Werckmeister and Cherubini. Compared with literature and music, visual art is of secondary importance in his intellectual activities at this time; Giotto and Michelangelo are the only artists to be mentioned briefly in the *Outline for a New Musical Aesthetics*. The little book deals with numerous problems of musical production and reproduction, technique and aesthetics, musical system and the creation of sound. It does not propose any solutions, but aims to stimulate, and rouse interest through criticism.

Busoni objects to programme-music every bit as much as he objects to absolute music. In connection with Eduard Hanslick, he speaks of the latter's 'audio-wallpaper patterns'. He completely rejects the legislators, with their faith in the letter of the law and their false ideas about accurate rendering.

In the last thirteen pages of the book, Busoni complains about the way a composer is chained down by the instruments themselves. What he is after, is abstract sound, unrestricted technique, and complete absence of tonal boundaries. Instead of the two keys, major and minor, he conceives of 113 scales of seven tones within the octave; and with this permutation and the 'kaleidoscopic re-shuffling of the twelve semitones', he comes very close to the dodecaphony of Hauer and Schoenberg. His intention is to enrich the musical system by means of sixth-tones, which is to say, two scales of third-tones separated by a semitone.

At the end of this pamphlet, Busoni mentions a new musical instrument that he had seen and heard in America. Its inventor, Dr. Thaddäus Cahill, calls it a 'dynamophone'. It uses electricity to create synthetic tones. Similar in type to the later Hammond Organ, the Dynamophone is an early ancestor of the electronic musical instruments that we are familiar with today. Busoni quite rightly sees the possibility here of creating 'scientifically perfect, utterly reliable sound'.

This short book, which appeared in 1907 through a small publishing-house in Trieste, was like a sudden flash of inspiration to the younger generation. On 7th July 1907, Busoni wrote to Gerda : 'A young student stopped me in the street, his voice trembling with excitement, to tell me how greatly impressed he had been by my little book. It was very gratifying, to find such whole-hearted and uncritical enthusiasm in a decent young man.'

In 1916, in the middle of the First World War, the Inselverlag in Leipzig had the courage to reprint the book written by the 'hostile foreigner' living in Switzerland, and publish it in their famous Inselbücherei edition. As a result of this, it had an extraordinarily wide circulation, as a sort of bibliophile's pocket-book. The composer and disciple of Schopenhauer, Hans Pfitzner (like many other German intellectuals of that period, embracing the most exaggerated form of Teutonic aggressiveness), replied with a pamphlet, *The Dangers of Futurism*, a title which in itself suggested a series of misunderstandings and even deliberate misinterpretations of Busoni's Utopia.

During the following years up till 1914, Busoni's literary output consisted mainly of analyses, essays, and articles for newspapers and magazines. Their intellectual range is wide, varying from the Mozart aphorisms written for the one hundred and fiftieth anniversary in 1906 to rough notes, such as those prepared for the preface to *The Well-Tempered Clavier*, in which Busoni sketches out a particular kind of mental biology. 'With human beings,' he notes, 'it seems as though, in order to progress, the various qualities have to develop in strict rotation. After the body, the mind, then the character, and finally the soul.' This hierarchy : body, mind, character, soul, is worth noticing; and is characteristic of Busoni's philosophy of organic development. This brief outline dates from September 1914; a few weeks later, he wrote the *Faust* libretto, in which the six spirits materialize one after another in a very similar way, building up towards a

138

climax. In his brief text, Busoni continues: 'With the artist, the first thing to assume any importance is intuition, then technique develops, is supervened by reflexion, and finally personality emerges. With a creative artist of any consequence, the first period consists of self-searching, the second of actually finding himself; while the third and final stages often seem in retrospect to have been periods of renewed searching.' Busoni is obviously describing his own creative activity, when he makes this three-part division.

Problems of composition were foremost among the purely musical subjects that preoccupied Busoni during the eight years preceding the outbreak of the First World War; they constitute the basic subject matter of: a self-confession, *How I compose?*; an article, *The Gothics of Chicago, Illinois*; a brief exposition, *The New Harmonic Language*; the account in *Pan* of the Schoenberg matinée in Berlin in 1911; a reply, *Futurism in Music*; and a series of aphorisms, *On the Future of Opera*. He is also concerned with problems of piano playing and interpretation in general; and is definitely in favour of playing from memory, in that no limitations are imposed on the consciousness of the player, particularly in the case of modern works.

Busoni's most important contribution along these lines is his *Introduction to the Etudes of Franz Liszt*, dating from September 1909. Also significant, is the article on *The Value of Musical Arrangement*, in which Busoni quite rightly points out, that the very fact of writing down an idea is in itself a kind of transcription; well worth reading is his commentary on *Pianistic genius*, in which he establishes that the things which seem difficult to one generation are accepted as a matter of course by the next. Here, as on many other occasions when he indulges in literary digressions, Busoni makes a comparison between something he has observed in the ordinary everyday world and something experienced on a higher cultural level: 'I know boys from simple, middle-class families—little more than children—who, in their own homes, perform pretty little tricks with electrical combinations, quite as a matter of course, like any other game. Where do boys of average talent find this sort of ability, which two hundred years ago only a "genius", a dare-devil, a magician would have had? It must obviously be a question of heredity and contemporary climate. A pianistic genius—like any other genius—is presumably the man of talent who embarks on a new path, and accomplishes unprecedented things; things that can only be learnt from him after a certain interval of time.'

In 1914 the *Phantastische Geschichten* of E. T. A. Hoffman appeared in an edition published by Georg Müller in Munich. Busoni wrote a preface for them, which revealed his deep understanding not only of the mentality of that great Romantic writer, but also of the sources upon which Hoffmann drew. The following lines provide a convincing resumé of Hoffmann's technique: 'In actual fact, Hoffmann very rarely abandons reality; and although we sometimes have the feeling that something improbable, illegal and supernatural is going on, it is almost impossible to put one's finger on a passage and say exactly when we first had this feeling. Hoffmann never states in so many words, that the witchcraft and magic are real events; he leaves the reader to draw his own conclusions. A chance word, unexpectedly overheard, can be infinitely suggestive without proving anything; unbelievable and hair-raising facts about a person's past can easily be construed from rumours reported at third hand, and introduced by Hoffmann in the correctest possible way. But in most cases, it is someone who is either dreaming, drunk, delirious or mad, who thinks he has seen or is seeing the apparitions and tricks that are described; and next morning, by the sober light of day, everything is back to normal, in a middle-class and commonplace environment, totally devoid of any element of fantasy or grandeur.'

This description also applies in many ways to Busoni himself, not only to his writing, but also to his music, particularly his magical piano playing.

The literary form of the operatic libretto continued to interest

140

Busoni. In 1912, the American, Louis Gruenberg, son of a Boston violinist, had begun studying with him. The two of them had many intellectual and literary interests in common. Somewhere about 1913, Busoni wrote a tragi-comic folk drama, based on the famous Indian story of Nala and Damajanti from the cultic play of the Mahabharata, which he called *Die Götterbraut* and handed over to Gruenberg to set to music. Gruenberg's opera, *The Bride of the Gods* (1913), has to my knowledge never been performed; Busoni's libretto was published in the pamphlet of the Staatsoper in May 1921, on the occasion of the first performance in Berlin of *Turandot* and *Arlecchino*. It shows the classic pair of Indian lovers at their first meeting, and overcoming the various forms of opposition that they encounter. In the first scene, two false prophets appear, who describe Damajanti's beauty and commend her to Indra and three other gods. Prince Nala, whom the gods want to send to Damajanti as their envoy, tries to evade this duty because he himself is in love with the princess. The second tableau shows him kneeling before Damajanti, who chooses him instead of her divine suitors. The setting of the comic third tableau is the court of the bride's royal father; he listens to the prophets, and would like to please all the suitors. At a state ceremony, the king tries to talk his daughter into a *mariage de convenance*, but fails to persuade her. She herself dismisses the gods, who are seeking her hand in marriage, and confesses her love for Nala. Finally, it is the gods themselves who bow to her sincerity and strength of purpose and lead her to Nala, as he rides forward to meet her.

The libretto has a good deal in common with the subject-matter of *Turandot*; while the prophets and the king are three comic types, borrowed straight from the Commedia dell' Arte. The third tableau in particular is reminiscent of various *Turandot* scenes, and there is even something of the irony of *Arlecchino* in the prophets' conversations and the suitors' chorus. Not even the gods themselves can avoid the mocking finger that Busoni points at them; for instance, one of them sings: 'I would give

141

the magic ring from my left toe, to be able to remove this pearl from the oyster!' and another continues: 'What wouldn't I give for a human adventure!' Finally, Busoni lets the three gods assume the appearance of Nala, with the result that poor Damajanti, faced with this three-fold apparition, is completely bewildered. Yet even in this test she emerges triumphant, and when she is deceived into believing that the real Nala is dead, her one wish is to die herself.

In spite of totally different themes, and the discrepancy in the forms that Busoni has chosen for them, there are nonetheless similarities between *Die Götterbraut* and *Doctor Faust*. Busoni, who was extremely subtle and imaginative, was well aware of the force of the folk wisdom contained in songs, fairy-tales and legends. In his dramatic writing, he is continually drawing upon his almost divine understanding of the folk spirit. His simple, reflective texts and dialogues may sometimes be sustained by irony, but they may equally well express the most profound ideas in a perfectly straightforward way. Just occasionally, wisdom and parody may combine; irony oversteps its own limitations, and becomes serious and tragic.* Many passages in Busoni's librettos are influenced by this folk spirit, which Goethe also appreciated and knew how to master. In *Doctor Faust*, Busoni follows up the introductory symphonia and the 'Pax' calls of the chorus with a prologue, 'The poet to the spectators', in which the style of popular verse is consistently sustained. In this, he gives an account of the various different stages that have led to *Doctor Faust*. Like a psychoanalyst, Busoni begins this self-analysis by recalling a puppet-play seen during his childhood. After drawing attention to the figures of Merlin, Don Juan, and Goethe's Faust, he ends up by admitting to the influence of the puppet-play:

* Vladimir Vogel wrote about this in an article for the *Schweizerische Musikzeitung* (March–April 1966): 'Thus Busoni was able to use the same creative roots for his writing as for his music. By re-establishing the original monumental quality of the language, yet retaining its dialectic clarity, he has given his librettos an extraordinary richness, and at the same time they are still within almost anybody's grasp.'

'On looking more closely at the simple images,
they seemed even more beautiful after all these years;
I was their varnisher, worked as a gilder—
(Time can equally well act as a destroyer)
one I softened, another I sharpened,
and from the chrysalis a butterfly emerged:
I wove new stitches into the old fabric,
you will be surprised to see the long-forgotten pattern
So my play appears new and alive,
Yet its puppet origins are still apparent.'

The mocking side of Busoni's nature reappears in the students' dispute in the Wittenberg tavern, when they quarrel about Platonic teaching, God and earthly possessions, to the rhythm of a minuet. Finally, the Latin *Te Deum* of the Catholics combines with the German chorale of the Protestants in a dialectic double chorus. The literary climax of the libretto is reached in Faust's final words, as he addresses the dead child, firmly convinced that he himself will rise from the dead : 'So I continue to operate through you, and you continue to procreate, and so until the end of time the impression of my being becomes ever more deeply engraved. What I did badly, you will put right; what I failed to do, you will do in my place; thus I transcend the law of life, embrace all epochs in one, and join the last members of the human race. I, Faust, an eternal will!'

The libretto of *Arlecchino*, the first draft of which was prepared in September 1913, could not and was not intended to reach such heights. Yet even in this, the hero of the title bids farewell with a sort of self-confession. 'Doesn't everything repeat itself, and in the same endless circles?' suggests Arlecchino. And he grants the right to the man who has heart and mind, and chooses an honest path. Busoni later maintained, that *Arlecchino* was something less than a challenge and more than a joke. He intimates that there are personal confessions and serious intentions, hidden beneath the surface of this apparently light-hearted, comic libretto. 'I have deliberately tried to sustain a style, that is

143

constantly fluctuating between grim humour and playful serious-ness, and I seem to have succeeded.'

The *Turandot* libretto is an arrangement based on Gozzi, as opposed to Schiller. Here again, we find the same individual combination of seriousness and irony, which is so characteristic of Busoni.

Yet another short dramatic libretto, *Das Wandbild*, was written during the same period as *Doctor Faust*. Busoni calls it a 'scene' and a 'pantomime'. The short text is dedicated to his friend and pupil, Philipp Jarnach, and was set to music by the Swiss composer, Othmar Schoeck. The scene, set in a Parisian antique shop, is disturbed by the sudden appearance of a mime, followed by a priests' song and a chorus of young girls. There is some-thing reminiscent of E. T. A. Hoffmann in the eerie moment, when the picture on the wall springs to life, and a silent dancer emerges from the torn canvas. It is a life-size painting of a girl in Chinese dress with loose, flowing hair. A student—Busoni calls him Novalis—had come into the shop in the Rue Saint-Honoré at eight o'clock in the evening with a friend. He falls in love with the picture, almost in the same way that Tamino falls in love with the picture of Pamina. He wants to know, who it is and what it means. He struggles with the centenarian antique dealer who, apparently quite unconcerned, tells him how he frightened his dead daughter by putting on a suit of armour, when she was being difficult. Eventually, Novalis rushes at the picture, and immediately finds himself in the spirit world of the Chinese, where the picture in some magic way belongs. He and the girl fall into one another's arms; as a symbol of her marriage, her handmaids arrange her hair in a wifely style. The couple are surprised in their wedding embrace by a black giant in golden armour, hung with chains and armed with a hammer. On seeing her changed hair-style, he binds the girl with chains and disappears into the ground with her. Novalis reappears in the shop. The girl in the painting has acquired the other hair-style. 'How do you explain that?' Novalis snaps at the old man. The answer uncovers a piece of typical Busoni philosophy : 'The appearance of a face depends entirely on the person who is looking at it!'

Busoni discovered this uncanny story in a collection of *Chinese Ghost- and Love-stories* that Martin Buber edited and wrote a preface for, in 1918. In June of the same year, he sent the libretto to Othmar Schoeck, with a poem dedicating it to him.

Das Wandbild appeared for the first time in July 1918, in René Schickele's Zürich monthly, *Die weissen Blätter*. For Othmar Schoeck's musical setting, which had its first performance in Halle in 1921, Busoni added another song for the old priest, which is reminiscent in every way of the spirit of the Faust libretto. In its extraordinary fantasy quality, the combination of the two settings: Paris in 1830, and a timeless Chinese spirit world; and finally in the moralizing note of his closing observation, the libretto is typical of Busoni's dramatic writing.

It is to some extent a synthesis of numerous themes that appear constantly in his operatic work, from the *Mächtiger Zauberer* and the *Brautwahl*, through *Turandot* to *Doctor Faust* and *Arlecchino*.

During his extensive travels, Busoni spent countless free hours reading. Consequently, it was not unusual for a book to remind him of his own literary projects; in the course of reading, a plot would occur to him, and he would jot it down, sometimes even work it out to some extent. On one occasion, he even wrote to Gerda from London about a ballet that he planned to write. The date was March 1913. Busoni was spending a lot of time with the dancer, Maud Allan, who had been one of his pupils in Weimar in 1900. ('Partly out of kindness, and partly for pleasure') he was working on a scenario for her: 'The idea is to tell the story of a girl in a series of tableaux, suitably entitled *The Dance of Life and Death*. The stage becomes a "music hall", in which a Beardsley-type scene is enacted—a Parisian dance-hall—and then there is a dance with a barrel-organ in the streets of London; the final tableau is (as I see it) mystical, and is set in a church, in front of a strange altar; on this altar stands a group, with the cross in the middle, and on the right and left figures

145

representing death and the angel of resurrection. There is a dance of death, and much else besides. It could turn into something very good, something vital and real; it's the kind of thing that lasts. But . . . (All kinds of dances are introduced, beginning with a sort of dance version of a game of tennis; then gypsy dancing, pantomime, a grand waltz and can-can, street dancing, a suicide dance on the parapet of a bridge, a religious dance and dance of death.)'

This subject, combined with Busoni's music, could have been the basis for a remarkable ballet. Dance music for its own sake appealed very strongly to this Tuscan musician. It plays as important a part in his operatic theories as in his actual compositions. Yet in spite of all his personal contacts with dancers, such as Maud Allan and Isadora Duncan, who was greatly impressed by Busoni when she met him in Bologna, he did not write any ballets. Nevertheless, his return to Berlin on 11th September 1920 served to stimulate him in various directions. A week later, on a Sunday, he composed his waltz after Johann Strauss—'just for fun'.

Many of his operatic projects were also left unfinished, some after years of work, others soon after the first draft. For a relatively long period, Busoni had plans for a libretto, *Aladdin*, based on the autobiographical fantasy of Adam Gottlob Oehlenschläger. He first mentions it in a letter written from London in 1902 : 'not as an opera, but as a work combining theatre, music, dancing, magic, if possible all in one evening . . . my original idea of a theatrical piece with music *where necessary*, but not otherwise interfering with the spoken word.' There is also some indication of the symbolism that is to appear in the later mature pieces, particularly when Busoni says, that he hopes the pieces may be similar to *The Magic Flute*, only 'with more sense and a less deadly theme'. Four years later, on 7th October 1906, he announces in a letter from Amsterdam, that he has finished the first act of *Aladdin*. Busoni is satisfied with his work; he has succeeded in introducing real cohesion into the act. All he has to do now, is go straight ahead. He speaks of the simplicity

146

of the ascending line. But he is critical of Oehlenschläger's original text, maintaining that it is clichéd and spoilt by its feminine gossipy quality. After this he does not mention *Aladdin* again.

Plans for writing a libretto with Karl Vollmoeller, famous at that time as the author of *Mirakel*, fell through even more quickly. On this occasion, the inspiration was a short story, *The Secret* by the French writer of fantasy, Villiers de l'Isle Adam. Busoni was busy working on this during the summer of 1912, but seems to have abandoned the project after completing three scenes. All these works have in common a 'rapprochment' of the real and metaphysical worlds. It is an essential part of Busoni's attitude to life, and is sometimes apparent in his restless day-to-day existence.

In the many articles, most of which were published in a collected volume in 1922, and appeared with some important additions in a new edition of the book in 1956, ideas of a totally non-musical nature do occasionally appear. The most original of these contributions is a piece of prose, dating from November 1914, on the subject of cigar-boxes. Busoni takes as his point of departure the idea, that objects are perfect, when the form has developed along with the function. The violin, the watch and the pencil are, in his opinion, fully-developed objects from this point of view. Then, with scholarly thoroughness, he goes on to describe the form of the cigar-box, its size, the way it is nailed and glued, the way the lid is fixed and how it operates, the condition of the wood and its decoration. He compares the label on the outside with the images of the saints and lottery tickets of the 'sixties. He mentions the palm trees, tropical landscapes and exotic ports, even the portraits of merchants that appear on them. His conclusion is, that a collection of these kind of cigar-boxes could be every bit as interesting and varied as many other collections. The piece ends with a few words about Swedish match-boxes, another example of an object that has attained perfection.

Even though in this short piece, Busoni's delight in describing

147

objects is almost indistinguishable from the ironic chuckle of a man raising objects he has despised into his own lofty field of vision, it is nevertheless typical of his pragmatic way of thinking. He had a strong natural bent for architecture and the architectonic, even though he sometimes maligned the use of architectonic symmetry in musical forms. Problems of cubically confined space interested him a great deal, just as the problem of space in general loomed large in his ideas and in his dramatic writing. Admittedly, the idea of the three caskets, which assume the role of destiny at the end of *Die Brautwahl*, is not original and stems from Shakespeare. Yet, in their shape and unimaginative decoration, they can be compared with the cigar-boxes, from which Busoni develops a certain concept of perfection. His interest in the architectonic problems of the theatre is revealed first in Zürich in 1918, and then in Berlin in 1922. The first thing to appear is a tryptich of drawings, then four years later the text, *Plans for a Three-part Stage Set*, with which Busoni promises to simplify stage production.

Another important but unfinished piece, dating from the Zürich period, is his *Ideas on Expression in Architecture*. In this, Busoni speaks of the importance of the functional element in architecture, which cannot successfully be induced by design. He makes a distinction between southern and northern architecture based on terraces and pitched roofs. With his theory of functionalism, Busoni is opposed to the idea of a Viennese station imitating a mediaeval castle, for example; the construction may be brilliant, but the form of expression is insincere. Within this definition of insincerity, Busoni includes all modern buildings that pretend to be older than they really are. At the same time, he mentions the powerful illusions created by this kind of faked styling. Finally, he considers three particularly typical architectural forms : the house, the temple and the theatre. As far as the house is concerned, his main requirement is that it should suit the stature and number of its inhabitants : 'In the same way that the format of a book is determined by the hand that holds it and the eye that has to take in its surfaces

148

and symbols, so the form of a house should be determined by the shape and natural movement of man.' He then goes on to say, that the house must be comfortable and inviting enough, to make the owner wish to return to it and inspire his guests with confidence. The front door and staircase are described as ways of making it inviting; the balcony and protective roof are considered as elements providing a link with nature and the open air. Busoni then goes on to talk about the materials used. He mentions iron gratings as a means of protection for the anxious, prudent citizen, and speaks of wood as a means of bridging the gap between man and nature. Wooden buildings are rustic in expression, and therefore further removed from the bourgeois. Attached to this piece, is a sketch of a symmetrical-type, Southern European country house, with the arcades of an entrance hall extending in front, rather like a smaller version of the *Loggia dei Lanzi* in Florence. At this point the fragment suddenly breaks off, without our discovering anything about Busoni's ideas about temples and theatres.

Another highly original piece, written in America in 1915, is concerned with the physical world of the blind. Busoni gives it the paradoxical title, *The Disadvantage of Sight*. He takes as his starting-point the true story of a girl born blind, who as the result of an operation performed on her as an adult is eventually able to see, and is deeply disappointed by the world that she discovers. Busoni puts himself in the position of this woman. He then tries to give a completely unbiased picture of the things that any seeing person is familiar with and takes for granted. For instance, he compares the impressions of someone, who for the first time is able to see his mother, with the imaginary image cherished by someone who is blind. The grimace of the smile, the uncanny searching of the eyes, must all seem quite terrifying: 'The arms hang down on either side, culminating in a series of smaller limbs, that are continually moving, writhing, clutching, and approaching him threateningly.' The blind person also has to learn to see in terms of perspective, to realize for example that a lighter area means that the surface is raised, that a dark one indicates a depression. Singing, which was a source of delight to the blind man, may revolt him when he can see; just as the sight of an orchestra, as opposed to pure sound, may well be disillusioning. After all, the appearance of a flower is crude and unsatisfactory compared with its perfume.

But the girl who gained her sight was disappointed by the very light. From this Busoni concludes, that the person who is born blind lives in a more perfect and less confined world than the person who can see. At the end of the essay he says: '. . . in people (and even in objects), that we have grown to love, we want to see nothing but good at any price, not realizing that it is our love that creates these qualities. Since a blind person is as susceptible to love as anyone else, he will be likely to endow the object of his love with even more perfect qualities, than the person whose eyes are continually reminding him of the imperfections.'

Fantasy and irony were always an important element in Busoni's literary work. In 1908, he wrote a short scene entitled *From the classical Witches' Sabbath* for the Shrovetide edition of the magazine, *Musik*. For this purpose, he used the transparent pseudonym, INO-SUB-F, which read backwards, spells F. Busoni. The scene is set in Limbo, that mythical region between Heaven and Hell, reserved for those souls who have not yet been redeemed by Christ. In the middle sits Felix Mendelssohn, surrounded by a little band of musicians, including Schumann, Niels Gade, Ludwig Spohr, Franz Lachner and other lesser figures. Schumann is talking mainly about himself and his protegé, Johannes Brahms, who (he reports) is in Heaven: 'he is sitting, somewhat on his own, in the German section—he would have liked to move closer to Beethoven—however, he is very comfortably installed, all very simple. A couple of soft cushions, a few horns on the walls, broken triads and a delightful collection of syncope. The Herzogenberg couple have been brought in to wait on him, and my wife is running the house.' Mendelssohn then asks, who else is 'up there'. Schumann replies, that the Italians, Palestrina, Cherubini and Rossini, are strutting about up there because they have not done anyone any harm. Whereas Donizetti is in purgatory, along with Meyerbeer and Marschner. Mendelssohn asks after Mozart. Schumann replies: 'That rascal has the right to go wherever he likes. He really belongs in Heaven, but when he wants to have a good time he goes down into Hell.' Incidentally, no one has so far shown himself worthy of staying permanently in Hell; Beethoven, Berlioz and Offenbach (who goes down every Easter Sunday) are only allowed in for short periods. Finally, Mendelssohn asks: 'And what about this Richard?' to which Schumann replies: 'He'll have to do his stretch in purgatory, but (maliciously) he won't get into Hell!'

A short contribution to the magazine *Signale*, entitled *A Magical Invention*, and dated 1st April 1911, is another of Busoni's ironical pieces. In this, Busoni dreams up a sort of microphone, that makes it possible to hear what is normally inaudible, but at the same time (by virtue of primitive sound-waves) transcends the barriers of time, so that it can produce impressions both of the past and future. He talks about phonographic symbols, which probably lie some hundred and forty years ahead of us, in other words, a form of music that will not materialize for another century and a half. But this short piece is as rich in ideas as the infinitely more serious *Outline for a New Musical Aesthetics* of 1906. A more sinister aspect of Busoni's powerful imagination is revealed in the sketch entitled *Dream*, which was written in Berlin on 17th September 1914, shortly after the outbreak of the First World War. It is a vision of war, in which an officer—a banker in civilian life—becomes involved in a mysterious crime. He plans a fake suicide, but is accidentally drowned at sea. Years later, fishermen bring his body to the surface, 'a human corpse, completely encrusted with pearls . . . like some exotic idol, made of mother-of-pearl.' This fantastic image alone is worthy of E. T. A. Hoffmann or Edgar Allan Poe. Busoni took an interest in Poe at various different times during his life. In 1900, we find him praising Poe for his perspicacity, for the consistency and Goethe-like clarity of his style, particularly of his descriptions. In 1907, when he is working on the libretto of *Die Brautwahl*, he frequently mentions Poe; he also quotes him in a study of Villiers de l'Isle-Adam in 1912, and again in 1919 when he describes him as the master of all modern fantasy writers.

Busoni was familiar with many languages. So he was inevitably concerned with the problem of translation. He had already undertaken a certain amount in early Mozart work, particularly in relation to *Don Juan*. In Zürich in 1917, he translated into German Charles Baudelaire's essay on Poe, and shortly afterwards Petrarch's 123rd Sonnet. Both translations are masterpieces in terms of thought transference from one language to another; and Busoni is able to formulate the subtleties of both the French and the Italian with all the assurance of a clairvoyant.

The fact, that Busoni considered Bach to be something more than the master of abstract counterpoint and soullessly constructed polyphony, was already evident in his early Bach editions. In this respect, he resembles Albert Schweitzer, who certainly attempted a thoroughly romantic interpretation of Bach's music in line with his own need for transcendental expression. Busoni went even further, when in Berlin at the end of 1921 he wrote down certain ideas for a dramatic production of the St. Matthew Passion. While on holiday with his father in Frohnleiten, the nineteen-year-old Ferruccio had written to his mother in Trieste asking her to send him the Bach Passion, which had been brought to his attention by Heinrich von Herzogenberg, a friend of Johannes Brahms. He was particularly interested in the recitatives, which had struck him as being intensely theatrical. He had apparently for many years, so he writes, wanted to see the St. Matthew Passion performed in a theatre. He does not overlook the problems involved in translating this idea into reality, particularly as Bach's way of illustrating the Path to the Cross does not correspond to the twelve stations of Calvary, but is more like a frieze on which the events are presented in rectilinear form. Busoni mentions the possibility of making cuts, in fact he would like to get rid of the arias altogether, because they hold

152

up the action, and with their pietistic words are nothing more than an imitation of the evangelical chronicle.

Busoni provides a sketch of a split-level stage, on which the various events are to be presented. The congregation is to sit on both sides, raised up half-way between the two levels of the stage, with the preacher in a pulpit between them. The scenery has the characteristic features of Gothic churches, with pointed arches and slender buttresses. The idea of making the St. Matthew Passion into a spiritual opera is strange enough in itself. The fact, that in order to do this Busoni wants to eliminate the arias, which are sometimes very dramatic, makes the whole project extremely puzzling. An equally idiotic idea was actually carried through at the end of the 'forties, when a film of the St. Matthew Passion was made in Rome, with Herbert von Karajan conducting, illustrated with religious paintings of the Italian Renaissance; in this case, musical forms were occasionally mangled in a similar fashion.

During the first winter of the war, 1914–15, Busoni became quite clear in his own mind as to the ultimate goal of his aesthetics. At that time he was working in America on the second part of *The Well-Tempered Clavier* for the Bach Edition. In March 1915, he added a *Conclusio* to this volume, written, as he puts it : 'at the time of the war-fugue.' In this piece he says : 'It is not the fugue, as a practical end in itself, but the importance in their own right of the techniques that give life to the fugue, which a present-day composer has to bear constantly in mind; with their help, he can realize his idea adroitly and exhaustively, and thereby give voice to his own age.

'It is the art of polyphony, which in the fugue appeared to have achieved its potential for the first time, that—having once gained independence—has become more precious than the fugue itself ever was, being simply a formal container.

'For the last time, I prophesy, that in music melody will triumph over all other compositional techniques : universal polyphony as the end-product of melodic writing, the mother of harmony, and bearer of the idea.

'New intervals, new means of producing sound, new, more powerful and more subtle minds will lead music along this path towards its ultimate goal which is: the expression of human sensibility, through technique being absorbed in an artistic totality.'

In 1920, Busoni made his important statements about the 'new classicism'. He was still in Zürich at the time, and the piece was addressed to the music critic, Paul Bekker, who had written an article criticizing Hans Pfitzner's exposition, *The New Aesthetics of Musical Impotence.* On many points, Busoni is in agreement with the champion of contemporary music, but he does draw the line at an expressionistic way of thinking, from which he would prefer to disassociate himself entirely. Busoni disputes the widespread use of exaggeration, made even by beginners. He rejects all experiments that lead to caricature, and dislikes the 'bizarre imitation of salient features in things that really mean something; defiance or rebellion, satire or foolishness'. Then he goes on to define the rules of the new classicism. He demands technical mastery; he wants every advantage to be taken of previous experimentation once this has been sorted out; he requires beautiful and tested musical forms, an art that is both old and new at the same time.

His view of the situation is expressed in very similar terms in a letter written to his son Benvenuto, who was living in Zürich. The letter is dated 18th June 1921, and serves as a reminder that Busoni had already mentioned a new classicism of this type more than two years previously. Yet at this stage, people wrongly assume, that his classicism is a backward-looking movement. This is entirely alien to his way of thinking; he is seeking in classicism, perfection, in two senses: impeccability and completion.

Busoni returns to these problems yet again in a letter published in a musical magazine. Written in January 1922, it is addressed to Fritz Windisch, editor of the magazine *Melos,* which had become the mouthpiece for a number of modernistic trends in music. In this, Busoni speaks of a form of art, which would be beyond all considerations of good and bad, and still be great at any period. In his opinion, a piece is not good just because it is new, and not new because it dispenses with all form and beauty. He mentions three characteristic features of neo-expressionism : its harmonic practice, hysteria, and temperamental gestures. Since the harmonic precludes the contrast of concord and discord, it must be limiting as a means of expression and devoid of individuality. By hysteria he means : 'short disconnected formulas, such as sighs, runs, the obstinate repetition of one or more notes, fading away, striking the very highest and lowest notes in the register, breaks in continuity, and the accumulation of various rhythms within the bar,' which would only be acceptable within the limits of a construction. By temperamental gestures, he means restless pseudo-polyphony in the orchestration. Then he goes on to protest about the way his own revolutionary requirements, as set out in his *Outline for a New Musical Aesthetics*, have been misinterpreted. 'By freedom of form, I never meant lack of form;' he insists, 'by unity of key, I did not mean an illogical and aimless confusion of harmony; by the right to be individual, I did not mean to sanction the presumptuous utterance of any clumsy fool.' Busoni requires the techniques employed to be aesthetically and meaningfully applied; the balance of time, sound and interval, to be distributed with artistry.

Between January and October 1920, an exchange of views took place between Busoni and the publisher, Gustav Kiepenheuer. It was primarily about the publication of the *Doctor Faust* libretto. This was followed by a number of very searching letters about the E. T. A. Hoffmann edition, that Kiepenheuer was planning. The publisher wanted to persuade Busoni to edit it, and Busoni suggested that his son, Benvenuto, should be the illustrator. Kiepenheuer also had plans for the Goncourt Journals. In both cases, Busoni revealed a truly encyclopaedic grasp of his subject, particularly with regard to the nineteenth century Hoffman illustrations. At the same time, he also tried to interest the publisher in an edition of Cervantes' *Don Quixote*.

To celebrate the sixtieth birthday of Gerhart Hauptmann, on

15th November 1922, the S. Fischer publishing-house was preparing a special anniversary edition. It never appeared, but Busoni's congratulatory address was found among his papers, and published ten years later in the *Neue Rundschau*: 'One of the many things for which Gerhart Hauptmann can take credit, is the fact that he has turned the German artists of his generation away from Wagner, and straightened up the literary standards of his day. As a musician, I feel that the final act of *Michael Kramer* is directly linked with the late Beethoven: it sticks in my memory, as the most genuine piece of contemporary German literature. I am deeply grateful to Hoffman for this, and consider it an honour, to be able to offer him today, not only my thanks but also my warmest congratulations.'

A few weeks before his death, Busoni dictated another article, *On the Nature of Music*, which was published in *Melos* in 1924. He returns to the idea, already suggested in the *Outline for a New Musical Aesthetics*, that all music, like electricity, has been present within the cosmos from the very beginning; and every composer has the possibility of 'observing, handling, and exhibiting only a fraction of the earth's total flora, a tiny fragment of the wealth of flowers that cover our planet.' In this aesthetic concept of the world, the creative artist becomes a discoverer, a person, who from among the countless possibilities available to him, selects according to a sympathetic process, those with which he has the closest affinity. If one pursues this idea, then the creation of music is a limited process of selection, dependent on taste and talent. With typically sceptical insight, Busoni deplores the fact, that the very process of selection means that musical matter is inevitably diffused. Nevertheless, music still retains enough of its divine origins, for it to appear to be 'the most exalted, noble, and luminous' element in our environment. And so the gifted creators of music are ambassadors from Heaven introducing us to beams of primeval light.

Busoni was not a religious man in the conventional sense. He visited churches for aesthetic rather than religious reasons; and on the question of education, he never mentioned God. But he was a man, who by reason of his spiritual make-up was constantly aware of religious and mythical ideas. His religion was an intellectual one, concerned with goodness and peace. He knew about the secrets of the supernatural; both his music and his writing testify most convincingly to the beneficent and daemonic powers that, he believed, operate beneath the surface of everyday life.

The Letters

'I am writing all this down quite deliberately. Separated by time and distance, it is all too easy to have the false impression, that a gulf exists between our very thoughts. I wanted to prove to you, that this is not so.' That is what Busoni wrote to Gerda from London on 20th November 1901. Twenty years later, on 3rd February 1921, he was writing also from London to his friend, Gisella Selden-Goth : 'I don't write this specifically for you (by which I don't mean any disrespect); it is just that I write it down to make sure of it, to get it off my chest, to clarify my own ideas. In this haze of uncertainty, it is a necessary exercise.' Busoni was a tireless and enthusiastic letter writer, even though he occasionally suffered from the sheer weight of correspondence that he kept up with countless people all over the world. Thousands of his letters have been preserved; most of them are privately owned and still unpublished, scattered throughout the world. But a large selection of them have been brought to light in various collections and individual publications. The largest and most illuminating of these collections appeared in 1935, edited and selected by Dr. Friedrich Schnapp. Out of the more than eight hundred letters, that comprise Busoni's entire correspondence with Gerda, this selection covers the period, 1895–1923. Two years later, Gisella Selden-Goth published twenty-five letters written to her between 1909 and 1922. In 1939, a slightly larger collection of letters appeared, addressed to Busoni's Swiss friend, the composer and Conservatory director, Hans Huber; they date from the period 1907–20. Busoni's letters also appeared in smaller numbers, sometimes only extracts, in newspapers, and books written either about him or his friends. They almost all date from the time of his maturity, after he had settled in Berlin in 1894. The recipients are friends of Busoni's, such as the Anzoletti brothers, Augusto and Emilio; the Swiss conductor and composer, Volkmar Andreae; the violinist, Felice Boghen; the critics, Rudolf Kastner and Marcel Remy; the great conductor and composer, Gustav Mahler; the violinist, Arrigo

Serato; the composer, Othmar Schoeck; the writer, Jakob Wassermann; and the versatile Richard Wintzer, who had appealed to Busoni in his various capacities, as writer, composer and painter.

Only very few letters dating from Busoni's youth have been published, virtually none from his childhood. A note, dated 1st December 1883 and addressed to 'the worshipful Philharmonic Concerts committee' in Vienna, is written in a stiff, formal style, obviously in no way typical of the seventeen-year-old writer. Much more characteristic is the love-letter that Busoni wrote from Weimar in July 1889 to the girl who was then his fiancée, Gerda Sjöstrand. In his own extraordinary way, he combines the passionate outpourings of a twenty-three year old with almost pedagogic turns of phrase, in which he reveals his unquestioning faith in art and intellect. A vision of Gerda, comparable with Raphael's images of the saints, is evoked by one of her letters, to which he is replying; and when, in conclusion, he praises the expression of her face, he adds, that it will become increasingly beautiful with maturity and further intellectual development.

Busoni's lengthy accounts of his first experiences in Finland, which he wrote between 1888 and 1890 to his friends Henri and Kathi Petri in Leipzig, are quite different in style. They are filled with shrewd observation, fantasy, biased judgements, rebellious attitudes, and descriptions of nature. It has often been said, that as a Latin and a confirmed townsman Busoni had no feeling for landscape. Certainly, as an artist, the man-made element always appealed to him more than nature in the raw. But he often looked at nature with the eye of a painter, and then his descriptions were very beautiful and highly perceptive. One example of this is his description of sailing into Reval in 1888, during the voyage from Lübeck to Helsinki : 'By the light of the setting sun, we saw the town, built on a hill, rise up from the water on our right . . . on our left, a green tree-clad coastline, with villas and little castles hidden among the shady foliage, climbing gently upward . . . But behind the spires of the town, the sun was sinking like a huge dark-red ball, and eventually it disappeared,

159

casting this unimaginable twilight spell over the entire scene . . .'
In his letters to Gerda, too, one frequently comes across these
kind of painterly renderings of the landscape through which he
has been travelling. On 4th March 1906, Busoni writes a
rapturous description of his impressions on revisiting his childhood home, Trieste : 'The sea is smooth, not a line to break the
surface, like the pale blue, tightly stretched fabric of an atlas,
a strong dark blue just at the extreme edge, where the contour
changes. On the right, the reddish-grey Karstberge, dotted all
over with little white shapes like dice approaching the cliff, their
outlines less distinct towards Miramar. Everything white stands
out, as if the edges had been sharpened. Sailing-boats and little
steamers with red, blue and black funnels, provide the only
mobile element in this unchanging scene.' Then in July of the
same year, he writes from Trent : '. . . reminded me of Bologna :
austere, sombre, calm, grey walls and tiled roofs; but the landscape is much grander here, really heroic in scale. And then there
are the cloud formations, which you only find in these mountain
regions, frequently stormy, but with unexpected patches of sun-
light illuminating certain parts while others never emerge from
the cold shadows; nostalgic views suddenly revealed at the end
of a valley.'

Clearly, it was the landscape of Northern Italy in particular,
that inspired descriptions of this kind, frequently combined with
comments on the towns as well, their colourful life, their endear-
ing but critically observed women. Sometimes he drops the
ironic, intellectual approach, and exclaims spontaneously : 'But
the country is divine . . .' He is equally enthusiastic about the
Southern states of America. In the spring of 1910, he writes :
'It is impossible to describe the ever-changing delights and
surprises. I have long become indifferent to changes of scenery,
but here it has made quite an impression on me again, and my
blood begins to tingle at the very idea of being at the Gulf of
Mexico . . . the soft, warm air, the steamy evenings, the eternal
summer, the curious little houses consisting of little more than
open verandas, the numerous black household servants, that

anyone can have, but which nonetheless still smacks of slavery. The women are beautiful and, I think, the centre of interest— apart from business . . .' And so it goes on, from New Orleans and Atalanta.

The sight of the industrial landscapes of England and America offends Busoni aesthetically, as well as rousing his sense of social injustice and his hatred of war. During the second year of the War, 1915, he writes from Chicago : '. . . the cult of machinery is just as stultifying, just as destructive and disastrous as war. The big employers are prepared to sacrifice for their own ends hundreds of thousands of human lives, in exactly the same way as the warmongers. If you really look into the heart of the English industrial area, you will find it looks every bit as hellish as a battle-field. There is nothing to choose between the lot of the workers and that of the soldiers. As for the artificial parks and recreation grounds, laid out by the well-to-do, they merely look pathetic and arouse feelings of hopeless melancholy.'

Naturally, descriptions of this kind appear less frequently in letters to other musicians and intellectuals than in those written to Gerda. Yet even in these, sentences are constantly cropping up which show that Busoni was vividly aware of the major changes continually affecting the countryside. In 1916, he writes, in a Christmas letter to Hans Huber : 'Let us be grateful, that you are still so very young; when your winter approaches, a new seed will be ripening beneath the snow. For me, the autumn was always the best time of the year, only I wanted peace as well.' He admits to the same correspondent on another occasion, 2nd April 1917, that he is attracted by the South, but it makes him feel melancholy and depressed, in Northern Italy more so than in France.

After music, the most frequent subject of discussion in Busoni's letters is literature. This corresponds with his own inclinations, but it also reflects the enormous amount of reading he did, to relieve what were often long days of travelling. From the numerous names mentioned in his correspondence, particularly in the letters to Gerda, a personal hierarchy emerges. First, by a wide margin, comes Liszt, followed by Beethoven, with Richard Wagner close on his heels. Then come Bach and Mozart, with Chopin and Brahms in sixth and seventh place. Among Busoni's own contemporaries, Debussy, Schoenberg, Stravinsky and Skriabin all follow some distance behind. In the realm of literature, Edgar Allan Poe and Goethe are the writers most frequently mentioned, and they come between Brahms and Mahler, followed by Bernard Shaw and Gabriele d'Annunzio, both of whom were close personal friends of Busoni. Villiers de l'Isle-Adam, Victor Hugo, Shakespeare and E. T. A. Hoffmann follow behind.

Leonardo da Vinci interested Busoni mainly from the biographical point of view, as a phenomenal example of an outstandingly creative personality, and more specifically, as the possible hero of an opera, which he also discussed with d'Annunzio. Rembrandt, on the other hand, fascinated him mainly through his actual work. Busoni was very impressed by the collections in Kassel and Amsterdam, and even more so by a Rembrandt Exhibition held in London in 1899. Among contemporary painters he was interested in the Futurists, and visited an exhibition of their work in London. On 18th March 1912, he writes about it to Gerda : 'I went to see the Futurists, and was very struck by one or two of the things there . . . this man, Boccioni, seems to me to be the best; he has one really great picture : *The growing town*. The other outstanding paintings are : *Leaving the theatre* by Carrà, and finally *The dance at Monico* by Severini, who seems to be a very uneven painter. I had to tell you something about it, while the impression was still fresh in my mind. (Unfortunately, I can already see even these people becoming "old-fashioned".) In any case, I found it refreshing and enjoyable.'

Busoni also takes an interest in painting with an eye to the title pages of his own compositions. For his Piano Concerto, he himself had done a sketch, which was then carried out by Heinrich Vogeler-Worpswede. In 1913 he writes to Gerda : 'For the *Nocturne symphonique* I wanted a really beautiful edition, with an etching and so on. But it does not seem to be possible. When I look round for etchers, I have to admit that Klinger is still the undisputed master . . . One can only know for certain what one thinks of a painter, when it comes to deciding on a purchase or a commission. Even though I very much admire Boccioni, I would not want to commission a title page from him . . .'

Occasionally, Busoni is haunted by dreams. He describes one in a letter to Gerda, written from Chicago on 12th March 1904 : 'I was in an old town . . . and had to climb down from the top of a Gothic tower, by means of an outside spiral staircase. I climbed through a window into the inside, and found myself in a chapel where a service was being held (in the "Catholic tradition", I think). Then, at a sign from the priest, three men, three demons, virtually flew in with a piano—and it was *le piano du Diable*. (I know that I imagined it all in French.) Then I had to play, as an accompaniment to the service, the most godless pieces that I could remember. I know that among other things I played the Kaspar song from *Der Freischütz* and Berlioz's Mephistopheles-Serenade. When there were difficult passages, the thing played of its own accord! Then, quick as lightning, it was borne away again—I was still calling : Stop! I must play something religious—but too late. I can only blame the Mephistopheles Waltz, which I am working on now and gradually perfecting.'

Accounts of his own concerts, the problems with pianos and rehearsals, the reactions of the public and the press, crop up constantly in the letters. One is always aware of the mixed feelings that Busoni experienced throughout his life, pleasure in his success combined with an aversion to the whole business of concerts, which were the source of his success. His distaste for it increased as he grew older. Incidentally, these accounts of concerts appear even in the early letters written to the Petris in the 'eighties, obviously in those written to Gerda too, and occasionally in the correspondence with Hans Huber.

We already know how Busoni scorned money. He always retained the sceptical attitude towards ownership, that dated from his Socialist days in Leipzig. After reading a story about a jewel robbery, he wrote to Gerda from Heidelberg on 8th April 1914 : 'It suddenly occurred to me as never before, that "ownership" is an empty, meaningless concept. The famous stones, that have names and histories, are inherited, given as presents, stolen, worn, kept in a cupboard—but at best they own one, because of the responsibility and risk they involve; however, generations die and the stones remain indestructible, are never lost, and as it were "visit" people from time to time. The same applies to estates and castles, because men . . . have to abandon them; land and castle continue to exist . . . The "owner" only has the negative right to destroy, and then only if no one else is concerned . . .'

Busoni's ironic sense of humour is also apparent in his descriptions of people, particularly in the letters to Gerda. When he went North, the young Italian took with him many of the prejudices of his nation, but also the ideas of any modern enlightened individual, who does not just accept the company he finds himself in without criticism. In one of the first letters, written in 1888 to the Petris in Leipzig, we find the following description of a colleague at the Conservatory in Helsinki : '. . . a mutton-head, and a business-man into the bargain; he gives lesson after lesson, just so as to be able to have a good time with the money he has earned.' Then he goes on : 'The female relationships here put one in mind of Gomorrah, they all lead the freest possible lives, but—look at hereditary disease in the ghosts of Ibsen !' This prejudiced view is immediately followed by the critical observation : 'The Jews here are limited by the regulations to a very small, prescribed number; are only allowed to live in their own quarter; and as soon as a family exceeds the given number through the birth of a child, they are expelled across the frontier. What a sad, mediaeval attitude !'

Busoni himself had described letter-writing to Gerda, as a dialogue between two minds similarly attuned communicating across a distance in time and space, a proof that it is possible to remain close to one another in spirit. Busoni's other motive

164

for letter-writing, the monologue, 'to get it off my chest', is always closely associated with the former. But these are conversational exchanges, which are only valid between relatives and friends. They generally lack any specific purpose. In letters of this kind, there may be disputes concerning points of view and questions of aesthetics; but at most, the recipient has to be convinced, not provoked into any kind of activity.

The other type of correspondence, teleologic, postulating, pleading, even fighting for a cause, is much less typical of Busoni, just as the functional is of less importance than the aesthetic in his entire intellectual make-up. But when he does have a specific objective in mind, then he writes with characteristic energy and determination. The earliest evidence of this appears in the letters written by the eighteen to nineteen-year-old boy to the Vienna Philharmonic. These are documents of artistic propaganda, personal descriptions dictated by adolescent pride. Busoni would like to appear as a soloist with the Philharmonic, because he knows how much this would mean to his career as a pianist. He offers his services, but in a letter dated 4th August 1884 he does not hesitate to say what he himself would prefer : '. . . I take the liberty of admitting, that I should prefer to play one of my own compositions; and with this in mind, I propose to submit to you at the beginning of September a *Konzertstück* for piano with orchestral accompaniment, for a run-through.' He gives, as a reference, the name of the artistic director of the Vienna Philharmonic Concerts, Hans Richter, who as 'hofkapellmeister' and well-known conductor of Wagner, had considerable influence. The reply from the Vienna Philharmonic was in the affirmative. Busoni brought his piece to Vienna on 7th September. When on 17th October there was still no reaction, the mortified composer asked them to return his piece, but left an orchestral suite with the orchestra. Hans Richter played it through with the Philharmonic; they took a vote on it, and by a majority of one the piece was rejected.

However, this in no way altered Busoni's determination to succeed. In February 1885, he made an appearance at the

165

Gewandhaus in Leipzig, on the recommendation of Johannes Brahms, and had an enthusiastic reception. From Frohnleiten in Styria, where he had already spent previous summers, he wrote to the Philharmonic yet again on 28th July. Once more he offered himself as a soloist, and referred to his recent success in Leipzig. He expressed the hope that they would not refuse him this honour, and promised them 'an artistically accomplished performance'. No answer. On 16th September, he repeated his request, and for the second time added that he would like to play his own concert-piece, in fact if possible, take part in the trial run-through. When there was no reaction to this either, he seems to have given up trying.

Even in his correspondence with friends, Busoni does not forget his own ambitions. In a long letter to Henri Petri in Leipzig, filled with descriptions of his experiences in Helsinki and of his fiancée, Gerda, he mentions a post in Breslau where Petri wished to intercede on his behalf : 'A post of this kind is the only "tie" that I would accept with real pleasure, and I could not be more grateful to you for your kindness in this matter. Therefore, would you please ensure for me an opportunity of appearing there on a trial basis. I must also take this opportunity of telling you, that my Orchestral Suite was performed here, myself conducting, and the general opinion was, that this was the best performance this orchestra has given; even the musicians themselves maintained that they had felt more assured and more lively under my direction. This is just to prove to you my aptitude for conducting; of course, I still need practice and experience.'

In an unpublished letter, written on 20th March 1897 to Liszt's pupil, Hans von Bronsart, who was then manager of the Weimar Hoftheater and had invited Busoni to a music festival, Busoni states what he would like to do. He does not want to play his *Konzertstück*, but instead his new arrangement of Liszt's Organ Fantasia after Meyerbeer's *The Prophet*. When one considers how insistently he offered his *Konzertstück* in Vienna in 1884 and 1885, it is not difficult to see how his taste has changed and to what extent he himself has developed artistically. The year

1894 was particularly decisive in this respect. As a composer, Busoni had branched out in new directions. In his letter to Bronsart, he goes on to say : 'Besides which, I wanted to suggest to you and the leader of the orchestra, Herr Petri, the possibility of his playing a violin concerto of my own composition at the music festival. By allowing this, my dear sir, you would for the first time be giving full credit to my individuality, whether as a pianist and performer, or as a musician and composer; such a concession on the part of the administration would mean a great deal to me on such an important and solemn occasion, and I should accordingly be particularly indebted to you.'

Here we find the same stilted and affected style, that we noticed in the letters written to the Vienna Philharmonic, and which is totally absent from Busoni's correspondence with his family or friends. The violin concerto, that he was offering them, was written between 1896–97 and at that time had not yet been performed; it was first published in 1899.

Busoni was always an enthusiastic teacher; the contact with pupils made him feel younger, and stimulated all kinds of ideas. One of the great disappointments of his teaching career was the master-class, which he had taken over at the Vienna Conservatory in 1907, at the invitation of the Society of the Friends of Music. In September, in a classroom overlooking the Karlskirche, he had got the students to audition for him. His immediate impression was obviously not encouraging. Shortly afterwards, he writes to Gerda from Bath, in the course of an English concert tour : 'More students will enrol, but will they be good . . . ?'

Work with the class began in October. Busoni was disappointed : 'The standard,' he tells Gerda, 'is about as high ("high" is a good word!) as that of my former class in Moscow. There is hardly one among them, with whom I could hold a conversation about a picture, a book, or a human problem.'

During the term, Busoni continued with his concert tours; there was no teaching from the middle of January until April 1908. This led, in February, to the dispute already described with the Society of the Friends of Music. Busoni was dismissed.

He considered himself innocent, even though he had acted in a high-handed fashion. In the struggle for his alleged rights, he sought publicity through the Viennese press. When accused of having repeatedly taught every day for a fortnight and then taken a fortnight off, instead of teaching the statutory twice a week, he replied that the teaching schedule could hardly have been organized any other way, even if he had been in Vienna all the time. Moreover, in his letters to the editorial staff, he was able to plead the fact, that the students were on his side, and that he was going to continue teaching them privately : 'I should like to feel that no one is missing, so as to be sure of fulfilling my duty to them all equally.' Busoni's self-defence is dictated by an arrogance which was justified by his phenomenal success at that time. Occasionally, this arrogance is exaggerated and verges on inordinate artistic pride. With regard to the Society of the Friends of Music, Busoni quotes the words spoken by the painter, James MacNeill Whistler, on being obliged to leave the British Artists' Association : 'The Artist has gone, the British remain !' Besides which, Busoni considered the incident 'as a challenging experience', which an artist ought never to underrate.

One can well imagine, that this handsome, elegant man of the world, familiar with many languages and cultures, seemed as arrogant to the average man of his time, as he was fascinating to his pupils and friends. In the years preceding the First World War, his personal and intellectual attitudes had a great deal in common with the aristocratic intellectualism of *Arlecchino*. The hostility felt towards these attitudes is apparent in every line of Hans Pfitzner's anti-Busoni pamphlet, *The Dangers of Futurism*.

Yet among his equals, Busoni showed a rare capacity for admiration and appreciation. Since he considered artistic talent and ability to be something exceptional, he had enormous regard for great musicians, poets and painters. Sometimes, in the course of a long friendship, he would have the opportunity to see an intellect, a personality, develop, as in the case of Gustav Mahler. He had known the great conductor and composer ever since he

168

was a young man in Leipzig, and in 1903 he told Mahler, that he would like his Fifth Symphony for the Berlin Orchestral Concerts. When Mahler replied, that he was prepared to conduct without any fee, not however the Fifth but the Third Symphony with Choir and alto solo, Busoni remarked jokingly to Gerda, that he had no alto, tenor or bass hippopotami at his disposal, nor chromatic snakes, nor pedal-birds of Paradise. In 1910, Mahler conducted the Turandot Suite in Boston. Busoni was delighted, and wrote to Gerda: 'What a shame that you did not hear Mahler's *Turandot* . . . what love and intuitive perception the man put into the rehearsals! Satisfying and gratifying both from the artistic and human point of view. The performance was perfect, better than ever before, its success enormous.' Before leaving America, he wrote to Mahler himself: '. . . I must tell you, how much love and respect I have for you, both as a person and as a musician; I feel that these weeks in America have brought us closer to one another (thanks to all we have gone through together!) than all the twenty years of our friendship . . . Please take these naïve remarks in the simple, affectionate way they are intended. Being with you has a sort of purifying effect, one has only to come near you to feel young again. That is why my language has become almost childlike.'

The world reflected in Busoni's letters is predominantly that of art and music. There is hardly any sphere of artistic creativity or reproduction that is not considered in these dialogues and monologues. Hardly a single creative person among the composers, writers and visual artists of his day, who is not mentioned. Whereas his interest in scientific matters and technical discoveries is relatively small. Busoni was by no means in favour of the technical comforts, which had made such a difference to human existence during his lifetime. He detested the telephone, and according to Gerda, only made three or four long-distance calls in his whole life. At the most, he accepted the motor-car as a comfortable means of transport, and also enjoyed travelling in comfortable trains. As for the first experimental flights, which took place during his life, he regarded them with admiration but without much interest. In 1909, in a letter to Gerda, he mentions Louis Blériot's flight across the Channel: 'I now know a good half-dozen names of *grandi ucelli* such as he, and my hope is, that modern youth will be distracted from piano playing by this new career (flying) . . . to return to the bird in question, it seems to me, that this flight across the Channel is a fine and important achievement—but no better than Wright's; just more impressive.'

Busoni's correspondence with Gisella Selden-Goth is distinguished from time to time by a particular tone that he adopts. He begins as a teacher with practical advice and examples, often as if his letter were a kind of detailed correspondence course in composition. Later, the letters more and more often take the form of a discussion of the artistic problems of the 'twenties, either as a dialogue, or sometimes even as a monologue. He begins by subjecting modern composers to critical analyses and comparisons, holding up for their inspection an operetta such as Franz von Suppé's *Fatinitza*. He knows that his young friend is much more at home than he in the revolutionary, intellectual world of Expressionism, and he wants to warn her and try to change her opinions. 'Look here, this man Suppé had talent. Among all the pieces included in *Der Anbruch* (Viennese avant-garde musical publication, author's own note), there was not one that revealed a talent anywhere approaching his . . . I must make an exception of a small fragment by Schreker. This gives the impression of being sincere, and of the composer being emotionally involved on a naïve level in his idea.' This letter was written in 1920. Busoni goes on to dispute the use of the word 'expressionism' as applied to music, which, he maintains, is *eo ipso* expressionist. Later, Busoni also turned against the word, 'atonality', which presupposes tonality in the same way that pacifism presupposes the existence of war.

Busoni repeatedly tries to dissuade his friend from various journalistic projects; he criticizes an article that she has written about him, whereupon it remains unpublished. Throughout the correspondence one is constantly aware of the determination to teach, the desire to shape another mind according to his own ideas. At the same time, there are ironical digs at many contemporary phenomena, which were causing a stir in Berlin at the time and did not necessarily meet with his approval: 'The Barber of Baghdad, Sarabande and Cortège, Servian Twins, Krschennek's Nonen und Chromosse, Petrifaxtaxen : 'don't allow yourself to be confused by all this variety!'

In 1922 in Paris, Busoni saw Robert Wiene's film, The Cabinet of Dr. Caligari, which fascinated Maurice Ravel so much at the time. Busoni was more sceptical : 'There is a splendid idea there and much that is successful. I learnt for the first time to appreciate an "expressionist" background and admired the character created by the actor, Krauss. The last third is an embarrassment. Besides which, I find too much in the subject antipathetic. Hoffmann would have made Caligari a demon or a god destined to a temporary life on earth, with a task to fulfil. To try and by-pass that sort of invention with dreams or madness is sheer literary faint-heartedness . . . Like a brilliant criminal offering his judges the excuse that he was drunk. All in all, however, the most interesting thing of its kind that I have seen.'

Psychological problems concerned Busoni very little, even in an academic context, where his teaching was involved. There is not so much as the faintest echo in his correspondence of the great discoveries made in the realm of modern psychology. The names of Freud and Jung do not appear in his letters, any more than in his famous library with its five thousand volumes. There is no evidence to suggest that he met Sigmund Freud in Vienna or C. G. Jung in Zürich. He clearly had the same aversion to psychopathic symptoms, and their being discussed in conversation or letters, as he had to dealing with erotic questions, which he excluded even from his views on opera.

Educational problems, on the other hand, had interested him ever since he was a child. Even as a boy of thirteen, Busoni wished to have the most comprehensive intellectual training possible, and he later transferred this ambition to other young people among his friends and acquaintances. When he himself was only twenty-two years old, he wrote from Helsinki on 14th October 1888 to the Petris in Leipzig, about their son, Egon, later Busoni's favourite pupil but at that time only seven years old: 'I like his liveliness, and am pleased to see it, even when it verges on naughtiness. Let us hope, that later in life, particularly during the dangerous period of adolescence, he will still have this healthy nature, which nowadays tends to disappear with childhood although there is no reason why it should not combine with a serious attitude to one's career. It is obviously both premature and superfluous (you know these things better than I do), to advise you to open the boy's eyes to the facts of life at the appropriate time later on. Reticence and modesty on the part of fathers, or strict supervision without any explanation or even justification, are harmful to budding masculinity; because nothing natural can be forcibly repressed, and anything that has to find an outlet, will simply do so in another artificial and more dangerous way. Forgive this moralizing outburst, which naturally has less bearing on you and Egon, than on myself and my own past . . .' It is easy to see from his recommendation of sexual enlightenment at the right time, and the reference to himself, what Busoni's parents failed to do for him.

Once again, on 3rd April 1890, he writes to Egon's father about the boy's education: 'One thing I can say, from my own experiences as an infant prodigy, is, that it was a great help having it impressed upon me from the beginning, that I could and should become a great man; however, no one ever appeared satisfied with my actual achievements. Young men, who were just making their name and appeared in the newspapers, were cited as successes; I know that these kinds of reports were always like a punch in the stomach to me. The idea was to rouse my already strongly developed sense of ambition. Nevertheless, the apparent dissatisfaction, the shaking of heads and the admonishing must not be overdone, or it can easily lead to discouragement or defiance. Even later, as a student, I was spurred on more by the desire to outshine my fellow students than by the subject itself. It was only with the beginning of manhood and the development of an independent personality, that I began to take things really

172

seriously. Until a few years ago, I hated playing the piano and tended to neglect it. When I was younger, I was more interested in reading than in music.'

Once Busoni himself had become the father of two sons, these educational problems became a matter of intimate concern. 'Benni', his firstborn, or 'chief heir' as he once called him, caused him most anxiety in this respect. For Christmas, 1900, he advised Gerda to buy the eight-year-old boy the *Märchenbuch des Jung-brunnen* : 'Training the taste and the eye, is every bit as important as cultivating the mind, as important as all dead knowledge is unimportant. This is the conclusion I have finally reached.' Nine years later, in Rome, he is worrying about the reading matter of his son, who by this time is sixteen. On 6th March 1909, he writes to Gerda : 'Lenau is not suitable for him to read; it is so much poison, like Schopenhauer and other engaging pessimists. He should only read things that stimulate, not discourage him. He should read more Shakespeare, which will develop his sense of form and his imagination, from a purely literary point of view. In fact, anything that is not pessimistic or erotic, and above all anything which (in addition to this) is artistically good.' Then he enumerates the things he thinks suitable, guided first and foremost by his own taste in literature : '*Don Quixote*, Goethe's poems, Kleist, Gottfried Keller, *The 1001 Nights* (admittedly erotic, but in such a way, that this is of secondary importance compared with its magical quality), the Life of Benvenuto, Dickens and Edgar Poe, the early Ibsen, the German Romantics; but not these gloomy melancholiacs and promoters of suicide, no Lenau, Schopenhauer, Werther, Leopardi—"the suicide club" of literature.'

Naturally, Strindberg does not appear in this list, even though Busoni had a high opinion of him and mentions him on several occasions in his correspondence. He clearly does not entirely share the enthusiasm, with which Arnold Schoenberg and Alban Berg greeted every new work by Strindberg and discussed it in their letters. The dark, psychopathic side of Strindberg appealed more to the Vienna School of composers than to the Latin mentality of the *Faust* composer, in the same way that they were more sympathetic to the ideas of Freudian psycho-analysis.

During an American tour, Busoni writes to Gerda on 14th April 1910, complaining: 'This Strindberg is a fearful man! I have read the "chamber plays" . . . and I must admit, that they kept me in suspense. But if the wisdom of old age only serves to make one bitter and angry, seeing nothing but bacteria in every drop of water, so that all enjoyment in the source of life is destroyed—then let us either remain simple or die young.' Eight years later, in the last year of the war, he writes to Hans Huber: 'My feelings about Strindberg have already been through three different stages: first he repelled me, then I became enormously enthusiastic about him, and now I am beginning to be more painfully aware of his weaknesses. But with his "fantasy" and his "chamber plays" alone, he has, after Schiller and Ibsen, succeeded in giving the theatre a new image once again, which is more than I could say of anyone else. I personally do not like the way he pries into and dwells upon *les petites misères* of everyday life, nor do I approve a certain artistic carelessness where form and expression are concerned . . . As with Voltaire and Heine, I recognize in him this great longing for love, goodness and beauty, and the intense exasperation of constantly failing to find these qualities in people.'

The crowning point in Busoni's revolutionary ideas about ownership is his scorn for money. It was scarcely permissible to speak about financial worries and problems in his presence; and they are very seldom mentioned in his letters. At the same time, it went without saying, that he should receive the remuneration usual for a virtuoso of his international standing. But there was never any need for vulgar discussions.

On one occasion only, there was a difference of opinion on this very point with one of his friends. During the First World War, Busoni was living as a voluntary exile in Zürich. His opportunities for travelling, and consequently his earnings, were drastically cut, since he avoided the countries at war, both on principle and from a feeling of bitterness. He had been connected with the Conservatory in Basle, on an artistic and personal level, ever since his master-class there in 1910. His friend, the composer Hans Huber, had been director there since 1896. At his invitation, Busoni had given the four famous concerts at the Basle Conservatory in January and February 1916, each devoted to a particular composer : Bach, Beethoven, Chopin and Liszt. At the beginning of 1917, Huber wrote to him about the possibility of a second cycle being held in the Neuer Konzertsaal in Basle. Busoni asked for an inclusive fee of 6,000 francs for the four concerts. On 16th September 1916, he replied to a letter from his friend, of which we have no knowledge, but which must have contained counter-proposals on the question of money.

It was a dismal period for Busoni; Italy had just come into the war, with the result that his two native countries were fighting one another. 'I have done no work for the last three days, and as you see, it does not agree with me at all. This brilliant action on the part of my fatherland has completely isolated me, and affected me economically as well. (This by the way, but serious nonetheless.) Therefore I am dependent on my ten fingers, to keep myself. If the Basle Conservatory embarks on a venture, which would appear to give them a certain amount of pleasure . . . they ought to be prepared to raise the money for it, and tell themselves, that they will provide the remainder of the proposed fee out of their own funds. Because these sort of evenings cost me more in time and money than a normal engagement, for which I am paid the same fee.' He defends his standpoint yet again on 25th September, saying that the Basle cycle sets him a 'worthless task' and takes a great deal of time. 'Which is why I am being so adamant about the fee, although to be strictly logical there is no association between spending a piece of one's life and receiving a thousand franc note. Will your treasurer understand that? Not a hope. Perhaps there is more chance among the wealthy people, who have been appointed Friends of Music.' Two letters written to Gerda from London in 1919 reflect his basic attitude : '. . . a very sympathetic trait, to want to have money in order to spend it. The guilt lies with those who make money for its own sake, who make money out of money. Also those who use money as a standard, by which to judge people's worth.'

A couple of days earlier in November, Busoni states his feelings even more precisely, and with pathological associations unusual in his writing, descriptions of haemorrhage, paralysis, nausea and pain : '. . . as soon as I want to do something for a purpose, from the moment there is a practical advantage in doing it, something inside me begins to bleed, a sort of paralysis overcomes me . . . I experience the same sort of feeling, when I see other people involved in art (and even those outside it) thinking and acting along purely utilitarian lines : a sort of nausea creeps over me . . . We only need money, because other people demand it of us as evidence of what we are really worth, which they themselves are unable to recognize.' This is almost a clinical self-diagnosis, one of the rare cases when Busoni observes pathological symptoms in himself.

Real illnesses are subject to an even stricter taboo. Busoni's friend, the poet, Jakob Wassermann, says in his obituary : 'He never once complained about his health; nor did he ever admit to a disappointment or frustration . . . The only time, there is so much as a hint of resignation and melancholy, is in his last letter to me, even though he is struggling to accept the illness which is already destroying him.' Then Wassermann quotes from this letter, which carries the date, 1st May, but with no indication of the year. It must have been 1924, the year of Busoni's death. 'I have not consulted a doctor for the last thirty years. My abilities have steadily increased . . . only bad art could throw me off balance, only a sterile period was capable of upsetting and depressing me . . . Even during the war, my state of mind remained unchanged. But at the end of the war I became aware of the devastation, and I was no longer strong enough to face up to this new situation, nor young enough to endure it. It suddenly became apparent, without any transitional phase, and was like a black line through my life, for which I was not personally responsible as I had usually been in the past. That is more or less the history of my illness . . .'

Wassermann has even described the external appearance of these letters, with all the perception of a poet and the affection of a friend. Everything written by Busoni was a little work of art from the graphic point of view, his writing exquisite. 'Each letter is added consciously,' Wassermann writes, 'almost as if it were painted.'

Large portions of the correspondence that Busoni left behind still remain undiscovered, and are not available for publication. His correspondence with Wassermann undoubtedly constitutes a large proportion of this. But Egon Petri, Philipp Jarnach and Eduard Steuermann also have in their possession letters from the master, which will have to be examined, when the sum total of his life and influence is eventually assessed. The published portions of Busoni's world-wide correspondence provide ample evidence of a great man, and a clear picture of the epoch that derived so much forward-looking stimulation from his work.

The Teacher

'The fact, that both as an artist and as a human being I prefer looking forward rather than backward, explains why I like having young people around me. So may it continue until the end—because if that ceases to be the case, it is very sad . . .' This passage from a letter written to Gerda in 1904 provides the clue, as to why Busoni, who frequently grudged every moment of his time and strength not devoted to work, and who considered giving concerts an insufferable waste of energy, was prepared to exhaust himself teaching. Human contacts were essential to him, he needed the exchange of ideas, and found in the company of young people eager to learn some source of energy. Transmitting knowledge, passing on his artistic discernment and experience was so essential to him, that the concept of the pedagogic Eros appears to have been coined with him in mind.

Between 1888 and 1924, generations of rising pianists and composers passed through his hands, people of various nationalities and different mentalities, both men and women. Nobody knows, exactly how many of Busoni's pupils there are; about thirty have become well-known as pianists, about ten as composers. Yet his spirit has outlived even them; pupils of his pupils continue to carry the flame that he kindled in the distant past. However different these frequently extremely individualistic members of Busoni's school may be, they almost all have one thing in common : they are musicians of a very high intellectual standard, often conspicuously creative themselves, many of them scholars and writers whose accounts and reminiscences have considerable literary value.

The earliest of these pieces written by students goes back to the 'eighties, and gives us a picture of the young Busoni, teaching the piano in Helsinki. The author is Adolf Paul, who became his pupil at the age of twenty-five, and was three years older than the Italian professor with whom he soon became friendly. Busoni's teaching-method was based on an authority, consolidated by a staggering knowledge of literature. It is characteristic of

Busoni, that even at that time he used visual ideas to explain to his pupils the feeling of a piece of music. Paul reports, that he was given the short C minor Fugue from *The Well-Tempered Clavier* (obviously from the first volume) to practise. He quotes Busoni from memory : 'I think of the Prelude as a thunderstorm sweeping across the meadow and then subsiding.' This is practical hermeneutics, as used by the successors of Wagner in the interpretation of Bach, and also employed by Albert Schweitzer in his book. But Paul then goes on to report Busoni's commentary on the Fugue : 'Then an elf shyly ventures forth with the subject of the Fugue, and dances round with it. A second one follows with the counter-subject, then a third with the subject, and they dance their way delicately and lightly through the entire Fugue. Until suddenly, with heavy octave passages, a clumsy gnome leaps in; there is a thundering roar, as he tosses the subject at the poor elves, who scurry away terrified. And he just stands there, making a stupid face.'

Poetic interpretations of this kind, in the style of the *Gartenlaube*, were popular towards the end of the nineteenth century. They spring from a heteronomous view-point, which can only conceive of music as the interpretess of non-musical subjects. A Romantic inheritance, that has become quite alien to us. Even Gustav Mahler in 1896 gives his Third Symphony movement titles, such as *What the flowers in the meadow tell me* or *What the angels say*. Busoni is in the thick of this movement, and it is only his Latin sense of irony that destroys the elfin idyll by introducing the clumsy gnome and the thundering roar of the subject. Whether or not Adolf Paul has exaggerated and added elements of his own invention, the broad outlines of his description of Busoni's teaching-method are undoubtedly to be trusted. But it is just as well, to compare this approach to teaching with the more analytical approach of the Bach Edition. This dates from 1894, which is only five years after Busoni wrote the following dedication in his Swedish pupil's copy of Bach, in 1889, at a time when he was busy teaching : '. . . in order that he may become really competent in the prelude, and technically

179

perfect in the fugue.' In the Bach Edition, the only thing it says about the Prelude (apart from purely technical observations), is that it is 'like a restless stream, reflecting the flames of a fire', its concluding section 'bursting through every dam'. Busoni interprets the Fugue as: 'a pleasing, almost dance-like rhythm; a theme, using the simplest of intervals, and therefore very easy to remember; great economy of contrapuntal means.' He insists that the working-out of this theme should be considered as a single large episode. He disassociates himself from the Czerny-type octave doubling in the bass, but lets it pass towards the end, with the entry of the subject.

It is essential therefore to make a distinction between Busoni's practical teaching, which is intended to stimulate his pupils' imagination, and his work as an editor, which admittedly on a higher level also embraces the work of a teacher. It seems that his teaching methods hardly changed during the 'nineties, even though there was such a marked change in his artistic attitudes.

We have very little information about the early years, when Busoni taught in Helsinki, Moscow and Boston. Gerda, his Swedish fiancée and later his wife, was never one of his pupils, as she did not study at the Conservatory in Helsinki. In fact as a teacher, he was remarkably tactless towards her. In her memoirs, she describes how, as a young girl, Busoni pressed her to play for him. She refused to be persuaded, but once when she was playing Bach he came into the room without her noticing and listened. After some considerable time he cleared his throat, whereupon she sprang up, and he took her place at the piano and imitated her 'most cruelly'. Gerda ends her account of the incident by saying: 'I was beside myself with rage, and hammered on the glass door of the adjoining room with my fists; Ferruccio burst out laughing. Since then I have never touched the piano again.' This episode serves to give us some idea of the price paid for the privilege of spending one's life with Busoni.

Among Busoni's earliest pupils were the Americans, Michael von Zadora and Augusta Cottlow. Both of them achieved success while still children; both had their definitive training with Busoni,

Zadora at the age of eleven in New York, Miss Cottlow at the age of eighteen in Berlin. It is to her that we owe one of the earliest and most perceptive descriptions of his teaching, and of his effect on young people. Augusta Cottlow was thirteen years old, when in Boston she heard Busoni play Beethoven's D major Concerto with orchestra, and in a solo performance Chopin's C minor Nocturne and Liszt's E major Polonaise. She later studied this same Polonaise, while she was taking lessons with Busoni between 1896–99. Before she had played so much as one bar of the piece, Busoni rose to his feet, gazed thoughtfully into space and said two words : 'With dignity !' Through his attitude and his words, the young American was able to grasp the spirit of the piece. It gave her the key to Busoni's rhythmic concept— he never approved of quick tempos, unless the music unquestionably demanded it. Furthermore, she claims to have learnt more about musical form from his playing than from all her composition studies. In his playing, there was never any aimless wandering about or standing still, just a clear forward movement towards a specific point, or away from that point. Both in his work and in his teaching, Busoni never conceived of form as something static, that could be thought of as inactive; it was an act of movement at every stage. Augusta Cottlow remembers studying Schumann's eighth Novellette with him. She was completely bewildered by the unconventional form of this piece, which seemed to her to present nothing but thematically and harmonically disconnected elements, and none of the traditional forms with which she was familiar. She asked Busoni, whether he could explain the piece to her. His reply was : 'Form in music can often be compared with form in architecture. Thus three-part form is analogous to the Greek temple. There are other Greek buildings that are not based on a central idea, but have decoration and motifs going right round, often in the form of a frieze in bas-relief depicting historical or mythological scenes, each one quite different, but all united on the same plane. The Schumann Novellette is similar in form.'

According to Miss Cottlow, Busoni did not call himself a

teacher. He refused to work out technical details with his pupils, expecting them to solve their technical problems themselves with the aid of a few basic principles. 'But,' she writes, 'the interpretations and examples he gave of the artistic side of technique were always so enlightening, his requirements, in the way of clarity, harmony, technical freedom and tone quality, so imperative, that there was no doubt as to the path one had to follow. It was also clear, that in this hard uphill climb not a single detail could be overlooked. The goal was nothing less than perfection.' Phrasing, tone-colour and tone quality were always Busoni's main concern. Even in the playing of chords, he demanded a singing, musical, pleasing tone, no matter what was to be expressed. Use of the pedal was an important feature of both his playing and teaching. He regarded rhythm as the heartbeat of a composition, inseparable from its character and message.

Miss Cottlow speaks highly of Busoni's deep respect for anything genuine and honest in human terms, as well as for all genuine feeling. But he ruthlessly rejected anything bordering on sentimentality or cheap sentiment. In this respect, he was a disciple of Bernard Shaw. He was always the first to recognize good work on the part of his colleagues, in the same way that he was always prepared to help young and struggling artists.

Busoni was inclined to measure the abilities of other people according to his own; consequently most of his pupils inevitably fell short of his expectations. 'He drew up an enormous schedule of work for those who studied with him; he never listened to any composition more than twice. Sometimes months would pass between the first and second performance of a piece, and on the second occasion he expected it to be at concert pitch. Lessons with Busoni could never be a regular weekly commitment, because he was frequently involved in concerts; but when there was a lesson, it was an event, and often lasted not only the entire afternoon but throughout the evening as well. Sometimes several lessons would follow in quick succession; then there would be a gap of one or perhaps two months. Naturally, this kind of teaching was only suitable for those who could think and work independently.'

Then Miss Cottlow describes an incident, that reveals a whole world of difference in teaching methods, and also the gap that exists between American and Slav psychology. However strict he may have been in the demands he made on them, Busoni was always very charming with his students. There was a young Russian girl, who studied with him in 1896 and gave it up soon afterwards. Miss Cottlow, who could not understand this, asked her why. 'Well, you see,' the Russian girl replied, 'Busoni is too much of a "gentleman". He is too kind. What I need, is a teacher who raps me across the knuckles, pulls my ear, and shouts at me.' She herself, Augusta Cottlow, was able to develop to her greatest potential, precisely because of his kindness; any other treatment would have completely suppressed her. His attitude was apparently always that of an elder brother.

She also mentions another characteristic episode. With his sharp wit and perpetual high spirits, Busoni always saw above, below, and through everything, frequently discovering comic elements at the same time. Even the Schumann Novelette already mentioned did not escape this kind of treatment. While Augusta Cottlow was playing the second Trio, Busoni suddenly called out : 'Doesn't that sound as if it had been written for a German male choir? One can actually hear the words.' Then, first in a falsetto and then in a rumbling bass voice, he sang in an indescribably comic way : 'How beautiful are the German woods, the German woods, the German woods. The beautiful, beautiful, beautiful, beautiful woods ! The woods !' Then he gave a rendering of the passage, that Schumann designates as a distant voice, singing in a trembling pathetic strain : 'Lonely, I wander . . . through the woods !'

From this it is clear that Busoni still had the same feeling for associated images, that Adolf Paul described for us in his demonstration of Busoni's teaching of Bach in Helsinki. Yet the programmatic, hermeneutic method of 1889 has now been intellectualized, and balanced by humour and sarcasm, at least as far as Romantic content is concerned. So it is possible to understand, although not to forgive, the cruel burst of laughter that stopped Gerda Sjöstrand from touching a piano again for the rest of her life.

In 1900 the eighteen-year-old Leo Kestenberg, whom Busoni had recommended as a pupil to his friend, José Vianna da Motta, was invited to take part in Busoni's master-class in Weimar. We are already familiar with his account of the happy time that the members of the class spent in Weimar that summer. Busoni was then thirty-five, a row of beautiful young women sat open-mouthed at his feet; and in a photograph of the master-class, taken in the garden in front of the Tempelherrenhaus in Weimar, we see the young bespectacled Kestenberg, literally crouching on the ground beside the master he idolized. 'We used to come to the Tempelherrenhaus twice a week for official lessons,' Kestenberg writes in his memoirs, 'sometimes the Grand Duke would be there too, but we were with Busoni almost every day for one reason or another . . . I played the Bach-Busoni Chaconne for him in front of all the students and many guests. After each piece there would be a general discussion; and this was the form of teaching—very different from correcting petty technical details—that best suited Busoni's personality. The work of art would be analysed mainly from the point of view of spiritual content; and each pianist had the feeling, that the observations Busoni made were meant specifically for him.'

Kestenberg has already stated, that Busoni never took a fee from a student for the lessons he gave. Money was never mentioned in these circles, they lived in a more exalted sphere. The actual teaching always took place in the afternoons; but afterwards, they and their master used to go out together.

The following summer, for the last time, there was another master-class in Weimar. Once again, a band of carefully selected young pianists (Kestenberg puts the number at twelve in 1910, but the photograph shows eleven of them, although admittedly

184

some may have been guests) gathered in the Tempelherrenhaus at the feet of Busoni, the handsome young maestro with the Romantic beard. Hermann Wilhelm Draber, originally a flautist, later a music publicist who organized music festivals in Germany and Switzerland, has written about this second Weimar course : 'Those who were lucky enough to be allowed to come, could consider themselves as free scholars, like the apprentices of the great Renaissance painters.' Draber describes the magical attraction that Busoni had for young people : 'a magician who, quite outside the sphere of conventional piano teaching, and without the slightest hint of pedantry, made young people see music as a boundless kingdom of Heaven, remote from the everyday world, his own life testifying to the fact, that first you must be a human being and an artist, then everything else will come right.' Apparently, Busoni never wanted to make ascetics of his students, but independent beings capable of participating in the art of life and austere priests of art, indifferent to the public and the scribes. 'Anyone irresolute he encouraged to go ahead, to those who were already doing so he gave confidence and conviction.' Busoni recognized and fostered anything approaching individuality.

Draber follows this up with a description of Busoni's classes, which serves as a confirmation and extension of the picture provided by Kestenberg : 'We would all meet twice a week in the Tempelherrenhaus. Anyone who had a piece ready prepared was allowed to play. The others sat on the simple chintz-covered sofas placed all round the walls and listened. They learnt as much from this as the performer. Once a student had finished his piece, there was either a general discussion about it first, or else people went outside onto the lawn in front of the house, with its marvellous view of the park, and smoked a cigarette. But everyone was affected with the indescribable sense of excitement that Busoni's comments aroused. It was as if the Holy Ghost had descended upon us. There was not a single person, who was not keenly aware of his future mission in music. Technical matters, incidentally, were seldom discussed. The

185

technical side was to some extent taken for granted. It was almost always the piece as a whole and its organization that came under discussion. Yet as soon as Busoni sat down and played, which happened at least once almost every week, each person realized how much he still had to learn in the way of technique, in order to render the meaning of the piece without any mistakes. Therefore outside teaching hours, technical problems were eagerly discussed by the students; and Busoni, if asked or indeed voluntarily, would express his views at considerable length.'

Draber is also deeply impressed by the fact, that both the conversation and teaching ranged far beyond the sphere of music. He is grateful but amazed at the number of precious hours the great man lavished on his students.

At the same time, Busoni never had any doubts as to the spiritual and intellectual gulf that separated him from the majority of his students. Not infrequently, and particularly in his letters to Gerda, he would sneer at the youngsters, the little ninnies that thronged about him, without even suspecting what it must have meant to any sensitive and sympathetic person just to be with him. This often applied even to the master-classes, although only the élite were admitted, students whom Busoni himself selected from the large number of candidates. His tendency, as described by Draber, to allow a musical discussion to trespass into other territories, is consistent with his basic aesthetics. For Busoni, the concept of art was a comprehensive one. Just as he himself compared musical and architectural forms, involved himself in both musical and literary composition, found stimulus in reading literature of every period and visiting museums and exhibitions, so he transmitted this attitude to the people with whom he associated. The sense of unity, which is characteristic of his attitude to music, has therefore simply to be extended to his artistic and intellectual outlook. In order to be and to remain Busoni's pupil, it was not enough to play the piano exceptionally well or be technically good at composition. One had to become an artist in his sense of the word, or else preferably drop the whole thing altogether.

Unfortunately, what had begun so auspiciously in Weimar in 1900 did not develop into a regular tradition. It was only reluctantly, that Busoni accepted teaching commitments during the summer months which, like Richard Strauss and Gustav Mahler, he wished to devote entirely to composition. When the idea of a master-class at the Vienna Conservatory eventually materialized, Busoni committed himself for the winter season 1907–1908, although admittedly this was extended to 15th July. In addition to this, the number of teaching hours was fixed at 280. Busoni was prudent enough to ensure, that the contract was initially for a trial year. It culminated in the dispute, with which we are already familiar, because Busoni was accused of not having taken his duties as a teacher seriously. He justified himself on the strength of his own particular method of teaching, which according to Augusta Cottlow he had practised as early as 1896, and which consisted on occasions of several lessons packed into a short space of time, followed by a gap of several weeks. He himself described this form of tuition in greater detail in a letter to the *Neue Freie Presse*, where he says : 'At the time, I was responsible for eighteen students, who prepared a considerable amount of work for each lesson. Three or four hours in the afternoon meant that I could only deal with three or four students. So I used to devote a whole week to going through their work for the first time, and during the second week I would hear it again in order to check on the alterations I had suggested; they had to produce a definitive version, to be able to move on to something new. The students needed time for this. Even if I had been in Vienna all the time, it would have been difficult to arrange the teaching schedule any other way.'

The fact that the students, both male and female, endorsed this method of teaching and wholeheartedly supported their teacher, is proved by a statement that they (which is to say, the entire master-class almost without exception) printed in the same newspaper. In this, they protested emphatically against Busoni's dismissal, and what they considered to be the injustice implied.

In their statement they point out : 'It is only fair, that the third party concerned in the Busoni affair should also have a hearing—namely, his students. As soon as they heard of his dismissal, they approached the administration, begging them to keep the master they loved and admired . . . this year, students from far and wide have joined the master-class because they wanted to study with Busoni (and with him alone). They have never found any disadvantage in his way of teaching, and have been only too glad to adapt themselves to suit the great artist . . . Almost all of us wish to continue our studies with Busoni, and no one else. Anyone who examines this case fairly must admit, that we have been badly let down both from the practical and the artistic point of view.' The students of the Vienna master class included Augusta Cottlow, Vera Maurina-Press, Georgine Nelson, Gregor Beklemischeff and Leo Sirota.

At about the same time Edgar Varèse moved to Berlin. He became very friendly with Busoni, whom he had greatly admired ever since reading his *Outline for a New Musical Aesthetics*. He did not become a pupil. But he did let Busoni look at his most recent compositions. Busoni read the scores and suggested certain alterations. The young Frenchman was obstinate, and refused to correct his work. As soon as Busoni realized, that he had encountered an indomitable artistic will, his attitude altered completely. He smiled, laid his hand on Varèse's shoulder, and said : 'From now on no more of this "maestro", call me Ferruccio and address me as "Du".' Varèse describes him as a man, who inspired others to think and act. He knew, that as far as he himself was concerned, Busoni had enabled him to crystallize ideas that were only half-formed, had stirred his imagination and given it an objective, determining the future development of his music. While treating him as a colleague and friend, Busoni had the same generative effect on him, as sun, rain and manure have on the soil.

There were also people, whose relationship with Busoni was not that of teacher/pupil, but who nevertheless derived inspiration from him in their own creative work. Gisella Selden-Goth met the famous man in Budapest in 1909, and showed him a score. In a letter dated 22nd June of that year, Busoni examined various details of this variation work and gave the young composer a résumé of his own ideas about composition. He compares the piece with another that had also been submitted to him, and detects a certain advancement in the overall plan and the realization, although he doubts whether it is any more original. He criticizes the tonal balance of certain passages, the too frequent appearance of one note played on several instruments, against only a single note in the bass. As far as instrumentation is concerned, he suggests that certain wind chords should be eliminated, in order to emphasize the horn, 'particularly as the low flutes should hardly be muted.' His final verdict is, that the variations ought to be perfectly balanced, as regards sequence, character, key and tempo, and the scherzo-character should not be too dominant. It is the practical musician in him speaking, when he insists, that it is more important to hear a piece once than to study it for a week. 'Just carry on working and enjoying it; and as soon as you have the technical skill (which, it seems inevitable, you will acquire), let us feel the blood racing through your work.'

In August 1910, Busoni held a master-class at the conservatory in Basle, and one of his students was Eduard Steuermann. However, this young Pole was not simply wanting to perfect his piano playing, which was only of secondary interest to him. He believed that his real talent lay in composition, so he asked Busoni to give him tuition. Although Busoni had every confidence in Steuermann's creative ability, he was unable to grant this request; but he did remain in close contact with Steuermann, both on a personal and artistic level, and Steuermann followed him to Berlin. Through Busoni he became a pupil of Arnold Schoenberg in 1911. Steuermann has provided very little information about Busoni's piano teaching in Basle. Yet his entire future development was strongly influenced by the Basle master-class and his association with Busoni. As an interpreter, he has constantly given Busoni his support, not only playing his Bach arrangements, but also giving sympathetic performances of the six Sonatinas and the great Toccata.

Busoni's American students included Louis T. Gruenberg, who came to him as an infant prodigy to study the piano, and over the course of a period of nineteen years eventually studied composition with him as well. Among Gruenberg's compositions, two pieces that appeared in 1923 and 1924, inspired by the spirit of jazz, caused quite a stir even in Europe : *The Daniel Jazz* and *The Creation*. The cosmopolitan, humanitarian quality of the pieces, and the clarity of their formal arrangement is reminiscent of Busoni. The literary awareness of Gruenberg, who in 1913 had written the music for Busoni's libretto *Die Götterbraut*, can easily be judged by his choice of Eugene O'Neill's *Emperor Jones* as the text for an opera. The negro problem of the United States, which is the subject of this play, had also roused Busoni's sympathy during his various trips to America.

One of the strongest personalities among Busoni's students was Philipp Jarnach. The son of a Catalan sculptor and a German mother, he studied piano and musical theory in Paris until 1914, and then during the war years became a student and close friend of Busoni in Zürich. What the two men had in common was the same Latin approach to form and the same sense of superiority in their artistic outlook, which manifests itself in all Jarnach's compositions.

Although Jarnach has not made many public statements about Busoni's teaching, he is nevertheless an important witness when it comes to testifying to the underlying spirit of Busoni's approach to teaching. 'What we call technique,' Jarnach writes in a work dealing with stylistic problems in Busoni's music, 'the result of a long and difficult struggle to come to grips with one's material, is the artist's personal concern and does not affect his relationship with the outside world.' We have already come across this same observation in statements made by Adolf Paul and Augusta Cottlow, and in later accounts from Kestenberg and Draber. Jarnach goes on to say : 'Busoni does not abide by any fixed rules; his universal talent mastered every known formula long ago, and his formal construction is no more tied to any existing system than his harmonic practice.' His techniques change according to the job on hand, at least that is more or less Jarnach's conclusion. Finally, he makes the important observation, that Busoni with his instinctive aversion to programme music was striving to remove all literary associations from music, and furthermore dreamed of capturing the sensuousness of sound itself through melodic expression. 'He never looked upon any achievement as final, whether recent or of the past; but he tried everything out, and used the various techniques consciously and systematically.' Although there may seem to be a contradiction between Busoni's universality as an artist, his passionate interest in literary problems on the one hand, and his steering music away from literature on the other hand, this is not the case. It was precisely because he accepted a comprehensive knowledge of the arts as a matter of course, that he was able to draw the line between the realms of music and literature, even—in fact particularly—when both arts were involved together, which is to say, in any vocal and dramatic composition. Jarnach's own work is to a large extent written for orchestra and chamber groups. At the early Donaueschingen music festivals at the beginning of the 'twenties, and in concerts given by the International Society for New Music, it stubbornly continued to appear alongside works by Hindemith and the Schoenberg school. Jarnach's musical thinking is predominantly polyphonic; his formal world is that of pre-classical music, his language often has a Romantic softness about it, but also a visionary strength. The most personal of his piano pieces is the sonatina which he calls *Romancero 1*, of his chamber music the Second String Quartet of 1924 and the *Musik zum Gedächtnis der Einsamen* of 1952, also written for a string quartet.

The period immediately preceding the First World War also saw Busoni as departmental head at the Conservatory in Bologna for a short while. After protracted negotiations, this venerable institute had eventually persuaded the great musician to begin work there on a trial basis in the autumn of 1913. It very soon

191

became apparent, that his primary duty was to solve purely administrative and practical problems. His outstanding ability as a teacher was of secondary importance. Despite the provincial backwardness of the institute, and of the town in general, he at first enjoyed the novelty of it all. Nevertheless he was disturbed by the traditionalism of the old Liceo: 'All the walls are hung with old gentlemen, some of whom do not invite a closer acquaintance . . .' Busoni listened to both young men and women playing and singing. He enjoyed the singing of the young girls most. But it was not the kind of situation to suit him for long. Even though his friends, the Anzolettis, lived nearby, he did not feel at home in Bologna. In May 1914 he still had not made up his mind. From Bologna he wrote to A. Dandelot: 'At this moment in my life I feel more undecided than ever before. For next autumn, I have to choose between Berlin, Italy, America and England. When faced with the proverbial *embarras de richesses*, one drifts to and fro between the four winds, until eventually the strongest wind blows one in that direction. At the moment I am like a blind man and cannot see my path. Wait until the summer when I shall be back in Berlin where I have always seen things clearly. This time I have quite an important decision to make, and I don't want to rush it . . . We will discuss the question of Madrid later. When one has just finished a meal, it is unpleasant to think about the next menu.' And this is as far as he goes in this important letter, originally written in French and translated literally.

Later, in a conversation reported in his memoirs by the violinist, Josef Szigeti, about the outcome of his activities as departmental head at Bologna, Busoni remarked ironically: 'One thing I am proud of: I succeeded in getting W.C.s installed.'

The war years in Zürich and the two years before he returned to Berlin also brought various teaching commitments. But by then Busoni concentrated his attention on a few musicians of kindred spirit, who enjoyed his company and up to a certain point his teaching. Himself a refugee from both Germany and

Italy, he became increasingly absorbed in those whose destiny had been shaped by war and politics. Wolfgang Hartmann, in his memoirs, has spoken of the 'peaceful haven', that Busoni's home in Zürich became. War and the problems relating to it were never discussed, and within this circle everyone was able to forget what was going on outside Switzerland. 'He was prepared to listen to anyone who came to him with something on his mind; he was always ready to give advice and help, where it was needed. He could take an almost childish delight in people and their achievements. He was like a kindly father to all these homeless emigrants, and he was sympathetic towards all artistic efforts and took an interest in everything that was new at that time . . . He had a chastening, purifying effect on everyone who crossed his path; and at the same time his brilliance outshone them all, without his even realizing it, because throughout his life he remained as modest as a child. Once he did begin to criticize a friend's work, he was never afraid of being completely frank, yet he never upset anybody.'

Admittedly, compared with his creative activities, which centred on the two one-act operas and above all his major work, *Doctor Faust*, Busoni's teaching receded very much into the background during the years in Zürich. It was not until he was back in Berlin in 1920, that he became once more the great teacher-magician, whose magic circle afforded protection to a small band of élite.

In 1918 a teacher-pupil relationship developed with Gisella Selden-Goth. She had sent him some recent songs, asking his opinion of them, and he answered with his customary thoroughness. In so doing he pointed out, that basically German song writing interested him very little, since for him the art-song was like a corsetted figure, strangled by the rhythm of the poem. As far as his friend's songs were concerned, he praised the fact that illustration was less important than emotion. But he criticized the way in which the piano frequently drowned the vocal part. He describes the harmony of the songs as acute but restless, betraying a lack of polyphonic training: 'If I may be so bold

G   193 as to assume the authority of a teacher, I would suggest that you practise a lot of counterpoint, and stand in your room and read your texts aloud before setting them to music; after that, think first and foremost of the vocal part!'

Three years later, in a letter written to Miss Selden-Goth from London, Busoni mentions the question of musical training once again. He recommends the following method: 'Take sixty-four bars of a good piano arrangement of Mozart, and orchestrate them without looking at the Mozart score beforehand. Then compare your instrumentation with that of Mozart. If you repeat this systematically, you will find it an invaluable exercise, and need no further proof of the extraordinary skill and accomplishment that lies behind Mozart's so-called primitiveness. Neither you, nor anyone else, will ever get it exactly right; perplexed, you will always be forced to admit his superiority. You (and anyone else) will always make it more primitive than Mozart.' We know from later students, that Busoni employed this method even when teaching the more advanced composition students at the Berlin Academy of Arts.

The circle of students that Busoni assembled in Berlin included a wide range of very different personalities. Among the first to be selected in 1920 was Vladimir Vogel, who has since written a great deal about Busoni's teaching. In the summer of 1923 a Bauhaus festival was held in Weimar, and Busoni was among those who appeared there. It was one of his last journeys. In the evenings he would sit, surrounded by friends and students, and in the course of conversation express various views, which Vogel recounts from memory. On one occasion they happened to be talking about fugues, and Busoni maintained, that not even Mozart and Beethoven had surpassed Bach in his use of this form. It was still possible, he said, to write fugues, using either traditional or modern techniques, but the result inevitably seemed old-fashioned. As a form, the fugue belonged to a specific period and was therefore transient. Polyphony, on the other hand, was a basic concept and therefore permanent. During the years he studied with Busoni, Vladimir Vogel did write a few

194

pieces, particularly vocal works, which show evidence of his moving away from the style of Skriabin, but very little trace of his teacher's influence, apart from his increasing control over form. One of the pieces belonging to this period is a musical setting of a poem by Goethe, *Die Bekehrte*, which Busoni referred to as an example of new departures being made in music. The three *Sprechlieder* for bass voice and piano, written in 1922, also date from the same period. They are important, not only because they establish Vogel's *Sprechstimme* technique, which he later elaborated so successfully, but also because of his choice of texts. The three poems are the work of August Stramm, the creator of an expressionist alogical form of lyric poetry, which had considerable influence during the 'twenties and affected all the German poetry of that period. The most important product of Vogel's years as a student is his composition for one and two pianos, more than an hour long, which, as far as piano composition is concerned, would have been inconceivable before the advent of Busoni's *Fantasia Contrappuntistica*.

In 1921 Kurt Weill joined Busoni's class. At that time, he was still very young and had come to music from the world of theatre; as a musician, he was developing into an exponent of linear polyphony and a tonally free idiom, clearly reflecting the influence of Mahler and the Schoenberg school in Vienna, particularly apparent in his String Quartet and *Frauentanz* and later in his Violin Concerto too. With Busoni, both Weill's sense of form and his polyphonic technique were crystallized. It was shortly after Busoni's death, that he began his operatic work, first using texts by Ivan Goll and Georg Kaiser, later collaborating with Bertolt Brecht. It is quite clear, that Kurt Weill was another who gained an enormous amount of technical confidence from Busoni's teaching, without ever imitating his teacher's personal style.

A year after the master's death, Weill remembered with admiration the 'spiritual European of the future' who, he says, never in his whole life told a lie. Honesty was the guiding principle of both his life and his art. 'But this same honesty,'

195

Weill goes on to say, 'which came so naturally to him, he also expected of the few people he permitted to approach him. This is where the unconscious, spontaneous process of education begins, this is where the first fruits of his personal influence will appear.'

The concept of an élite was a dominant factor in Busoni's world, increasingly so as he became more mature. Weill speaks of the 'distorted image of beauty', which the artistic youth of Germany had doggedly fostered during the years of isolation imposed by the war. He describes the way they suddenly leapt into undiscovered territory, rejected everything traditional, and confined themselves ascetically to new techniques. But they had not yet discovered a form. Then they were confronted with Busoni : 'He was different from what we had expected : more mature, more controlled—and younger.' He had passed by all the fuss and bother, gone much further than these young people, without their realizing it. 'He called us disciples and there were no actual lessons, but he allowed us to breathe his aura, which emanated in every sphere, but eventually always manifested itself in music. These hours spent daily in his company are still too recent for me to be able to speak about them. It was a mutual exchange of ideas in the very best sense, with no attempt to force an opinion, no autocracy, and not the slightest sign of envy or malice; and any piece of work that revealed talent and ability was immediately recognized and enthusiastically received.'

Strangely enough, in a memorial article written in 1926, Jarnach maintained that Busoni was not a teacher in the narrow sense of the word; he had no vocation for teaching, besides which he lacked the necessary cool impartiality. Having himself undergone a detailed theoretical training, he did not believe in teaching systems. What he required of an artist, was not that he should rely upon what he had learnt, but that he should allow his techniques to grow out of his original idea.

The German-American pianist, Edward Weiss, sees Busoni as a teacher quite differently. He was with him a great deal during Busoni's last years in Berlin, where he did so much to champion his work, that he gained the master's confidence. Weiss describes him as an exceptionally conscientious teacher. He respected him so much, that there was never any question of a discussion. 'The basis of his teaching,' so Weiss wrote in a letter to me, 'was physical relaxation combined with mental tension. He used to say, that playing the piano was like the work of ants. Outwardly absolute calm, not a single unnecessary movement that might distract the audience.'

In 1922 the Rumanian pianist, Theophil Demetriescu, was preparing a Busoni recital, which was to include only original works, that is to say, no transcriptions. During this time, he used to play for Busoni every two or three weeks. At these sessions the composer stressed the importance of following his instructions for the use of the pedal. If Demetriescu tried to moderate the harshness of certain passages, Busoni became annoyed. Among the specific techniques that Demetriescu learned from him were : 'pointed staccato, martellato, wrist-octaves, the habit of crossing-over and wherever possible avoiding crossing under, playing chords from the wrist as well; steering clear of so-called vibrato, which is to say, being scrupulously careful about finger-changes on repeated notes; sitting in front of the region of the piano where one has to play, which means a quick movement of the body in the direction in which the arm is about to drift or make a leap.' This description completely contradicts a statement made by Busoni, in which he said that he had given up finger-changes on repeated notes. Perhaps it was not advisable to teach this new way of repeating notes.

Another pupil to come to Busoni during the last years of the master's life was Dimitri Mitropulos, who had already received his training in Greece, but wanted to perfect his piano playing. So impressed was he by the writing and music of the great Italian, that he fell completely under his sway; and his entire future development, particularly as a conductor of the highest standing, was based on this period 1921–24 when he studied at Viktoria-Luiseplatz. As an interpretive artist too, that is to say, as a pianist as well as conductor, Mitropulos often referred to Busoni's music.

In his correspondence with Hans Huber, Busoni very seldom mentions the problems of teaching. Only once, in 1910, did he actually direct a master-class at the Basle Conservatory. However in September of that same year, he gave a cycle of concerts spread over four days, at the invitation of the Institute. In 1916 he repeated the venture, but with slightly different programmes The final evening, 2nd February, was devoted to Liszt. Busoni obviously felt that the young students were particularly in sympathy with him that day. On 7th February he wrote to Huber and asked him to convey the following message to the students: 'My dear young friends, young people and mature artists provide mutual support and draw upon one another in the constant process of give and take between experience and the invigorating freshness of youth. To be understood by the young and to have their confidence was a source of great pleasure, and provided me with the essential interrelationship. I therefore thank you for showing and indeed expressing your encouragement and sympathy. In return, I am working towards your future.'

Nevertheless, he could not bring himself to teach the piano again. When Held, the director of the Geneva Conservatory, got Huber to ask him, whether he felt disposed to take up a post there, Busoni confided to his friend the reasons against it: his desire for independence; his aversion to listening to laborious piano playing; his determination, that if he was to undertake a mission of this kind at all, it should be in his own homeland, by which he meant Germany and not Italy. Furthermore, his 'complete lack of confidence in young women, where real art is concerned, and they are the backbone of the conservatories.' But above all he felt the need to account for every day of his life, in order 'to accomplish much that still remains to be done'. The Geneva professorship did not offer enough money, fame or stimulating work, to make up for virtual imprisonment.

Among the Swiss students who studied composition with Busoni during his last years in Berlin, Luc Balmer and Robert

Blum both have clear memories of his teaching. Another pupil recommended to Busoni was Erhart Ermatinger, although admittedly he never actually studied with him. In 1921 Jarnach arranged a meeting between the two, and Busoni was so impressed by the score of a symphony that he wrote to Volkmar Andreae, enthusiastically acclaiming Ermatinger's work. It does not give the impression of being a beginner's work, he writes, even though it is. He praises his assurance in disposition, his continued skill in the construction of lines, as well as the finished product 'which commands respect even from an expert'.

Ermatinger wrote a long letter to me, expressing his views on Busoni's piano playing and his whole stylistic approach. He also described visiting the master : 'I have a rather curious memory of that first meeting . . . I met Busoni, surrounded by a swarm of people of all types . . . This was so different from what I had imagined in what was then my naïve and idealistic way, that I took my leave at the very first opportunity, without having exchanged much more than a handshake with Busoni, who asked me in a friendly way to call in again some time.' On the second visit, Busoni said something complimentary to him about the symphony. On the last occasion, Ermatinger was alone with the sick man. He describes him as aged and tired, speaking slowly, and not laughing as he usually did. The conversation was entirely about the past. Ermatinger himself had always fought shy of studying with Busoni, because he considered himself unworthy of approaching someone he so greatly admired.

Reinhold Laquai, who had begun studying with Busoni in Zürich in 1915, achieved great success with a piano trio at one of the Donaueschingen Chamber Music Festivals. He has not published anything about his experiences as Busoni's pupil.

Luc Balmer wrote a very brief reply to my letter asking him about Busoni's teaching. He maintains, that where orchestration was concerned, Busoni always referred to Mozart whom he admired more and more. Balmer apparently had the impression, that Busoni was shocked by the effect that his earlier visions of the future had had on the younger generation. He could not help being reminded of the sorcerer's apprentice. 'For him (Busoni), the first essential was a masterly craft, the composer taking full responsibility for every note, and the technique corresponding to the sound he has heard within.' Balmer also claims, that unlike Ernst Krenek, Busoni became increasingly conservative and sceptical towards all innovation. This description confirms what we have already gleaned from various passages in Busoni's correspondence with Gisella Selden-Goth.

I received a much more detailed letter from Robert Blum, who also joined Busoni's class in Berlin in 1921. It appears that he was a shy young man and usually awestruck when in the presence of the master. Only once, when Busoni somewhat disparagingly called Franz Schubert a rustic composer, did Blum presume to protest, maintaining that surely, some of Schubert's work had meaning. Busoni was annoyed by the young man contradicting him and left the room. Yet, in Blum's opinion, he nevertheless played Romantic music superbly well.

On the subject of Busoni's teaching method, Blum praises his 'desire to explore and develop the possibilities of composition along the path of evolution'. He attached great importance to composing with ease, and not allowing the effort to become a hardship. He once remarked on the pleasure it gave him, to think that he had written his Concertino for Flute and Orchestra as easily as a letter. Blum then goes on to make an important observation about Busoni's desire to achieve continuity: 'He criticized those composers, who would finish a page of music and write it into the score, without having any idea at the time as to what was coming next.' It appears that in this case, Busoni is applying his concept of unity to the process of composition.

Blum then describes an incident that happened during an actual class. His fellow-countryman, Walther Geiser, brought Busoni an overture. The master read it through, and found a passage that he did not like. He 'took the score and disappeared into his study (the class was held in a big music-room), reappearing after a short while with an entirely new passage already orchestrated.' Blum concludes by saying, that he 'thinks of him in the way that a child might feel, who has grown accustomed to accepting unquestioningly the security of his parental home.'

When one considers the diverse evidence produced by students over three decades, the image of the great teacher appears infinitely varied rather than consistent. Not only as a composer and pianist, author and aestheticist, but also as a teacher, Busoni changed and developed in ways that cannot always be explained in terms of the stark individuality of his mind and character. Many of the changes in musical outlook, that occurred during the time he was active and productive, are reflected in his work. The naïve programmatic interpretation of Bach, described by witnesses of the Helsinki period, was soon rectified and developed into a much more objective, one might almost say technical, insight. The days of experimenting with almost every aspect of sound, harmonic practice and counterpoint, which his students also shared before the First World War, were later superseded by a more ponderous and conservative attitude. This is something which can be traced in the work of Vogel, Jarnach and Weill, as well as in all the Swiss students. It is also clear, that Busoni indulged in literary and visual associations in his piano teaching more than in his composition classes. However, both aspects of his teaching reflect his uncompromising and unequivocal attitude to art. He was never concerned with teaching according to a strict timetable. Whenever he passed on to younger people his own immense experience and insight as an artist, he did so with all the generosity and prodigality that distinguished his private life. The hours became afternoons, the afternoons stretched into evening—this is the impression we gain of the master-classes in Weimar, Vienna and Basle, as well as of the later years when Busoni, already a sick man, was teaching in Berlin. There was not a single person who, once under the spell of this teacher, went away unchanged or untouched. Much of the energy, that must have lent such incredible force to Busoni's teaching, has had a lasting effect. Thus the testimony of his students confirms what Busoni himself said, echoing the words of his own Doctor Faust : 'The symbols contained within this potent core are not yet exhausted; the work will produce a school, which as the years go by will become increasingly productive.'

The European

'He is quite unjust when he argues, that in criticizing the stereotype use of the words "musical" and "deep", my intention is to
educate the Germans. Quite the reverse. I am someone who, ever
since childhood and even now as a mature man, has constantly
been gaining knowledge in Germany; and any music copyist,
any provincial music master could and indeed had the right
to intimidate me with those two words and take precedence over
me. A similar thing happened with the current use of the word
"emotion", and people succeeded in pinning on me the label of
an intellectual without a soul.'

This letter, written to Huber in the year 1917, refers to Hans
Pfitzner's pamphlet *The Dangers of Futurism*. Busoni, who had
chosen Germany as his home in 1894 and taken up permanent
residence in Berlin, could not be touched in a more sensitive
spot, than by being denounced as a threat to German music.
When Italy entered the war, he saw himself as 'totally isolated'.
During the years that followed, he was considered in his native
country, which he had left for ever almost thirty years previously,
as a hopeless Germanophil. Between the frontiers of nationalistic
world-shapers, there was no longer any place for people of his
intellectual stature. Busoni was one of the first supporters of the
future concept of a united Europe. The Italian virtuoso, whose
compositions reflected the spirit of Bach and Mozart, married
a Swedish girl from Helsinki in Russia. His greatest successes
had been celebrated in America, his first prize for composition
won at a competition in Moscow. He spoke five languages
fluently, and in his correspondence used German, Italian and
French with equal assurance.

As a creative musician and as a writer, he had grown up with
and had a mature knowledge of all these cultures. Ultimately he
reached the lonely position, where he could no longer accept
national viewpoints as criteria for quality, and took them merely
as indications of ethno-psychological peculiarities.

Moreover, this great European was exceptionally critical in

his judgement of national characteristics. He recognized all too clearly certain weaknesses in the Italian mentality, particularly the provincialism and the resulting backwardness in social and artistic matters. He was equally aware of the many strange attributes of German life and thought. He was always ready to make sarcastic remarks about his countrymen on either side of the Alps. This was what won him the reputation among Nationalists in both places of being on the opposite side. He was naturally drawn to the French temperament. His favourite authors included Voltaire and Villiers de l'Isle Adam. Yet even in France he found a good deal to criticize, as soon as he spent so much as a couple of days there. He wrote ecstatic letters from Paris. But he hesitated about deciding to settle there whenever he thought of Berlin.

As a Latin and an individualist, he had very little understanding for the Slav temperament. Although the Moscow professorship of 1890 was a great honour for a young musician, he gave it up after only a short time. In spite of all the admiration that he expressed for the beauty of Moscow, he felt constricted and ill at ease in the Russian environment.

Busoni had got to know America early in life; 'her culture came over from Europe, and produced (along the coast) people like Franklin, Lincoln, Poe', he observed in 1913. He found his most enthusiastic disciples among the young American musicians. He struck up countless friendships with Americans of all ages and every walk of life. He spent months travelling through the towns and countryside of the New World; he was captivated by it and described it in many of his letters. Yet the American way of life remained so alien to him, that even in the critical situation produced by the First World War, he did not want to stay there and preferred to seek asylum in the much more restricted environment of Switzerland.

Dent, Busoni's close friend and later biographer, repeatedly observes that during the course of his life Busoni developed into a world-citizen. This is not really the right word for him. For a true cosmopolitan, he lacked the ability to accept the Slav culture and also the American way of life. If after long years of considering Italy and Germany as his dual home, he did in fact develop, it was towards a European awareness defined in cultural terms. It embraced both the Latin and Germanic cultures, considering the English culture as something slightly apart, which appealed to him more and more as he grew older.

Busoni's ideas about nationalism and European unity occasionally came into conflict with his political convictions. As a very young man in Leipzig, he had been strongly influenced by socialist doctrine and had even acted as spokesman for the Marxists from time to time.

At that period in his life, nationalistic viewpoints were of no significance whatsoever in his way of thinking. But during his travels as a successful virtuoso, he came into such close contact with the various nations, that he was forced to consider their peculiarities. His letters are full of observations about the social life, the architecture, the theatre, the women and the customs of the countries through which he travelled. Consequently, many preferences and dislikes become apparent, without his ever allowing them to become generalizations. What he appreciated in every nation, was what he called sincerity. Whenever emotion overstepped certain limits and failed to come up to his ideal of genuineness, Busoni rejected it. He has said many biting words on the subject of German sentimentality; but when necessary he was equally ready to criticize Italian mawkishness.

During a trip to London in January 1913, we find him worrying, as he frequently did after thought-provoking occasions such as the New Year or a birthday, as to what path he should follow in the future. He mentions it to Gerda, saying that because of his age and maturity it is time he embarked on a major work. Then immediately afterwards he comes round to the subject of his ambiguous position from the point of view of nationality: 'At the same time I would like to bend the course of the stream back towards its source and attempt to make my major work have equal meaning in Italy. But it means doing a thorough

205

job, in order to be sure of its impact both intellectually and emotionally.' Busoni maintains, that Wagner planned his *Nibelungen* along these lines, but only indirectly achieved this effect with his own people. On the other hand, Dante, he claims, is a figure cherished by all Italians, a popular poet in spite of his stature even outside Italy. Busoni envisages a Dante opera written in Italian.

With his peculiarly ironic wit, Busoni inevitably had a fellow-feeling for Bernard Shaw, and during a visit to London in 1919 he enjoyed entertaining the sixty-three year old Irishman to tea. But even Shaw did not escape his criticism, particularly where his relationship to music was concerned.

The aspect of human behaviour that Busoni understood least of all was opportunism. To do a thing for purely utilitarian reasons was so totally alien to his way of thinking, that he was more likely not to do things that were practically advantageous, and to do things which (at any rate in the eyes of the world) could be damaging to him. The intellectual sphere, to which he considered himself totally committed, was way above utilitarian considerations. The poet, Jakob Wassermann, who saw a great deal of Busoni during the last years of his life, has said of him, that the mixed blood of his Italian father and German mother determined his whole personality, but at the same time caused the most profound spiritual conflict. Wassermann also quotes the significant phrase, 'Asiatic lubricity', which Busoni used when speaking about the bad aspects of the Russians.

On the other hand, there is a passage in a letter written to Gerda in 1910 which sheds light on his attitude to the problem of Americanism. Busoni is in Toledo, a small town in the United States, with his piano tuner, Hochmann, and is having a talk with him: 'I tried to explain to Hochmann, how in older civilizations industrial inventions had to spring from growing needs. Whereas in America, the invention comes first and then a use is found for it, so that the public will regard it as a necessity.' The conversation continues, and Busoni elaborates his point of view, which is that industry in America is an end in itself, and not merely a means of achieving certain practical goals. There is virtually no need for millions of automatic shoe-horns, the real motive in producing them is to employ thousands of workers. He maintains that Americans are only interested in politics as the power behind the Stock Exchange. He even mentions the typically American patriotism in this context. He had always found patriotic thinking too restricting, and even in the *Arlecchino* libretto he scoffs at the fatherland, calling it 'the quarrel in one's own house'.

One has only to glance at the programmes of the orchestral concerts that Busoni organized in Berlin between 1902–9, to be immediately aware of his European attitude to music. The contemporary composers that he introduces to the German public are Englishmen, Frenchmen, Norwegians, Finns, Danes, Czechs, Belgians, Dutchmen, Germans, Hungarians and Italians. In spite of the fact, that many of the names on these programmes have since been forgotten, the pioneer work carried out on behalf of Elgar, Sibelius, Delius, Debussy, Carl Nielsen, Hans Pfitzner, Johan Wagenaar, Bartók, and finally Busoni himself, is no less significant. One has only to compare these programmes with contemporary programmes produced for the music festivals put on every year by the Allgemeine Deutsche Musikverein, to realize how much greater in scope Busoni's selection was. The fact that *Neudeutsch* symphonic writing came off relatively badly corresponds with his marked sense of social justice. Busoni knew that the *Neudeutsch* composers did not need any publicity from him, since in any case they spiritually dominated the entire sphere of progressive music in Germany. This also explains his support of Pfitzner and exclusion of Richard Strauss, whom Busoni in fact admired very much and considered to be the cleverest musician of his time apart from Toscanini. Gustav Mahler would have fitted in very well with the spirit of these programmes. Busoni did intend to get hold of him for a performance of one of his symphonies, but for some reason or other the plan never materialized.

207

Another striking feature of Busoni's European outlook is his strong, sometimes passionate taste for exotic cultures. In his Berlin apartment on the Viktoria-Luise-Platz a large gilt Buddha occupied a commanding position, and a considerable section of his famous library was devoted to Oriental literature. Sometimes in his letters to Gerda, he mentions how enormously impressed he is by Indian literature, and quotes pages of Indian prose that bring tears to his eyes. Exotic subjects are also a feature of his operas and projects for operas.

The choice of musicians who have determined the form of Busoni's musical writing and thinking reflects an unequivocally European attitude. Three masters are of prime importance: Johann Sebastian Bach, Wolfgang Amadeus Mozart and Franz Liszt. Three German masters, one might say. Three European masters, it would be more correct to add. His choice would be German, in an entirely different sense, and not European at all, if instead of these three names we had mentioned Beethoven, Wagner and Brahms, for example. Neither Bach nor Mozart, not to mention Liszt, were German musicians in the exclusive sense, as the other three were.

In Bach's work, the currents of German, Italian and French tradition flow more or less side by side; Bach is a European phenomenon, no less than Goethe or the great artists of the Renaissance, the Dutch musicians, the Italian poets and painters.

Mozart was certainly as strongly affected by the Italian influence as by the Austro-German. This is obvious not only in his operatic work, but also in his sacred music and symphonic writing.

Franz Liszt is the most striking example of the European type in the nineteenth century. A German from a Hungarian milieu, he long considered France as the homeland of his choice, and the French language as his natural means of expression. His whole life seems in many ways to have been the model for many phases in Busoni's own life. It is only in their religious attitudes that the two men are radically different; throughout his life Busoni admittedly practised Christian virtues, but he was not a practising Christian; whereas Liszt, at the age of fifty-five, took minor orders and became an Abbé.

There were three crucial points in Busoni's life, three occasions when he made decisions that typified his attitude as a human being and as a European-minded artist: the first was in 1894, when after disappointments in Russia and America he took up residence in the go-ahead metropolis of Berlin. The second time was in 1915, when he was obliged and in fact wished to avoid the inner conflict brought about by the World War. Busoni went to neutral Switzerland, even though he could not foresee that Italy, the land of his birth, and ultimately even the great America, which would have offered him asylum, would enter the war against Germany. The third time was in 1920.

Already once during the war, when there was a question of accepting or refusing a teaching post in Switzerland, he had spoken of Germany as his homeland where he might conceivably take on such a mission. Germany lost the war, and in 1918 was virtually ostracized by the entire world. In his commemoration speech, Jakob Wassermann speaks of the 'seething impatience' with which Busoni was consumed during this waiting period in Switzerland. The poet then goes on to praise Busoni's decision in 1920, to obey the voice calling him back to Berlin: 'Once he regained the freedom to move about, without which he had felt so angry and helpless, that he had frequently been driven to seek comfort and insensibility in wine; once his imprisonment in a country, which was in every way too constricting for him and whose mountains enclosed him like walls, finally came to an end, then instead of throwing in his lot with the victorious nation—as he could well have done, and as most people would have done in his place—he chose without a moment's hesitation, and without even thinking of his own interests and comfort, the nation that was defeated, poverty-stricken, and virtually ostracized. This, in my opinion, was the most important thing he ever did as a human being, and once it is recognized as such it will be praised accordingly. The poverty in which he died, after living thirty years as a *grand seigneur*, is like a transfiguration of this gesture.' There is no finer testimony to Busoni's attitude than these words, spoken by the poet, who himself a German and a Jew and consequently in a similar situation, was a close friend and admirer.

As he grew older, Busoni changed in accordance with his natural disposition from a socialist into an aristocrat. This attitude to life becomes abundantly clear whenever he speaks about his art or aesthetic matters in general. He was the opposite of a mass man. Even though he was accustomed to producing music in the largest concert halls in the world, frequently in front of enthusiastic audiences of several thousand, he set very little store by popular patronage of the arts. Not even his pupil and most devoted friend, Leo Kestenberg, who even before the First World War, was closely associated with the People's Theatre movement in Berlin, could change his opinion in this matter. The Schopenhauer epigraph that Hans Pfitzner, Busoni's adversary of 1916, applied to the text of his *Palestrina*, might well apply to his entire work, in fact to his very existence as an artist : 'This intellectual type of existence floats way above the bustle and stir of the world, the truly real and purposeful life of the people, like some ethereal luxury, a fragrant perfume rising out of the ferment; and alongside world history, the history of philosophy, science and art, marches forward without guilt or bloodshed.'

As a young man, Busoni already knew something of the nature of victorious monarchism. Even later, he continued to take an interest in the traces of Napoleon that he found throughout Northern Italy. The name of Napoleon Buonaparte crops up remarkably often in his correspondence with Gerda. In Trieste, Busoni remembers the prosperity that the town enjoyed during the Napoleonic era, the trade between 'the colourful Orient and grey, strait-laced Hamburg'. While in Trent, he buys a book and discovers in it a poem on the nomination of Napoleon as king of Italy; he sends it off to his delighted father. Whenever he himself was subject to attacks of particularly aggressive, individualistic behaviour, such as the occasion when he suddenly

210

cancelled a concert in the little Dutch town of Enschede, he would laughingly speak of a Napoleonic gesture.

Although he was by no means drawn to Chauvinism, Busoni was nonetheless patriotic about one thing; and that was his Tuscan background. For him, Tuscany was the most important breeding-ground for culture and genius. A visit to Florence in 1909 convinced him of this, and filled him with pride. He named the great men to have emerged from this landscape : poets from Dante and Boccaccio to Carducci; painters from Giotto, Michelangelo and Leonardo da Vinci, down to a 'milky way of lesser stars'; scholars such as Galileo; musicians such as Monteverdi, Cherubini and Puccini; statesmen such as Machiavelli —'even Napoleon Buonaparte can be counted as a Tuscan.'

During the latter years of his life, Busoni's aristocratism increased in inverse proportion to his worldly prosperity. Erhart Ermatinger, the Swiss composer, who visited him for the last time during the summer of 1923, mentions what for him was an unforgettable moment in their conversation. Clearly, Busoni could not express wholehearted sympathy with the new political situation in Germany. Ermatinger told him, that he was intending to travel to Holland the next day. Whereupon Busoni suddenly brightened up 'and praised the monarchical regime there, maintaining that it was the only social system in which artistic activity could really flourish. This was the confirmed aristocrat speaking, which is what he really was, not by birth but intellectually. Even if this frank confession was not entirely true in the case of Holland, it seemed to me nonetheless remarkable, spoken as it was, there right in the middle of the newly established German republic. He must have thought so too, although for different reasons, because he found it necessary to apologize, believing me to be a Swiss arch-democrat. He need not have done so . . . And so I couldn't do other than agree with Busoni.'

To think and feel as a European is unusual even today, more than four decades after Busoni's death. Even the realization, that from the economic and political point of view everything speaks in favour of a united Europe, has made no difference. The fact that Busoni's music is still not understood, although the idiom is nothing like so esoteric as that of many other movements that have emerged in the musical world since 1900, is undoubtedly because it transcends any specifically national characteristics. It is too German for the Italians, too Italian for the Germans. In Anglo-Saxon countries, particularly in England, it has had a more profound and wide-reaching influence than in Busoni's two native lands. The fruits of his teaching have been most apparent in North America and in Switzerland.

Busoni often spoke of the frequent misunderstanding, that every creative artist has to expect from even the most well-intentioned public. The final misunderstanding, provoked by his own creative work, consisted of equating his 'new Classicism' with the Neo-classicism, which was spreading throughout France, Italy, and to a certain extent Germany too, during the same period. The aesthetic conclusions that Busoni reached in the final years of his life had nothing to do with looking back to the past. During those important years after the World War, he never wrote *pasticcios*, never for a moment supported mere stylistic imitation. His classical idom, breaking away from the thematic approach and conceding new rights to melody, demanded an extremely involved polyphony, and had nothing to do with traditional classicism. In a letter written to his son Benvenuto in 1921, Busoni protests against the popular misconception, that his teaching is essentially backword-looking. He borrows an example from the world of painting, and mentions the reinstatement of Jean Ingres, whom Pablo Picasso rediscovered at that time and used as a model for a short period; Busoni says of Ingres, that although he himself is a master, as a model he has nothing to offer but dead forms.

Works such as *Doctor Faust*, the Piano Toccata, the late Goethe Songs, have nothing in common with the Neo-classicism, which in France was degenerating into an artificial vogue. European in spirit, and in the way they combine the best

212

techniques from every culture and every period of Western music, they bridge the gap between German and Italian music. They embody the concept of unity, which throughout his life as a creative and thinking artist Busoni envisaged as the goal of music.

Acknowledgements

The basis for this book was provided by: Hugo Leichtentritt's biography (1916); Gisella Selden-Goth's monograph (1922); Edward Dent's important book (1933); as well as other lesser German and Italian publications. Apart from the published collections of letters: Letters to his wife (1935); Twenty-five letters written to Gisella Selden-Goth (1937); Busoni's letters to Hans Huber (1939); I have been through numerous letters printed in periodicals such as *Die Neue Rundschau, Schweizerische Musikzeitung, Zeitschrift für Musik, Die Musik, Allgemeine Musikzeitung, The Score*, etc., as well as unpublished ones, either privately owned or in public collections in Germany, Switzerland and the United States.

Among more recent essays, those of Ronald Stevenson and Terence W. Gervais were particularly important for me; among the consistently valuable contributions to the Busoni number of *L'Approdo Musicale* (1966) I would single out that of Roman Vlad.

Other sources of information were: Hans Jelmoli's memoirs, *Ferruccio Busoni's Years in Zurich*; Gerda Busoni's *Memories of F.B.* and Jakob Wassermann's *In Memoriam*.

I received endless help and information from Dr. Willi Schuh and Dr. Erwin Kroll, also Gisella Selden-Goth, Philipp Jarnach, Dr. Friedrich Schnapp, Vladimir Vogel and Edith Stargardt-Wolff. Also invaluable were conversations with Hanna Busoni and Benvenuto Busoni, Olga Demetriescu, Heinrich Kosnick and Daniel Revenaugh.

Helpful and informative letters were sent to me by former pupils and members of Busoni's circle, such as Luc Balmer, Robert Blum, Erhard Ermatinger, Heinz Joachim and Edward Weiss.

The Busoni archive in the West Berlin Academy of Arts was placed at my disposal by the director, Dr. Walter Huder; other archives too, such as the *Stiftung Preussischer Kulturbesitz* in

Berlin and the former Prussian State Library in Tübingen, have provided me with important material.

Busoni's work and his particular style of playing were interpreted for me most vividly by Eduard Steuermann.

I am deeply indebted to all the people I have mentioned for their encouragement and help.

H. H. Stuckenschmidt

For the kind permission to reproduce the photographs in this book, the author and publishers are indebted to the Berlin *Staatsbibliothek*, Dr. Willi Schuh, Walther Geiser and the pianist Amadeus Schwarzkopf whose father, the photographer Michael Schwarzkopf, was a close friend of Busoni.

Index

217